Fake News – What's the Harm?

Fake News – What's the Harm?

FOUR IDEAS FOR FACT-CHECKERS, POLICYMAKERS AND PLATFORMS ON COUNTERING THE CONSEQUENCES OF FALSE INFORMATION AND DEFENDING FREE SPEECH

Peter Cunliffe-Jones

University of Westminster Press
www.uwestminsterpress.co.uk

Published by
University of Westminster Press
32-38 Wells Street
London W1T 3UW
www.uwestminsterpress.co.uk

First published 2025

Cover design by Newgen North America
Print and digital versions typeset by Newgen North America

ISBN(Paperback):978- 1-915445-36-0
ISBN(OpenAccess):978- 1-915445-38-4
DOI:https:// doi.org/10.16997/14614695

The full text of this book has been peer-reviewed to ensure high academic standards. For full review policies, see: http://www.uwestminsterpress.co.uk/site/publish.

Suggested citation: Cunliffe-Jones, P. 2025. *Fake News – What's the Harm?* London: University of Westminster Press. DOI:https:// doi.org/10.16997/14614695 License:CC- BY-NC-ND 4.0

To read the free, open access version of this book online, visit https://doi.org/10.16997/14614695 or scan this QR code with your mobile device.

CONTENTS

Acknowledgements vii

INTRODUCTION 1

PART 1 WHAT IS 'FAKE NEWS'? 13

Chapter 1 Defining Terms: Fake News, Misinformation and Disinformation 15

Chapter 2 Where and When False Information Has Effect: Why Setting and Context Matter 37

Chapter 3 Rethinking the Nature and Drivers of Information Disorder 54

PART 2 WHAT'S THE HARM? 79

Chapter 4 Media Theory and Evidence of False Information Consequences 83

Chapter 5 How Changes In Factual Understanding May Cause or Contribute to These Consequences 104

Chapter 6 The Specific Substantive Consequences of False Information Examined for This Study 114

PART 3 PREDICTING THE WEATHER. PREDICTING HARM? 139

Chapter 7 A Model for Identifying the Potential of False Information to Cause or Contribute to Specific Consequences 143

Chapter 8 A Model for Identifying the Potential Field and Weight of False Information Consequences and Information Disorder 176

CONCLUSION 194

Suggested Further Reading 203

Appendices 207

Appendix 1 – Link to the Database and Guidelines Used for This Study 207

Appendix 2 – Fields and Evidence of Specific Substantive Consequences 208

Appendix 3 – Factors Affecting the Field and Weight of Consequences that Occur 229

Notes 231

ACKNOWLEDGEMENTS

This study is one of two books published with University of Westminster Press in 2021 and 2025 on the nature and drivers of information disorder in Africa and around the world, and the nature and consequences of different policy responses to it.

The first work, which examines the primary public policy responses to the spread of false information in Africa between 2016 and 2020, was divided into two sections. The first part,[1] a study researched with the help of media and Internet rights researchers Assane Diagne, Alan Finlay and Dr Anya Schiffrin,[2] identified a near doubling in the number of laws and regulations related to false information in eleven sub-Saharan countries between 2016 and 2020.[3] This work found no evidence that, despite a chilling effect on freedom of speech, the new laws caused any substantive change in the nature, volume, or effects of misinformation and disinformation in circulation. We proposed a new regulatory approach promoting, on the one hand, a proportionate response to the spread of false information, in line with international human rights laws, and, on the other hand, easier public access to accurate information.

The second section,[4] a study conducted with the support of media literacy researchers Dr Sahite Gaye, Wallace Gichunge, Dr Chido Onumah, Cornia Pretorius and Dr Schiffrin,[5] assessed the extent to which media literacy was included in the curricula offered in state-run schools in seven African countries in the second half of 2020 and its potential to reduce students' susceptibility to false information. This found only limited elements of media literacy offered in school curricula and almost no correlation with the knowledge and skills required to reduce learners' vulnerability to false information. We proposed that a new sub-set of media literacy – which we dubbed misinformation literacy – be provided in state schools to furnish learners with knowledge and skills in six specific domains: the contexts in which false information emerges, who creates it, the types of content, where it circulates, how and why individuals consume it and the consequences it does and does not cause.

This second book, published in 2025, explores the nature and drivers of information disorder more broadly and, within that, examines what it may and may not be possible to say about the nature and effects, or consequences for individuals and society, of different forms of false and misleading information in circulation today.

I developed my interest in this field, joining the University of Westminster's Communications and Media Research Institute (CAMRI) as a visiting research fellow in 2019, after more than 25 years as a news journalist. Most of that time was spent as a reporter and editor with the AFP news agency in Europe, Africa and Asia. In 2012, working as deputy director of the agency's then media development arm, the AFP Foundation, I led a project to found Africa's first fact-checking organization, Africa Check, in Johannesburg, South Africa, in partnership with the Journalism Department of the University of the Witwatersrand. Over the next five years, the small initial team and I set up three more offices in Senegal, Nigeria and Kenya. And in 2017, we launched a programme to encourage and support the development of a wider network of new independent fact-checking organisations across the continent, some of whose work is used in this study.

When the International Fact-Checking Network (IFCN) was set up in 2015 to promote common standards in the emerging field, I became a member of its advisory board. I stepped down as director of Africa Check in 2019 and became senior advisor to the IFCN director, leading a review in 2019–20 of the Code of Principles it uses to assess fact-checkers' adherence to its five core concepts: non-partisanship, transparency of funding, transparency and rigour of sources and methodology, and willingness to correct proven errors. In 2022–3, I worked as strategic advisor to the Arab Fact-Checking Network (AFCN), which supports the growth of non-partisan fact-checking in the Arabic-speaking world.

I describe this personal history to explain my experience in the sector and acknowledge any potential professional biases.

I have been grateful, while researching this book, to receive editorial and academic advice from Dr Peter Goodwin, Principal Research Fellow at CAMRI. I am thankful both to him and to other colleagues who gave generously of their time to review the evidence used in this study and comment on my findings. The list of everyone who provided assistance in this work since 2020 is too long for me to mention but I would particularly like to thank my colleagues Dr Daisy Hasan of University of Westminster, Dr David Corney of the UK fact-checking organisation Full Fact, Professor Lucas Graves of the University of Wisconsin-Madison and Professors Jean Seaton and Tom Buchanan of University of Westminster for their kind assistance reading and commenting on different aspects of the research.

I owe thanks to colleagues at the University of Westminster Press, who have supported and assisted the publication of this book, and especially to Richard Baggaley for his careful guidance of the book through the publication process. I owe thanks also to a wide range of colleagues in this sprawling, inter-disciplinary field, past and present, whose research has been invaluable in researching this book – even where I disagree with their specific findings. And I owe special thanks to my wife Nicola and son Sam, whose love, forbearance – and healthy interest in other topics – helped me keep perspective while I worked on the research on too many evenings, weekends and holidays.

I would like, above all, to thank the many diligent fact-checkers and their editors at six leading fact-checking organisations – Africa Check, AFPFactCheck and AFPFactuel, BBC Reality Check, Congo Check, Dubawa and ICIR/FactHub – whose painstaking work, sorting fact from fiction over the last six months in 2019 in Africa, I examined for this study.

Thanks are due, in this regard, to: Allwell Okpi, Alphonce Shiundu, Amanuel Neguede, Ange Kasongo, Anne-Sophie Faivre Le-Cadre, Brett Horner, Butchie Seroto, Cayley Clifford, Charlotte Durand, Charlotte Mason, Daniel Garelo Pensador, David Ajikobi, Dawit Endeshaw, Duncan Bwire, Eileen Jahn, Guillaume Daudin, Grace Gichuhi, Jennifer Ojugbeli, Kate Wilkinson, Kunle Adebajo, Marie-Ange Makadi, Mary

Alexander, Mary Kulundu, Mayowa Tijani, Monique Ngo Mayag, Motunrayo Joel, Naphtali Khumalo, Rabiu Alhassan, Rachel Yan, Remi Banet, Rodriguez Katsuva, Sam Kisika, Sammy Mupfuni, Segun Olakoyenikan, Silas Jonathan, Taryn Khourie, Temilade Onilede, Tendai Dube, Valdez Onanina and Vincent Ng'ethe, with apologies to anyone I missed.

While I learned from many in researching this second book, I am the sole author responsible for its flaws and weaknesses. Some initial funding used to support the research was provided in 2020 by the Facebook Journalism Project, the Google News Initiative and Luminate. They neither sought nor had any influence over the scope or findings of this book. All errors of style or substance are mine, and mine alone.

INTRODUCTION

In the wake of political upheaval and unrest in 2016 – with upset elections from the Philippines to the United States in 2016, and civil unrest in countries from Myanmar to Brazil – concern has risen worldwide among politicians, the public and academia at the potential consequences of fake news, misinformation and disinformation for individuals and society. In January 2024, the World Economic Forum declared information disorder – a phenomenon I define, in Chapter 3, as a threefold disruption of the information system (the circulation of false and misleading information, the lack of access to and trust in accurate information, and the distorted focus of the information to which people are exposed) to be the 'gravest threat' to global stability facing the world over the following two years.[1] Of particular concern has been the potential of false and misleading information to disrupt democracies,[2] sow unrest and violence,[3] and harm public health.[4]

In the years since 2016, this alarm has given momentum to a series of political and civil society interventions from new laws and regulations, brought in either from genuine concern or as an excuse for censorship in Africa,[5] and around the world,[6] to growth and change in the practices of fact-checking,[7] and 'pre-bunking',[8] and the teaching or calls for the teaching of media literacy in schools in Africa[9] and worldwide.[10]

While many of the concerns expressed about the events described above are well founded, I argue in this book that a striking disconnect exists between the nature and consequences of false and misleading information, and lack of access to accurate information, that I observe through this study, and the approaches taken to countering these phenomena by fact-checkers, policymakers and platforms. A series of false assumptions and misconceptions by fact-checkers, policymakers, platforms and researchers undermine the efforts made to counter the negative consequences these phenomena do or may have, leading to the adoption of approaches to the regulation of information that are, often, thus, both ineffective in curbing potential harms and restrictive of freedom of speech, as a result.

The false assumptions, which I detail in the first three chapters of the book, start, as computer science and Internet researchers Chico Camargo and Felix Simon noted in 2022,[11] with the ahistorical understanding, common to many practitioners, that false or misleading information is a fundamentally novel problem that emerged only recently with the advent of online media. This misunderstanding is compounded by false assumptions widespread among those unfamiliar with this history, about the way that information does and does not affect the understanding and behaviour of individuals and society and about the nature of information disorder as it affects society as a whole.

*

The result of four years of research, this book is based on both a close reading of numerous earlier studies of the nature and effects of information and a detailed investigation of 250 case studies of information identified by fact-checkers in Africa in 2019 as in some way false or misleading: examining the nature, drivers and consequences, or lack of consequences, of these examples. These cases are displayed in boxes, and referenced numerically in the text as, for example (**Case** 1.1) – which would be the first case in Chapter 1. Judging the effects, or lack of effects of these examples of false information, I recognise, of course, that the human behaviour they describe almost always occurs as a result not of just one, but of a combination of factors. I identify the cases of false information, studied in this book, as causing a consequence where credible evidence available in the source material shows, beyond reasonable doubt, that an understanding caused by the claim was an essential factor in bringing about what followed. Not necessarily the sole cause, but an essential element.

Setting out my arguments in three parts, I first offer a discussion and definitions of four, key contested terms, essential to understanding the nature of false information we discuss: fake news, misinformation, disinformation and information disorder. I explore, in Part Two, the factors that drove the creation and spread of the examples of false information examined in the book and the consequences they may or may not have caused or contributed to. Having considered the differences between cases of false information that the evidence available suggests did and did not contribute to specific negative effects, I identify in Part Three a series of factors that shape the potential of false or misleading claims such as these to cause or not cause substantive negative consequences for individuals and society. Through this, I put forward four ideas that can help fact-checkers, policymakers, platforms and researchers to better counter the harms done by information disorder without unduly limiting freedom of speech.

In Part One of the book, I start by considering the history and evolution of the key terms and phrases used in the field and the trouble that researchers, fact-checkers and policymakers have found defining them in a clear and consistent way. The failure of the field to do this to date is, at least in part, the result of what the communications scholar Lucas Graves terms the narrowness of the current theoretical paradigm used by many researchers and practitioners alike.[12] To address this, I first review the history of these terms from their earliest appearances in print to the way they are used today.

I consider the existing, widely used definitions in the light of evidence I draw from a database I created between 2021 and 2023[13] of 250 examples of information identified as in some way false or misleading by one or more of half-a-dozen fact-checking organisations operating in sub-Saharan Africa in the second half of 2019. I identified this period as one of 'business as usual' on the continent, coming as it did between six months during which national election campaigns dominated the news in some of Africa's biggest countries and the two years starting in 2020 during which the Covid-19 pandemic disrupted the normal flow of news and information worldwide. Drawing on both past and recent literature and the evidence available from this sample of false and misleading information in an important but under-researched part of the world, I seek to present a clear understanding of the nature, and history, of these different phenomena. It is this combination of literature and empirical evidence that provides the basis for the findings I put forward.

*

The merits of a literature review are well understood. The merits of fact-checking reports as a source of evidence may be less well appreciated. To consider their worth, it may be useful, first of all, to understand the nature of fact-checking organisations and the way they work. From the start of the nineteenth century, proofreaders were employed at a growing number of newspapers in the United States and Europe to check spellings and grammar in news reports and commentaries prior to publication. This was not, however, enough to cut out factual errors and in the 1920s, a new type of specialist staff were employed to check the accuracy of facts in reports yet to be published: 'fact-checkers'. In journalism, the role was not generally seen as a prestigious one. 'The women's section of the classifieds in mid-century newspapers advertised for fact-checkers alongside typists, secretaries, file clerks and "his girl Fridays,"' Lucas Graves noted in the first proper history of the field.[14] All the same, the new practice was considered essential to strengthening trust and it stayed.

Quality news media do not, in theory, report only their own claims and observations but also claims and observations made by public figures and organisations. And in the first years of this century, a new and different practice emerged in the US media; one less concerned with the accuracy of facts the journalists reported – covered by existing practices – and more with the accuracy of the claims by politicians and others. Distinguishing itself from the earlier practice, this was known as 'political fact-checking'.

The first political fact-checking operation launched was FactCheck.org, founded as a non-profit venture at the University of Pennsylvania in 2003. It was followed in 2007 by the *Washington Post*'s Fact Checker column, and PolitiFact, launched by the Florida newspaper the *St Petersburg Times*. In London, the UK fact-checking site Full Fact was set up in 2009. In Argentina, the fact-checking site Chequeado was launched in 2010. Africa's first fact-checking organisation, Africa Check, was launched in 2012, in South Africa. Over four years, the team and I opened a network of additional offices in Senegal, Nigeria and Kenya.

By 2014, more than three dozen fact-checking organisations had been set up worldwide and, after a meeting which I attended in London, the US-based Poynter Institute established the International Fact-Checking

Network (IFCN) to foster communication between members around the world. For most of this first wave of operations, the focus of attention was firmly on false claims made by politicians and public figures in speeches, political debate and the media. Concern about information spread online by the public would come later.

Practices and standards varied and, at a meeting in Buenos Aires in June 2016, the community agreed to establish a Code of Principles to enable the public to judge the impartiality and rigour of work carried out.[15] By 2019, members' adherence to the Code's five core principles – (i) quality and transparency of sourcing, (ii) quality and transparency of methodology, (iii) operation of a clear and open corrections policy, (iv) transparency of funding and staffing, and (v) non-partisanship and fairness – would be reviewed annually on thirty-one criteria by independent assessors from senior positions in journalism and academia.

As part of the assessment, fact-checking organisations would have to show that they focus their attention not unduly on any one side of public debate but rather select claims to check primarily on the basis of their potential to impact society, if false. All reports must provide the sources of evidence they use and set out how they reach their conclusions. In his 2016 study of fact-checkers in the United States, professor of journalism Lucas Graves identified the fact-checkers whose work he studied as operating in a field of 'institutional facts': 'Unlike the "brute facts" of the material world, these concern things – like money, or borders, or last month's joblessness rate – which exist and have meaning only by virtue of some institutional rule-making apparatus.'[16]

The nature of the claims used in this study is more diverse than those identified by Graves in 2016, relating to both 'institutional' and 'brute' facts – a reflection of changes in the focus of fact-checking organisations over this time. Some claims do, indeed, relate to socially constructed 'facts' such as the number of employment opportunities that a government programme in Nigeria created (Case I.1), or the artistic intentions of a sculptor (Case I.2). In such cases, the evidence of an individual's statements or institutional data may be considered the most reliable evidence to judge the accuracy of the claims. Other cases relate to more material questions such as the location of a particular bridge (Case I.3), or the health effects of a purported medical treatment (Case I.4), and were assessed using material evidence.

The Nature of Claims Examined in the Fact-checks in the Study

Case I.1 Employment figures – a statistical claim

Allwell Okpi, 'No evidence for big millions of jobs claim by Nigerian senior official', *AfricaCheck*, 27 August 2019 https://africacheck.org/fact-checks/reports/no-evidence-big-millions-jobs-claim-nigerian-senior-official

Case I.2 Intentions of an artist – a claim about an individual

Monique Ngo Mayag, 'Non, ces sculptures ne sont pas une découverte scientifique et n'illustrent pas une prière musulmane', *AFPFactuel*, 3 December 2019 https://factuel.afp.com/non-ces-sculptures-ne-sont-pas-une-decouverte-scientifique-et-nillustrent-pas-une-priere-musulmane

Case I.3 The collapse of a bridge – a material claim

Ange Kasongo, 'Non, le pont qui a cédé en RDC n'a pas été fraîchement inauguré par le président congolais', *AFPFactuel*, 5 November 2019 https://factuel.afp.com/non-le-pont-qui-cede-en-rdc-na-pas-ete-fraichement-inaugure-par-le-president-congolais

Case I.4 The effects of a stroke treatment – a claim about health science

Mary Kulundu and Rachel Yan, 'Doctors warn against "dangerously misleading" posts claiming you can treat a stroke with a needle', *AFPFactCheck*, 7 August 2019 https://factcheck.afp.com/doctors-warn-against-dangerously-misleading-posts-claiming-you-can-treat-stroke-needle

Fact-checkers' selection of which claims to verify reflects, of course, not only their judgement of which claims are feasible to check, affect the public interest, or even draw an audience, but also their capacity to monitor and verify the multitude of claims in circulation. In interviews with the author in 2020, leaders of the six operations whose work I use in the study all acknowledged that their capacity to monitor public information was limited by the size of their teams and the means available to them: even large organisations being able to identify only the 'tip of the iceberg' of false information in circulation, one leader of a fact-checking organisation said. Moreover, while claims that circulate on open social media platforms, or in national print and broadcast media, may be easy to monitor and check, all my interviewees noted that claims spread in closed messaging networks, on local and community radio stations, and in offline community settings such as prayer meetings or social gatherings, can have effects but are hard or impossible to monitor at all or consistently.

*

There are, of course, other means available to researchers to understand the different types and effects of false information in circulation than the evidence to be found in fact-checks, and, before proceeding with this study, I considered several different research avenues. One approach, taken in recent years to understand the challenge false information poses, has been to measure public perceptions of exposure to misinformation. In 2018, for example, a study by the distinguished media scholars Herman Wasserman and Dani Madrid-Morales examined perceptions of exposure to 'fabricated news' in three African countries – Kenya, Nigeria and South Africa – and compared this to levels reported in the United States.[17] In 2020, the polling institute Afrobarometer provided further evidence of public perceptions, finding that almost three in four respondents across Africa believed they were subjected to false and misleading information frequently on social media.[18]

While offering valuable insight into public perceptions of the spread of false information, such studies do not, however, provide evidence of the actual prevalence of false information in circulation, but only of public perception of the problem. This is partly a function of most individuals' limited ability to correctly distinguish between different sorts of accurate and inaccurate information they receive. A 2023 study which argued that aggregating the judgements of large groups of individuals could be used to correctly identify news sources as 'low' or 'high' in quality, recognised that the assessments of what information was false or misleading was often flawed.[19] Meanwhile, if false information spreads not on social, print, or broadcast media but in channels accessed only by members of elites – from internal government communications to think-tank reports – it may still cause or contribute to substantive consequences without being recognised in research based on public perceptions.

With this in mind, an alternative approach to understanding the spread of false information that I considered was to survey the news and information intake of a representative sample of both elite and grassroots populations, over a period of several months, then to assess the accuracy of information to which they were exposed. While this approach could have provided valuable insight into the nature and spread of false information such a broadly representative group receives, it was not feasible, with the means available, to conduct such a survey and assess the accuracy of all the information the audiences received.

Fact-checkers' reports have limitations, of course. The evidence they provide is not, and cannot be, exhaustive. Fact-checkers do not check every claim they see and do not see all claims in circulation. The selection of claims they check reflects, at least in part, their judgement of claims that are feasible to check and have potential to draw an audience. Nevertheless, I argue, the evidence available from the reports examined in this book, all laid out in a database, provides a useful, credible means to identify a broad range of types of false information to which both elite and grassroots populations in an important region of the world were exposed over a six-month period. And the reports provide sufficient evidence on the claims examined to understand the type of claims and the consequences they caused, or may have caused, for individuals and society.

*

Though working now at the University of Westminster, in London, I decided to ground this book in an examination of false and misleading information seen in circulation in sub-Saharan Africa, a region long under-represented in misinformation research. It is a part of the world in which I have spent several years of my life, first working in Nigeria as a journalist for the AFP news agency from 1998 to 2002 and then, from London, as the founder-director of Africa Check, from 2012 to 2019. And while the political, socio-economic, cultural and historical context of every country and continent differs in ways that influences the nature, drivers and consequences of false information that occurs, the evidence from this study provides lessons of a wider pattern of information effects that apply internationally. For this reason, for this book, I both draw on evidence from research undertaken in Africa and around the wider world, and argue that many of the lessons I learned can, and maybe should, be applied elsewhere.

*

To arrive at the set of examples used in the database, I first established a set of 1,600 claims examined in 2019 by the fourteen fact-checking organisations I found then operating on the continent. After assessing all entries, I excluded more than 400 claims which had been found by the fact-checkers to be true, and were thus outside the study's remit. I then excluded just over 800 more for – whatever the interest of the topics – providing insufficient quality of evidence in the fact-check to enable me to reach a clear conclusion about the nature of the claim, its drivers and its actual or potential consequences. Having reduced the database to 402 cases, I examined all remaining claims, breaking evidence down into thirty fields, from the topic of the claim, to the country or countries in which it was observed, the channels or settings in which it appeared, the way in which the claim was false or misleading, and the apparent capacity and motivation of the audience to act on any false understanding caused. In the database, which can be seen on a link set out in Appendix 1, I provide details on 250 of these cases and links to 152 more which were similar to cases already examined.

This process limited the sample to fact-checks from six organisations. Two of the six – AFPFactCheck and Africa Check – provided the most detailed reports and therefore accounted for a large majority of the fact-checks examined in detail. The BBC's fact-checking unit, Reality Check, had just one full-time fact-checker in Africa at the time and I used only two of its fact-checks. I used three reports from Congo

Check, an independent organisation set up in the Democratic Republic of Congo, two from Dubawa and three from ICIR/FactHub, which both operate in Nigeria. And one from Ghana Fact, which operates in that country. All the organisations whose work I used had been found to adhere to the IFCN code of principles, save for the BBC which operates to its own published editorial guidelines.

*

Based on this review of existing literature and the cases of false information examined in the database, I thus, in Part 1, discuss the history, evolution and definitions of 'fake news', 'misinformation', 'disinformation' and 'information disorder' used in the field, explain the terms I use in the study, and identify factors that drive the spread of false information of the types examined in the database.

In Part 2, I briefly review the evolution of media effects theory from the 1920s onward, and set out evidence from both studies and cases examined of wider forms of information effects in particular fields and in its broad societal effects. To do so, requires me to touch on longstanding differences in approach taken in different schools regarding the nature and effects of communication, diverging as they do between viewing communication as either, primarily, the transmission of information, shaping or influencing factual understandings and attitudes, or, primarily, as social or cultural sharing of information for social or cultural ends.[20] And I argue that cases examined in the database show information can be both – different forms of communication contributing, in different contexts, for different audiences, to different forms of factual and representational or symbolic beliefs.[21]

*

Using evidence set out in the fact-checks, I identify more than a dozen cases in the database which evidence shows caused or contributed to specific, substantive consequences for individuals, groups, or society, and the factors common to those and to other similar claims which failed to do so. The cases examined range from a false claim which, evidence from witnesses and participants shows, caused or contributed to the killing of two health researchers and the maiming of a third in Ethiopia in 2018 (Case 1.5), to false claims of an AIDS vaccine that caused or contributed to authorities in the Democratic Republic of Congo changing policy and approving the product for sale (Case 1.6).

Two of Many Fields of Consequence Identified

Case I.5 False information causing or contributing to vigilante violence

Dawit Endeshaw, 'Mob action costs two researchers' lives', *The Reporter Ethiopia*, 27 October 2018 https://www.thereporterethiopia.com/6682/

Case I.6 False information causing or contributing to negative effects for public health

Charlotte Durand and Monique Ngo Mayag, 'Un médicament pour guérir du sida? Un faux, depuis interdit dans plusieurs pays,', *AFPFactuel*, 5 July 2019 https://factuel.afp.com/un-medicament-pour-guerir-du-sida-un-faux-depuis-interdit-dans-plusieurs-pays

In the final part of the book, I draw on this combination of earlier studies of information effects in a wide range of fields and evidence from the cases of false information examined to propose a model of how the different factors I identify shape the potential of cases of false and misleading information to cause or contribute to specific substantive consequences for individuals or society. And I identify factors that shape the field in which such consequences may occur, who may be affected, and the severity and duration of the effects – if caused.

Doing so, I present four ideas that may help fact-checkers, policymakers, and platforms to better understand the nature and consequences of information disorder and promote information integrity. First, is the idea that information disorder, itself, should be seen as a broader phenomenon than the notion adopted among practitioners and policymakers since 2017 suggests.[22] I argue the disorder in information systems around the world encompasses not simply the existence of false and misleading information – misinformation and disinformation – but also lack of access to and trust in accurate information. It follows, I suggest, that the phenomenon requires a broader range of responses than those currently applied.

Second, while false information may spread more easily, and be easier to detect, online than in offline settings, this does not necessarily equate with greater consequences for individuals or society. And I argue it is important for fact-checkers, researchers and others to pay attention to the nature and effects of false information spread in offline platforms and settings as well – from print and broadcast media to parliaments, business meetings and community gatherings.

Third, while the overwhelming majority of research and initiatives in recent years have focused on the effects of false information on public understanding,[23] serious consequences for society also come from false information directly affecting the factual understanding and attitude of members of the elite, not the public. And to properly understand and respond to the potential consequences of false information it is necessary to address also its effects in elite circles – be that in business, among health or social policymakers, or what twentieth-century philosopher Hannah Arendt called 'the internal world of government'.[24]

Fourth, I argue that the model I propose – a series of questions and criteria that I set out in Part 3, and detail in the Appendices – can be used by fact-checkers, researchers, platforms and others to go beyond stale twentieth-century debates about 'strong' or 'weak' media effects to better identify specific false claims and types of false claims with the potential, subject to a variety of factors from audience to context, discussed in detail in Part 3, to cause or contribute to specific negative consequences, directly or over time.

Having set out these ideas, I describe a trial undertaken in the middle of 2024 by senior researchers at three leading, international fact-checking organisations – Africa Check, AFP FactCheck and Full Fact – proving the practicality and utility of the model that I propose. And I provide evidence from an independent assessment of the trial carried out by doctoral researchers at University of Wisconsin-Madison, and proposals for how it might be developed.

Part 1 – What Is 'Fake News'?

In November 2017, the dictionary publisher Harper Collins announced its word of the year: 'fake news'.[1] Given the frequent use of the term by both media and the successful candidate in US elections twelve months earlier, it could be argued that Collins was a year late making its selection. But, late or not, the choice recognised a huge surge in public attention to a once little-known phrase that is, today, widely used and misused by media, the public, politicians and academics alike. In the years since 2016, the term has entered popular and academic discourse. It has been applied by both the public and scholars to blatantly false reports on social media and low-quality news sites. And it has been attached by politicians and their supporters to reports they disagree with in traditional or mainstream media.

Governments, media organisations and online platforms have since 2016 denounced those they say propagate 'fake news' and launched a series of initiatives to counter its spread and effects. These efforts have ranged from changes in laws and regulations[2] to the teaching of media literacy.[3] Other responses have included the growth of fact-checking[4] and 'pre-bunking', the practice of training audiences to identify anticipated types and patterns of false information.[5]

Scholarly research into the nature and effects of the spread of false and misleading information has surged to an unprecedented level.[6] As the computer scientists and Internet researchers Chico Camargo and

Felix Simon noted in 2022, the research of fake and false information is now 'firmly entrenched in various academic disciplines' with numerous courses and entire academic conferences devoted to its discussion.[7] The study of false and misleading information is not, however, a cohesive field. And despite the growth in attention, both policymakers and practitioners still today 'lack good information about the nature of the problem they seek to solve', a review of scholarly literature found in 2021.[8] Laws and regulatory frameworks drawn up, at least in theory, to counter its effects 'often struggle to properly define categories of "harmful content" they seek to regulate'.[9]

In June 2024, a debate about the best means of identifying the effects of false information broke out in an online group of misinformation researchers, cognitive scientists, and others, to which I belong. The debate, one eminent researcher argued, 'arises from people defining the term "misinformation" in different ways'. He was not alone in thinking this. 'There is no consensus' on the definitions of misinformation and disinformation, the head of research at the Cambridge Centre for Science and Policy, Magda Osman, wrote earlier in 2024.[10] And this has severely undermined efforts to counter their spread and effects.

In this first part of the book, I therefore consider the history, usage and meaning of the terms 'fake news', 'misinformation', 'disinformation' and 'information disorder' to seek to answer some of the questions posed.

Chapter 1

DEFINING TERMS: FAKE NEWS, MISINFORMATION AND DISINFORMATION

In works such as *Democracy Hacked*[1] and *This is Not Propaganda*,[2] Dr Martin Moore, the director of the Centre for the Study of Media Communication and Power at Kings College, London, and Peter Pomerantsev, a Ukraine-born British journalist and author, paint a troubling picture of the effects of different forms of false information for society. Identifying an online problem, Moore writes: 'Technology has fractured democracy, and now there's no going back … After years of soundbites about connecting people, the social media giants are only just beginning to admit the scale of the problem.' Pomerantsev agrees: 'We live in a world of "influence operations" run amok, dark ads, psy-ops, hacks, bots, soft facts … We've lost not only our sense of peace and democracy, but also our sense of what those words even mean.'

In earlier works, from 'Lying in Politics',[3] written in 1972 by the philosopher Hannah Arendt, to more recent studies such as *Not Born Yesterday* published in 2020 by cognitive scientist Hugo Mercier,[4] others dismiss concerns about the potential of exposure to false information to significantly influence public attitudes. Such alarm overestimates the gullibility and manipulability of public opinion, they argue. And in an article in *Nature* in 2024, a group of prominent social and political scientists argued many of the concerns expressed are misplaced for a different reason. In the United States, average voters have limited exposure to blatantly false information – 'fake news' – online with exposure highest among a 'narrow fringe', they wrote.[5]

Which of these two schools of thought about the nature and effects of different types of false information is closer to the truth, is one of the main questions that this book seeks to answer. The differences arise in part from the different forms of information that researchers study, the different ways that scholars perceive communication,[6] how they understand the nature of beliefs that are or are not affected by this communication[7] and the attention given to the different processes and contexts in which decisions are made.

To determine the consequences of false information, it is therefore necessary first that we disentangle these three related but distinct phenomena seen as causing negative effects: 'fake news', 'misinformation' and 'disinformation'.

Fake News: An Overused Term for Fabricated News in a Pseudo-journalistic Format

The term 'fake news', which erupted into public discourse in the middle of 2016, is thought by many to be a modern expression. Other languages have long had similar terms. '*Lügenpresse*', (or the lying press), first appeared in the media in Germany in 1914 and was later adopted by authorities in Nazi Germany to undermine trust in their critics in the media.[8] In 2017, then US President Donald Trump falsely claimed credit for the first use of the term in English.[9] It was, however, in June 1890 that the *Cincinnati Commercial Tribune*, a newspaper in the Midwest of the United States, became the first English-language publication known to have used the term, reporting a speaker's complaint that 'fake news … is being telegraphed over the country',[10] applying fake as an adjective to 'news' in an original way.

The person who can most credibly claim responsibility for the term's initial popularisation in English this century is *Buzzfeed News* journalist Craig Silverman who used the expression in 2014 to describe a new form of social media content: 'written in the journalistic style, but … all fake'.[11] Others in the media and public debate, from Trump in the United States to Rodrigo Duterte in the Philippines, then picked up the term and, more than a century after its first recorded use, the expression entered the public mainstream. It rapidly became ubiquitous in both popular culture and academic debate as a catch-all term for inaccurate or disputed information of all sorts.[12]

The way the expression has been used since its widespread adoption has drawn much rightful criticism. First, the critics say, the term is often loosely applied to very different forms of information, causing confusion in public and academic debate about the phenomenon. Second, the term has been adopted, by elites and the public alike, to delegitimise credible reports, and trustworthy media.

Following a pattern set by populist politicians such as Trump and Duterte, the military in Myanmar, for example, used the term to undermine international pressure to respond to reports of ethnic cleansing and genocide in 2017, declaring all such reports 'fake news'.[13] In Nigeria, the army did the same in 2020, using the expression to dismiss accurate reports of a massacre of protestors in Lagos,[14] as 'fake'. Around the world, conspiracy theorists and others have similarly adopted the expression to dismiss accurate information that contradicts their particular worldview.

Concerned by its misuse, academics and policymakers in many countries have called on colleagues not to use the term to avoid giving legitimacy to its propagandistic value.[15] 'This term has been appropriated and used misleadingly by powerful actors to dismiss coverage that is simply found disagreeable,' a high-level working group of the European Union declared.[16]

Compelling as such criticisms are, however, it is evident the term has entered both the popular and academic mainstream and to not recognise it at all would be to ignore reality. Moreover, if used in the purely literal sense, the expression can in fact help distinguish between a form of false or misleading information distinct from others in ways that can be helpful in understanding and countering its negative effects. In 2018, a group of leading US media researchers proposed just such a definition of 'fake news' as 'fabricated information that mimics news media in form but not in organizational process or intent'.[17] Analysing the cases in this study, I identified more than one in five entries as meeting this definition – false or misleading information that is presented in a pseudo-journalistic or news format, with intent to mislead. It is a clear part of the phenomenon of false information.

Of the claims that met this definition, some were 'clickbait' reports created to attract an audience, for revenue or gratification, not to achieve a wider social or political effect. This type of fake news is, in a sense, analogous to that described in a famous 2005 essay by the analytical philosopher Harry G. Frankfurt, who identified what he termed 'bullshit' as information aimed not at persuading an audience of any particular understanding, but 'unconnected with … unconstrained by a concern with truth'.[18]

The second form of fake news identified in the database comprised entries using false information in pseudo-journalistic format to further a political or social goal. One case, for example, was a faked version of a newspaper front page in Cameroon, crafted by supporters of an insurgency to make it appear the newspaper was supporting their separatist agenda. A majority of the 'fake news' entries in the database were created for just such political or social reasons.

While the cases of fake news studied thus differed in their motivation – financial or political – they all used traditional journalistic language and formats either to draw an audience, or to harness or affect the credibility of a real or fabricated media house to meet their goal. This use of a pseudo-journalistic format is what distinguishes fake news from information fabricated in other formats. Since 2016, however, the label 'fake news' has been liberally applied by academics, politicians and commentators to diverse form of false information – both to blatantly fabricated information distributed on social media and low-quality news websites, and to false or misleading claims from public figures and organisations spread in traditional media and in offline community, business and political settings. And this imprecision in the use of these labels, not only in the media and among politicians but also among scholars, has contributed to some of the disagreement about misinformation consequences referred to above – that is, researchers using similar terms to refer to research effects of very different things. Only if restricted to being used as it should be will the term serve a useful purpose, exposing both the intent to deceive with false information and how it seeks to achieve its goals.

Misinformation: A Term for False Information Created by Mistake, False Assumption

While the expression 'fake news' is disputed by many scholars, academics and practitioners are accepting of the term 'misinformation', at least in English. From its first known appearance in print, in a text written by an English clergyman in 1587,[19] the term misinformation has always connoted false information. What has not always been clear is the basis on which the judgement of falsity is made, how and by whom. The challenge for those who study the phenomenon has been, as communication researchers Emily Vraga and Leticia Bode noted in 2020, defining it in a 'consistent and coherent way'.[20]

An important step toward a useful definition came more than twenty years ago when the political scientist James Kuklinski and colleagues identified people as 'misinformed', as distinct from 'ignorant', when they 'confidently hold wrong beliefs'.[21] Misinformation by this definition is information that causes or reinforces a 'confidently held wrong belief'. But who might establish a belief to be 'wrong' and on what basis, remained unclear, however. And as English moral philosopher Bernard Williams noted in *Truth and Truthfulness*, in 2002, while society may, on the one hand, show 'an intense commitment to truthfulness – or, at any rate, a pervasive suspiciousness, a readiness against being fooled', at the same time, it demonstrates 'an equally pervasive suspicion about truth itself: whether there is such a thing; if there is whether it can be more than relative or subjective'.[22]

In 2010, the American political scientists Brendan Nyhan and Jason Reifler took a step toward addressing this, defining misinformation as a factual claim or claims 'not supported by clear empirical evidence and/ or expert opinion'.[23] Seven years later, misinformation researchers Claire Wardle and Hossein Derakhshan went further, identifying misinformation as information shown to be false but 'not created with intention of causing harm'.[24] And since that time, broadly similar versions of this definition have been widely, but not universally, adopted by practitioners and academics in many parts of the world.[25]

The primary area of disagreement remaining is over the presumption of the intention, or lack of intention, of those who create the information to deceive. In a report for the UN's education and cultural agency UNESCO in 2020, computer science and journalism researchers Kalina Bontcheva and Julie Posetti disputed the very concept of misinformation. Even if false information is 'on occasion' shared without intention to mislead, 'it is evident that the content at hand often owes its origin to others' deliberate acts of disinforming citizens with harmful intent,' they argued.[26] For those, like the author, who believe false information is often created and shared more through error or false assumptions than malign intent, Bontcheva and Posetti's argument points, nevertheless, to two notable difficulties with the term misinformation. Firstly, the intentions of those who create false information are not necessarily the same as those of the people who subsequently spread it. Secondly, information accuracy can change over time.

In many languages, just one word is used for different types of false information defined in languages such as English, Arabic, or Indonesian by two. Spanish, for example, uses the term '*desinformación*' to refer to false and misleading information regardless of whether or not it is intended to mislead. Portuguese uses '*desinformação*' the same way. 'We do not find misinformation and disinformation useful distinctions,' a leader of one Latin American fact-checking organisation told the author. French fact-checkers use the terms *désinformation* for false information, and *intox*, which best translates as 'fake news'. The term *misinformation* is 'a very English concept', one French fact-checker told the author.[27] Persian also uses just one term, normally translated as 'incorrect information'.

The Arabic term – 'الخاطئة المعلومات' – translates as '**misinformation**' and 'المضللة المعلومات' translates as 'disinformation'. **Persian** uses just one term – 'نادرست اطلاعات' – for both, and translates as 'incorrect information'. **Indonesians** use multiple different words from *misinformasi* and *disinformasi* to *kabar kibul* and *hoaks.*

Examining evidence about those who created and spread the cases of false information studied for this book,[28] I found that, though they may not have been intended to deceive by those who promoted the claim, several had originated in disinformation, as Bontcheva and Posetti suggested. In Nigeria, for example, news website *Sahara Reporters* reported as fact a false claim about Nigerian President Muhammadu Buhari that had indeed been fabricated to deceive. While it is, of course, possible that the website knew the claim it published was false, there was no proof this was the case. A few days later, news sites in several countries reported as fact, again with no proven intent to mislead, a claim fabricated by a network of fake news sites about Rwandan President Paul Kagame. Again, there was no evidence that the genuine news sites which published the claim knew it was false, but it had, indeed, originated on fake news sites set up to mislead (Case 1.1).

In total, in eleven of the 250 cases I studied, I identified the claim as misinformation which had originated in some form of 'fake news' or disinformation. The phenomenon thus does occur, when disinformation is originated to mislead, and then actively promoted by individuals or organisations who do not or may not know it to be false. And in many cases, while such false claims are not actively promoted by news groups or website they are shared online by ordinary individuals. However, given the eleven claims I identified amount to under 5 per cent of cases examined, the claim that most false information 'often owes its origin to others' deliberate acts of disinforming citizens with harmful intent' is not supported by the evidence.

In around one-sixth of the cases, in fact, evidence in the fact-checks suggests simple errors or failures of understanding caused or contributed to the creation and sharing of the false claim. In July 2019, for example, a newly appointed minister in South Africa gave an interview to a broadcaster about what officials term 'bogus marriages', a loosely defined category that comprises both marriages of convenience – agreed for an ulterior motive – and fraudulent marriages – obtained without the knowledge or consent of one of the parties. The new minister referred to the data as showing all suspect marriages as 'fraudulent' but when the difference was pointed out, admitted he had used the wrong term. There was no evidence of intention to mislead (Case 1.2).

Other database entries examined were proven incorrect but considered *essentially* true by those who spread them, even after facts revealed the claim to be inaccurate. The distinction between what can be considered true or not in such cases is less concerned with literal definitions and more with what constitutes 'real truth'. Since the 1970s, French philosopher and cognitive scientist Dan Sperber has argued for a distinction between what he terms 'factual beliefs' that reflect verifiable strict reality and 'representational', 'cultural', or 'symbolic beliefs' that could be called an 'opinion' and are not held to the same epistemic standards.[29] In a case in the database, a Kenyan journalist shown evidence a video that he believed showed poor conditions in Kenyan schools was actually filmed in Nigeria, insisted his belief was still substantively correct. 'Fact is, there could be worse cases in Kenya, and it does not matter where it is … I stand by my tweet,' he wrote (Case 1.3).

Misinformation – Factors That Play a Role in Origin of False Claims

Case 1.1 – False claim that originated as disinformation shared with no proven intent to mislead

Tendai Dube, 'No, Rwanda's Paul Kagame did not tell journalists that South Africa should be removed from the African Union', *AFPFactCheck*, 20 September 2019, https://factcheck.afp.com/no-rwandas-paul-kagame-did-not-tell-journalists-south-africa-should-be-removed-african-union.

Case 1.2 – Inadvertent error in a broadcast interview

Taryn Khourie, 'Over 2,000 phoney marriages reported in South Africa, but only 1,160 "truly fraudulent"', *Africa Check*, 16 July 2019, https://africacheck.org/fact-checks/reports/over-2000-phoney-marriages-reported-south-africa-only-1160-truly-fraudulent.

Case 1.3 – Source recognises claim in accurate but sees it as broadly true

Mary Kulundu, Monique Ngo Mayag, and Mayowa Tijani, 'Social media posts have located this flooded classroom in various African countries. It was actually filmed in Nigeria', *AFPFactCheck*, 31 October 2019, https://factcheck.afp.com/social-media-posts-have-located-flooded-classroom-various-african-countries-it-was-actually-filmed.

Case 1.4 – Lack of clarity by source causes false inference by audience

Mary Kulundu, 'Protesters set fire to Burkina Faso's parliament in 2014. Why is it trending in Kenya now?' *AFPFactCheck*, 12 July 2019, https://factcheck.afp.com/protesters-set-fire-burkina-fasos-parliament-2014-why-it-trending-kenya-now.

Case 1.5 – Lack of transparency by source causes false inference by the audience

Anne-Sophie Faivre Le-Cadre, 'Ces photos ne montrent pas des détenus au Sénégal mais les conditions de détention y demeurent "extrêmement préoccupantes"', *AFPFactuel*, 6 September 2019, https://factuel.afp.com/ces-photos-ne-montrent-pas-des-detenus-au-senegal-mais-les-conditions-de-detention-y-demeurent.

Case 1.6 – Potential motivation but intent to mislead unproven

Tendai Dube, 'An old image of the trial over the Zuma assassination plot is circulating online again', *AFPFactCheck*, 23 July 2019, https://factcheck.afp.com/old-image-trial-over-zuma-assassination-plot-circulating-online-again.

In total, I found clear evidence in more than 60 per cent of the cases examined suggesting that the information was false or misleading either as the result of an error or false assumption, or, at the most, was not proven to be intended to deceive.

During a heated political debate in Kenya in 2019, for example, a well-known radio host posted a link to a news report published five years earlier on the BBC about a violent protest in Burkina Faso. The message did not claim the report was recent, however, many readers inferred the incident had just occurred: a false assumption by an audience, not proof of the radio host's intent to deceive (Case 1.4). The same happened months later when a prominent Senegalese opposition leader illustrated a blog post about prison conditions in Dakar with a photo of prisoners crowded in a cell. The politician did not state that the photo – of similar scenes in a prison in Malawi – had been taken in Senegal but many readers assumed that it did: again a false assumption by the audience and not proof the politician intended to mislead (Case 1.5).

Other fact-checks provide examples of claims that may well have been created with intent to mislead but proof of intention was lacking. In South Africa, for example, supporters of former President Jacob Zuma circulated courtroom photos they said showed South African media were censoring news of the trial of four men for plotting to assassinate the former president. The media had, in fact, provided coverage of the trial when it took place five years earlier. While those who claimed an ongoing trial was not receiving due coverage may have known their claim to be false, there was no proof this was the case. As the response of the Kenyan audience to the post about earlier events in Burkina Faso showed, people make mistakes and a potential motivation is not proof of intention to mislead (Case 1.6).

Taking evidence from the database as a whole it is clear that, as Bontcheva and Posetti suggest, false information shared without intention to mislead does, on occasion, originate as disinformation. More commonly, however, it originates and is shared in error, false assumptions are made, or it may be intended to deceive but this cannot be proven. This matters, first, because since 2016, governments across the world have introduced or amended legislation to penalise publication of information they find to be false, with intention to deceive assumed, often wrongly.[30] Second, understanding the intention of those who create and spread false information helps make for effective responses. Other things being equal, if false information spreads through error, not intent, interventions that cause audiences to pause and think may reduce its spread. Individuals who make mistakes may be persuaded to correct their mistake in a way that those who spread false information to deceive will not. On this basis I argue that, misinformation – a term considered misleading by some and redundant in many languages – is neither of these things, and, if precisely defined, can be useful in explaining the phenomenon.

'Disinformation': False Information Intended to Deceive for Political or Social Effect

While disinformation is defined, in English, as false or misleading information intended to deceive, not all information intended to deceive is disinformation. A magician deceives to entertain their audience. A satirist makes a false claim to reveal a perceived deeper truth. Disinformation is different. It is false information intended to deceive an audience for political or social effect.

The word 'disinformation' first appeared in English as a transliteration of the Russian word '*dezinformatsia*' (or 'дезинформация') – used by Soviet officials for a programme of covert information activities post-Second World War, aimed at influencing public and official opinion abroad.[31] The first known appearance of the Russian term in print came in 1949. The first known use of the term in French came five years later, followed a year later in English. Whatever its origins, there was nothing remotely new about governments disseminating false information to mislead officials and influence public opinion.

In recent years, many have conflated the term disinformation with others such as 'propaganda', defined in 1927 by the American political scientist Harold Lasswell as 'the management of opinions and attitudes by the direct manipulation of social suggestion'.[32] This overlaps closely with many people's definition of disinformation. For professors of communication Garth Jowett and Victoria O'Donnell, however, the term propaganda refers to 'the deliberate, systematic attempt to shape perceptions, manipulate cognitions and direct behavior to achieve a response that furthers the desired intent of the propagandist'.[33] While this definition would fit many people's understanding of disinformation, there is nothing in it that requires that propaganda is false or misleading. To avoid confusion, I thus use the term propaganda sparingly in this study.

For fact-checkers, researchers and platforms, the hardest aspect of identifying information as disinformation is often not establishing the claim as false or misleading, but identifying who originated the claim and whether or not they understood it to be false. In many cases, false information comes from an unknown source and they must use a variety of methods to identify those behind covert campaigns.

These range from informed speculation, based on establishing *cui bono*, or who might benefit, from the false understanding caused to use of technical forensics and analysis of the particular tools and techniques used to spread the claim.

Whether or not it is possible to identify the origin of a false claim, a review of the database reveals two broad forms of disinformation that can be established by content analysis alone – both involving one or other form of fabrication or doctoring of the content published. The first is imposter content; false or misleading text or images presented to impersonate the name, brand, or style of an individual or organisation, without their knowledge or consent. When a middle-aged man dressed in a Red Cross uniform to declare an Ebola outbreak, in a video posted online in 2019 in the Democratic Republic of Congo, he dressed in a fake Red Cross uniform to deceive his audience (Case 1.7). Those who mimicked the look, name and style of an opposition website in Eritrea and used the platform to publish pro-government reports also knew what they had done, and intended the deception (Case 1.8).

Disinformation – Evidence of Intent to Mislead

Case 1.7 – Video of man in fake Red Cross uniform – intended to deceive

Monique Ngo Mayag, 'Le virus Ebola arrivé à Kinshasa? La Croix-Rouge et les autorités démentent', *AFPFactuel*, 1 August 2019, https://factuel.afp.com/le-virus-ebola-arrive-kinshasa-la-croix-rouge-et-les-autorites-dementent.

Case 1.8 – Activists create lookalike website – intended to deceive

Amanuel Neguede, 'Popular "Eritrean Press" Facebook page warns readers against copycat version', *AFPFactCheck*, 11 December 2019, https://factcheck.afp.com/popular-eritrean-press-facebook-page-warns-readers-against-copycat-version.

Case 1.9 – Activists fabricated polling figures – intended to deceive

Mary Kulundu, 'Ignore these "polling figures" on the popularity of Kenya's possible presidential contenders – they didn't really come from IPSOS"', *AFPFactCheck*, 3 July 2019, https://factcheck.afp.com/ignore-these-polling-figures-popularity-kenyas-possible-presidential-contenders-they-didnt-really.

Case 1.10 – Activists doctored video– intended to deceive

Mayowa Tijani, 'No, London buses are not carrying adverts saying that Buhari rigged Nigeria's election', *AFPFactCheck*, 14 August 2019, https://factcheck.afp.com/no-london-buses-are-not-carrying-adverts-saying-buhari-rigged-nigerias-election.

Case 1.11 – Activists fabricated quotes – intended to deceive

Jennifer Ojugbeli, 'Obasanjo did not say there will be a second war in Nigeria', *Africa Check*, 5 July 2019, https://africacheck.org/fact-checks/meta-programme-fact-checks/obasanjo-did-not-say-there-will-be-second-war-nigeria.

And today, with developments in artificial intelligence enabling the creation of increasingly realistic video, audio and human-like text, the creation of this sort of deceptive imposter content is easier than ever before.

A second type of disinformation identifiable by content analysis alone, is information this is fabricated or doctored to distort audience understanding of the facts. Reviewing the cases in the database, the intention to deceive of those who fabricated polling data about political candidates in Kenya, and presented this under the logo of a respected company, is clear (Case 1.9). The same is true of those who doctored a video of a London bus to suggest it had carried a political advert about recent Nigerian elections. The doctoring of the video was inherently intentional (Case 1.10). This was also the case for those who fabricated quotations or descriptions of events that had not occurred (Case 1.11). Evidence of the fabrication or doctoring quotations or descriptions is also proof of intent to deceive.

Other means to prove intention to deceive are more complex. One indicator of a source's possible intention to mislead may be the refusal to correct claims when presented with indisputable evidence a claim was false. While many studies show that individuals can persist in holding false beliefs for months or years,[34] research indicates that most people will, while not changing their overall view, change a false factual understanding if presented with persuasive corrective information.[35] In such cases, persisting in a false factual claim may be inferred to be intentional. This does not, however, amount to incontrovertible proof.

Other forms of proof exist, however. Three decades ago, documentary evidence emerged that tobacco companies that disputed the carcinogenic effects of smoking knew that their claims were false.[36] Similar evidence emerged more recently showing energy companies have understood the role of fossil fuels in causing climate change for decades yet have sown false doubt about the science.[37] This sort of proof of a source's knowledge is hard to obtain but, when found, can provide evidence of disinformation.

Even in cases where it is possible to identify the origins of false information and prove it was known to be false, establishing motivation may still be complex, however. In 2018, a high-level group of experts brought together by the European Union declared disinformation to be false information designed 'to intentionally cause public harm or for profit'.[38] The definition is flawed in two ways. First, identifying false information created with intent to profit financially as disinformation would also cover other types of false information – such as frauds and scams – which most would not identify as disinformation. Second, while it may be the intention of disinformation campaigns to sow division or unrest in enemy states to cause what they would recognise as 'public harm', disinformation has long been seen by many protagonists as a legitimate tool used for the good of a justified cause. It can be right for rulers to use falsehoods 'when helpful' the philosopher Plato argued in *The Republic* in 375 BCE.[39] German-American philosopher Hannah Arendt, in 1972, argued: 'Truthfulness has never been counted among the political virtues and lies have always been regarded as justifiable tools in political dealings.'[40] Social and political movements spreading false information often "genuinely believe that they are working for the greater good," journalist Peter Oborne wrote in 2005.[41] Allied commanders in the Second World War believed themselves justified using false information to deceive German commanders about plans for the D-Day landings that turned the course of the war in their favour.[42] They, and many since, viewed their actions as spreading disinformation for the public good.

Noting these reservations, it can still be useful to recognise disinformation as intentionally deceptive, and aimed at a political or social goal. In a study published in 2023, the communication researchers Xinyan Zhao and Stephanie Tsang showed that audiences perceive information that has been fabricated to deceive as 'more false' than claims that are merely 'misleading' or taken out of context.[43] Identifying information as not merely false, but false and intended to deceive may, thus, be more effective in correcting a false understanding, than calling everything misinformation. For this reason, I thus define disinformation as information that, according to the best evidence and expert opinion publicly available at the time, is false or misleading, and can be shown to have been known to be so by those who created or spread it for political or social effect – leaving aside the question of whether they considered the effect to be beneficial or harmful for society overall.

Identifying the Ways That 'False' Information Misleads Can Counter Its Effects

As useful as they are for understanding both the basis on which information is identified as false and what is or may be known about intention to deceive, the terms misinformation and disinformation, both however share one flaw in common with the label *fake news* so criticised by many academics and practitioners. All three identify information as being false or misleading but do engage with the way in which the claim creates a false or distorted understanding, or what it is that is false or misleading about it.

Assessing cases examined in the database of this study, I identified ten ways in which information that is in some way false or inaccurate may undermine audience understanding, starting with what we might call 'known unknowns'. When public figures present an **unproven claim** as known fact, they misrepresent what is or was known about the situation or event, at the time. When Nigerian Women's Affairs minister Pauline Tallen told an audience in November 2019 that two million rapes occur every year in Nigeria, there was no reliable data to back up the claim. Whether the figure was an over- or under-estimate the minister caused a false understanding about what was and was not known about the level of sexual violence (Case 1.12).

If properly understood, satire is not disinformation but, rather, makes a false or exaggerated claim to reveal a deeper truth about an individual or society. However, when a false claim that originated as **satire is taken to be true**, the effect can be to cause or reinforce a misunderstanding. When a social activist in Nigeria deliberately misidentified a group of individuals arrested by police in south-east Nigeria to satirise southern attitudes to northern Nigerians, for example, her point was lost on many readers. Among these readers, her satire reinforced the false understanding she sought to expose (Case 1.13).

Authentic content that is labelled, attributed, or identified in a false or misleading way – **mislabelled, misattributed or misidentified content** – is one of the most common forms of false or misleading information identified by fact-checkers. When two French military helicopters crashed in Mali in 2019, killing thirteen, for example, critics of the former colonial power circulated photos from previous crashes and images taken from video games and labelled them as showing the crash site to create a false understanding of the event (Case 1.14).

Other forms of misinformation contain an element of truth but lack crucial details or context and reframe meaning in a way that is substantively **misleading**. In September 2019, for example, a wave of violence broke out in South Africa targeting African nationals. Days later, a video of a former minister making negative remarks about foreigners circulated widely and was presented as the government's view. The video was authentic but the events shown dated from two years earlier, the minister had since been dismissed, and the views he expressed had been repudiated. The video was authentic but the understanding it caused was wrong (Case 1.15).

Claims may also contain an element of truth but, if **overstated or understated**, create an understanding that is false. In 2019, for example, officials in Kenya claimed that all Kenya's forty-seven county governments had allocated more than 20 per cent of their spending to public health. Most had done so, a few had fallen far short, and the claim created a false understanding (Case 1.16). Other claims **conflate situations** to create or reinforce a false understanding. When two road accidents took place one weekend in Bloemfontein, South Africa, for example, news reports conflated the accounts and created a false understanding that preferential treatment had been given to a politician involved in one of the incidents (Case 1.17).

Not only is much authentic content mislabelled or misidentified. It can also be partially or entirely **fabricated or doctored**. At one end of the spectrum, this means entirely fake video and audio can be used to distort understanding of the people and events shown. More commonly, at the moment at least, it means the use of doctored still images and videos and fabricated quotations that change the content's meaning. In 2019, for example, separatists in Nigeria doctored a 2006 photo of then Georgian President Mikheil Saakashvili addressing the European Parliament, replacing his image with that of the main Nigerian separatist leader (Case 1.18). As described above, **imposter content** can be used either to harness or harm the reputation of an individual or organisation, such as the copycat version of an opposition news website in Eritrea, created to spread pro-government reports about events in the country (**1.19**).

For all that most of the different forms of false or misleading information described above thus contain at least an element of accurate information, presented in a way that distorts the understanding caused, many claims are simply false – claims sitting in total contradiction with clear 'brute facts'. In numerous cases I examined, no element material of the claim was accurate. For example, for two years from 2017 onward, separatists in Nigeria spread an entirely false claim that the country's

President Muhammadu Buhari had died and been replaced in government by a foreign body-double, a man identified as 'Jibril from Sudan', thereby making the government illegitimate under the constitution. The claim was entirely made up. Buhari was alive. He ran for office and won again in 2019. There was no stand-in from Nigeria or Sudan (Case 1.20).

As essential as our understanding of the effects of false information in this granular form – the specific false or misleading claim – is to our understanding of misinformation, it is important also to understand the cumulative effects of false claims and narratives made through what online platforms term **coordinated inauthentic behaviour**: the operation of a disinformation network of inauthentic online accounts – or 'sock puppets' – that repeat and spread multiple claims to increase their potential for effect.[44]

Numerous studies, conducted over decades, have shown that repeating information and creating cohesive narratives increases the effect of distinct and related claims, whether true or false, on factual understanding. During the Second World War, the psychologists Floyd Allport and Milton Lepkin established the first clear evidence of the power of repetition to persuade an audience a particular claim is true: identifying what became known as the 'illusory truth effect'.[45] Such findings have been replicated in multiple studies since, showing that repeated exposure to false information 'can increase belief in that misinformation',[46] including belief in highly implausible statements such as that 'the earth is a square' or that 'elephants run faster than cheetahs.'[47]

The false claim that President Buhari had died in 2017, for example, was not a unique false claim, but was repeated via hundreds of linked, coordinated online accounts, operated by supporters of a separatist movement opposed to the Buhari government. Understanding the coordination is key to understanding the spread and effect (Case 1.21). In total, the 250 cases studied in the database fed into more than forty broad false narratives, ranging from claims exaggerating the threat of crime in South Africa, to claims overstating the health risks of vaccines or identifying foreign powers as supporting the separatist movements in Nigeria and Cameroon.

Different Ways in Which a Factual Claim may be False or Misleading

Case 1.12 – Unproven claim

Kunle Adebajo, 'Are 2 million Nigerians raped every year? Here's what we know', *ICIR/FactHub*, 3 December 2019, www.icirnigeria.org/fact-check-are-2-million-nigerians-raped-every-year/.

Case 1.13 – Satire seen as true

Mayowa Tijani, 'These are not Fulani herdsmen captured for armed robbery in southeast Nigeria', *AFPFactCheck*, 22 August 2019, https://factcheck.afp.com/these-are-not-fulani-herdsmen-captured-armed-robbery-southeast-nigeria-its-satirical-post.

Case 1.14 – Mislabelled content

Anne-Sophie Faivre le Cadre, 'Tour d'horizon des infox sur le crash d'hélicoptères au Mali', *AFPFactuel*, 28 November 2019, https://factuel.afp.com/tour-dhorizon-des-infox-sur-le-crash-dhelicopteres-au-mali.

Case 1.15 – Misleading claim

Mayowa Tijani and Tendai Dube, 'This video of a South African minister blasting immigration was filmed in 2017 and he's since been replaced", *AFPFactCheck*, 4 September 2019, https://factcheck.afp.com/video-south-african-minister-blasting-immigration-was-filmed-2017-and-hes-been-replaced.

Case 1.16 – Over/understated

Alphonce Shiundu, 'Claims on Kenya's counties: fact-checking the State of Devolution Address', *Africa Check*, 25 July 2019, https://africacheck.org/fact-checks/reports/claims-kenyas-counties-fact-checking-2019-state-devolution-address.

Case 1.17 – Conflated facts

Vincent Ng'ethe, 'ANC official not arrested for hit-and-run in viral video – but he was arrested for crash on same weekend', *Africa Check*, 26 July 2019, https://africacheck.org/fact-checks/spotchecks/anc-official-not-arrested-hit-and-run-viral-video-he-was-arrested-crash-same.

Case 1.18 – Doctored content

Mayowa Tijani, 'This photo has been edited to falsely show Nigerian separatist leader Nnamdi Kanu addressing the European Parliament', *AFPFactCheck*, 20 September 2019, https://factcheck.afp.com/photo-has-been-edited-falsely-show-nigerian-separatist-leader-nnamdi-kanu-addressing-european.

Case 1.19 – Imposter content

Amanuel Neguede, 'Popular "Eritrean Press" Facebook page warns readers against copycat version', *AFPFactCheck*, 11 December 2019, https://factcheck.afp.com/popular-eritrean-press-facebook-page-warns-readers-against-copycat-version.

Case 1.20 – Outright false claim

Temilade Onilede, 'Picture on Buhari's Death Is False!' *Dubawa*, 26 August 2019, https://dubawa.org/picture-on-buharis-death-is-false/.

Case 1.21 – Coordinated inauthentic behaviour

Mayowa Tijani, 'A separatist group said images of Buhari arriving in Japan were fake. But AFP photos show he did attend Yokohama summit', *AFPFactCheck*, 2 September 2019, https://factcheck.afp.com/separatist-group-said-images-buhari-arriving-japan-were-fake-afp-photos-show-he-did-attend-yokohama.

Why These Definitions Matter

If fact-checkers, researchers, policymakers, platforms wish to understand the nature of the challenge posed by information disorder, it is essential to start by defining terms in consistent, coherent ways. While I agree with many that the terms 'fake news', 'misinformation' and 'disinformation' are all flawed, I argue they can and do serve a useful purpose, if carefully defined and applied.

Properly understood, the term 'fake news' can serve a useful end in establishing both the intentionality and nature of a deception, while the terms 'misinformation' and 'disinformation' establish the basis on which information is identified as false or misleading and may, in some cases, assist understanding of the factors that drove the claim's creation and spread that make it easier to counter.

All three phrases, however, suffer the flaws of overuse and imprecision; they declare information to be false or misleading with no requirement for those that use them to engage with the way in which the claim is false. And if the goal is to counter the negative effects of false information, it is necessary to clearly identify not only the way in which it is false but also the way in which it distorts our understanding, from claims that are unproven but stated as fact to claims that mislabel or lack context or conflate facts. Identifying not only the way in which it is false but also the way in which it is false requires those who dismiss it to engage with the evidence about the claim made and this makes it harder for people to dismiss information that is true or mostly true as something that is false or fake. Acknowledging the element or elements that are accurate in a false claim, and explaining why the claim is still misleading, is also a more effective way of correcting a false understanding than simply stating that it is misinformation.

At the same time, to understand the nature and effects of false information, it is also important to understand the history and evolution of false information – what we know of the tools used now and over time to disseminate false claims, the topics on which false claims can and do occur, and the different channels and settings online and offline in which different forms of false information spread, why and with what effect. And it is important to understand the range of extra-communication factors from the status of the source, the channels or settings in which it appears, the different responses of different types of audiences, and the context to the mechanisms by which decisions are made, that influence whether false information has a substantive potential to cause or contribute to particular consequences for individuals and society.

Chapter 2

WHERE AND WHEN FALSE INFORMATION HAS EFFECT: WHY SETTING AND CONTEXT MATTER

If fact-checkers, policymakers and platforms define false and misleading information with care, but take a narrow view of where and how it circulates and has effect, they will still fail to understand, and counter its negative consequences for individuals and society. Responses to misinformation have broadened in recent years but the field still demonstrates both a lack of historical grounding and a narrow focus on false information spread on a small number of important online platforms, as researchers such as Camargo and Simon, among others, have noted.[1]

The historical view of misinformation tells us false and misleading information has circulated as long as people have communicated, starting with falsehoods daubed in paint on cave walls, voiced in conversations on street corners, printed in books and pamphlets, emerging in talks and speeches at political assemblies, in information fed into government and business meetings and spread widely in print and broadcast media.

Since the political upheavals of 2016, from the Philippines to the United States, governments around the world have introduced or amended dozens of laws and regulations to penalise the spread of what they declare 'false news' online. This has happened in countries from Malaysia and Russia[2] to Ethiopia and Brazil.[3] The European Union and United Kingdom have each introduced legislation aimed at countering harm they say is caused by false and malicious information – respectively the Digital Services Act[4] and Online Safety Act.[5]

Addressing false information online is seen as an effective, overall response to the challenge posed by information disorder. In June 2022,

EU Commission Vice President Věra Jourová declared the European bloc's new code of practice for online platforms a 'comprehensive answer to disinformation', though it related only to digital misinformation.[6] Fact-checking organisations, which once focused on accuracy in political debate in elite settings and traditional media, pivoted after 2016 to put debunking false online claims at the centre of their work.[7] Many media literacy initiatives took the same approach, focused on training students to identify the tell-tale flaws in fake websites, and the teaching of OSINT skills such as geolocation of images and reverse image search.[8] The creation and spread of false information is, however, a much older phenomenon than this approach suggests and its history holds lessons for how we might better understand the situation we face today.

An Evolution In Misinformation: From Artwork and Books to Fax and Digital Messaging

If art historians are to be believed, the first false or misleading images made by our distant ancestors may date back 30,000 years, or more, to the 'ferocious bison on the cave wall … an audacious boast on the part of a prehistoric hunter'.[9] Since the development of cave paintings, society's means of communication have evolved a long way, passing through the emergence of the written word to the invention of the printing press and on to print and broadcast media. And with each evolution, these new tools have been used to spread information, true and false, further and faster than ever before.

In 33 BCE, Octavian, the adopted heir to Roman general Julius Caesar, was vying with his rival Marcus Antonius to succeed Caesar. Antonius was seen by many Romans as a hero and Octavian decided to use false information to undermine support for his adversary. First, he read aloud in the Senate a document, the true origins of which are still disputed, that suggested falsely that Antonius planned to leave his lands to three children he had fathered with Cleopatra, the queen of Egypt – an act regarded as treachery in Rome. Second, Octavian had silver coins made with the heads of Antonius and his lover shown on either side and messages hammered into the rim depicting his rival as a womaniser and drunk. The false claims stamped into every coin used were an early example of a disinformation campaign.[10]

While silver coins were used for disinformation in ancient Rome, a Franciscan preacher named Bernardino da Feltre used sermons to his congregation to disseminate antisemitic falsehoods in Trento, northern Italy, centuries later. Following the disappearance of a two-and-a-half-year-old child in 1475, the Franciscan falsely claimed members of the local Jewish community had abducted and murdered the missing infant. Lay authorities in Italy believed da Feltre's falsehoods and acted on them: detaining, torturing and executing fifteen Jewish men at the stake – victims of a false claim spread by spoken word in a religious setting.[11]

A few years earlier, German craftsman Johannes Gutenberg had changed the history of communication with a seemingly simple invention: the moveable-type printing press. Over the course of a few years, the revolutionary device spread to a dozen European countries, greatly increasing the speed and ease with which publishers could produce books and pamphlets. Between 1462 and 1500, the number of printing workshops using the new technology across Europe rose from four to 1,700. Over the course of five decades, print shops produced more printed books than had been published in total until that time.[12] When a German clergyman, Heinrich Kramer, wrote a book, the *Malleus Maleficarum*, in 1486, laying out a series of false factual claims about witchcraft and prescribing ways to identify and punish witches, the publisher's ability to print and distribute the work across Europe caused Kramer's delusions to have great impact. For two centuries, the writer's false claims gave village heads and church authorities across Europe excuse to persecute, torture and murder thousands of marginalised people, mostly women, whom village and church leaders wanted rid of. In total, an estimated 45,000 people were killed for this reason.[13]

When the first regular daily newspapers began to be transported by railway as trains replaced carts in the nineteenth century, the information they published could travel further, faster than ever before. When it did so, newspapers became a faster and more effective way to deliver not only information that was true, but also false news. And, then as now, those responsible were not always journalists. In 1782, Benjamin Franklin, one of America's founding fathers, ordered a mocked-up image of a newspaper, the *Boston Independent Chronicle*, featuring a false report crafted to undermine support for a peace deal that he opposed.[14]

Just over fifty years later, New York newspaper *The Sun* published what is now considered the world's first large-scale 'fake news' hoax, printing six articles it claimed falsely were based on research published in the *Edinburgh Journal of Science* by respected astronomer Sir John Herschel. Beautifully illustrated with drawings of batlike humanoids, bearded unicorns and bipedal beavers, the reports – which became known as the 'Great Moon Hoax' – claimed falsely to reveal the discovery of life on the moon and caused a huge surge in sales.[15]

Evolution in communication continued with the emergence of film and radio. When US radio stations broadcast a 1938 radio adaptation of H.G. Wells' book *War of the Worlds*, the simulated news reports of a planetary invasion were understood rightly to be entertainment by all but a few hundred of the listeners. Those who took the simulated news reports seriously, however, were duly alarmed. Media reports of the alarm the programme caused then exaggerated the impact of the event and reinforced fears among politicians and others that the new medium was a powerful tool capable of reaching and influencing the understanding and behaviour of millions of people, live.[16] Over the following decades, film, radio and television would all come to be used for disseminating news and propaganda for governments of all colours, from radio broadcasts by Nazi authorities in Germany, and across Europe, during the Second World War, to Russian state-run television promoting the Kremlin's view of the war against Ukraine that began in 2022.[17]

Around the world, authorities have long expressed concern about the effects and potential effects of false information on public opinion and behaviour, and responded by banning and punishing publication of information they deem untrue. Publication of reports that 'scandalized the King or the great men of the realm' were criminalised in England in 1275. In 1536, a later English king, Henry VIII, decreed a ban on writings containing 'open and manifest errors and slanders'. The same approach has been taken again and again, before and since, by authorities around the world.[18]

One source of comfort to authorities alarmed by the spread of false information was, nevertheless, that the different tools of communication described above – from false claims displayed in wall paintings, hammered into coins, or spread in books, or on film, radio and television – all required either considerable time or resources or both to publish and distribute their claims. The fantastical delusions of a witch-hunting cleric or the political propaganda of a radio station took time and resources to bring before a wide public. The ownership and operation of newspapers, film, radio and television was beyond the reach of most members of the public, and could be quite easily controlled by the authorities. The development of telecommunications and devices such as the fax machine and photocopier in the late nineteenth and early twentieth centuries, however, enabled members of the public to communicate directly with ever wider audiences, at greater speed, than ever before. And then emerged the changes of the digital era.

Effects in Africa: From the Banal to Apartheid, Genocide and Harm to Public Health

False claims and misleading narratives have emerged, over time, in every part of the world, from political falsehoods to myths about subjects ranging from daily life to history, the fourteenth-century Arab historian and polymath Ibn Khaldun famously recorded. 'There are various reasons that make this unavoidable … Prejudice and partisanship obscure the critical faculty and preclude critical investigation,' he wrote.[19] The same is true in the spread of false information both online and offline today. And, in Africa, from which much of the evidence for this book comes, the consequences of false claims have ranged, over the years, from mundane grievances to shoring up the apartheid regime in South Africa, contributing to genocide in Rwanda and catastrophic effects on public health in South Africa and Nigeria.

*

In 1978, South African Prime Minister Balthazar Johannes 'John' Vorster was obliged to resign, first as prime minister and then, a year later as president, over revelations that he had authorised a secret disinformation campaign targeting domestic and foreign opponents.[20] In what became known as 'Muldergate', or 'the Information Scandal', it was revealed that the South African government had operated an unauthorised slush fund of $72 million (equivalent to around $300 million in 2024) to run a covert programme of disinformation aimed at shoring up the apartheid regime. Undeterred by fears of a new scandal, no sooner had outrage died down than the new government established a new secret unit with orders to use false information and rumour to undermine the reputation of and support for those hostile to the apartheid authorities; planting false reports in domestic media and fabricating statements by anti-apartheid activists that would undercut their credibility with supporters and the wider public..

The 'disinformation … libel and manipulation [was] of such a mischievous type that, in situations of acute unrest, they could lead to murder and other bloodshed,' the Leiden University historian Stephen Ellis noted in 1998, following revelations about the new unit's operations.[21] Much effort went, with some reported success, into influencing attitudes among foreign leaders and the public overseas 'smearing the ANC by means of a calculated dirty-tricks campaign, while image-washing the National Party', Paul Erasmus, a former deputy commander of the unit, known as Stratcom, acknowledged many years later.[22]

*

In the months leading up the genocide in Rwanda in 1994, leaders of the extreme-nationalist Hutu Power movement used managerial roles in prominent media outlets to spread false factual information and hate speech and to incite genocide and crimes against humanity.[23] Chief among these were directors of the ill-famed *Radio-Télévision Libre des Milles Collines* (RTLM) radio station, found guilty in hearings of the International Criminal Tribunal for Rwanda which took place in 2003, of using false information and hate speech to build support for the genocide that followed.

In February 1994, for example, the radio warned Hutu citizens that the opposition Rwandan Patriotic Front (RPF), a military force led mainly by ethnic Tutsi soldier-politicians, was poised to attack the capital, and murder the majority of its Hutu residents. While it was true that the RPF had advanced on the city, it had no such plans for an attack and mass murder, but the false claims spread alarm and were found to have been instrumental in motivating public participation in the killings of Tutsis that followed. 'What RTLM did was almost to pour petrol, to spread petrol throughout the country little by little, so that one day it would be able to set fire to the whole country,' the international tribunal heard.[24]

*

In 2003, the World Health Organization launched what it hoped would be a final push in a global initiative to eradicate the last world's last major reservoirs of the poliomyelitis virus, then found in northern India, Pakistan, Afghanistan and Nigeria. The initiative failed after false rumours spread in the community in northern Nigeria that the vaccine had been doctored to add HIV, anti-fertility and carcinogenic agents, and the whole campaign was, in fact, not aimed at tackling polio. It was part of a wider attempt by Western powers to reduce the world's Muslim population.[25]

Given negative experiences in the past, and the fact that the four areas where the campaign was taking place had mainly Muslim populations, the rumours convinced a group of powerful northern Nigerian state governors. Nigerians were naturally sceptical about Western firms after past controversies including an ethically flawed trial conducted by US drug company Pfizer in Nigeria in the 1990s, and many in northern Nigeria were suspicious of Western institutions more widely.[26] 'We believe that modern-day Hitlers have deliberately adulterated the oral polio vaccines with anti-fertility drugs and contaminated them with certain viruses which are known to cause HIV and AIDS,' the head of the Supreme Council for Shariah in Nigeria told Nigerian media.[27] The state governors banned the vaccination campaign and by the time the ban was reversed, hundreds of thousands of Nigerians had missed their vaccinations. An outbreak of polio spread rapidly across Nigeria and beyond, leading thousands of people to contract the disease in Nigeria and eight formerly polio-free West African countries. Eventually, the Nigerian strain of the virus was recorded in countries as far away as Yemen, Saudi Arabia and Indonesia. This happened because politicians changed policy on the basis of a false claim. The outbreak changed the lives of thousands of people around the world.[28]

*

While the rumours that distorted health policy in Nigeria emerged in community settings, the claim that changed health policy in another country first appeared in scientific journals and was debated at a round table before becoming policy. The false notion concerned the links between HIV and AIDS.

In 2000, as the AIDS pandemic was sweeping through South Africa, President Thabo Mbeki discovered an academic paper published more than a decade earlier by a German-American molecular biologist, based at Berkeley, in California. In the paper, Professor Peter Duesberg argued that HIV is not the cause of AIDS. The condition, he argued, the result, in the West, of recreational drug use and in Africa of reduced immunity due to malnutrition and poor drinking water. Attracted by the false claim, Mbeki invited the professor to South Africa and asked him to sit on a 44-member Presidential Advisory Panel on HIV and AIDS.

Days later, Mbeki publicly endorsed Duesberg's flawed claim. South Africa would not provide antiretroviral drugs (ARVs) to treat AIDS and prevent mother-to-child transmission, the president announced. The country would focus, instead, on poverty eradication and diet instead. The new policy was disastrous. Looking at treatment and mortality data for the period 2000 to 2005, public health researcher Pride Chigwedere and colleagues, at the Harvard School of Public Health, found that 'More than 330,000 lives … were lost because a feasible and timely ARV treatment program was not implemented in South Africa.'[29] And comparing mortality data in provinces run by the ANC with data from the province run by the opposition, another study came to similar findings. 'If the national government had used ARVs for prevention and treatment at the same rate as the Western Cape … then about 343,000 deaths could have been prevented,' the study found.[30] Both reviews attributed the catastrophic change in public policy to the president's acceptance of a false health claim.

*

One common element, to all these false claims, is that they all emerged and caused consequences for individuals and society long before the emergence of social media and messaging platforms. And all used primarily non-digital means of communication which are still used to spread false information today. As the philosopher Harry Frankfurt noted in 2005, it was then, 'impossible to be sure that there is relatively more ['bullshit'] nowadays than at other times. There is more communication of all kinds in our time than ever before, but the proportion that is bullshit may not have increased.'[31]

The situation has changed. Since that time, the new tools of online communication that have been developed have done more than simply change the volume of communication. They have changed the rules of public communication, enabling individuals to create and spread information rapidly, often anonymously, and reduced incentives for accuracy. They have added whole new spheres of communication to those used previously, and this explains, at least in part, the focus of research and responses on false information in the digital field.

That said, the primary lesson of the brief history set out above – just a few examples from just one region of the world – is that the dominant focus of research and responses to the spread and effects of false information in the digital space alone, to the exclusion of false information in other settings and contexts, fails to reflect the clear evidence that false information circulating offline – in print and broadcast media, community and religious settings, and parliamentary and official meetings – can and does cause or contribute to serious consequences for individuals and society. And understanding the nature of this false information and its effects requires equivalent levels of research to that on false information spread online.

*

Settings and Contexts of False Information Examined for the Study – From Online Platforms, to Media, to the Street, Business Meetings and Parliaments

Examining the claims studied for this book, I identified twelve different types of channel, platform, setting, or context in which claims circulated – ranging from social media and messaging platforms, to print and broadcast media, placement on street posters and product labels, religious settings and parliamentary meetings. The claims that circulate in these different channels and settings vary not only in terms of format but also in the nature of the communication, the type of claim made, the audience reached, the perceived authority of the source of information and the capacity of the audience to act on the understanding caused and, thus, the potential for consequences to occur.

Since interest in the field of false information surged post-2016, by far the most attention has been paid to the spread of false information on a relatively small number of large social media and messaging platforms – particularly Alphabet's Google and YouTube, Meta's Facebook, Instagram, Threads and WhatsApp, Telegram, ByteDance's TikTok and X, formerly known as Twitter. False claims posted on these platforms also accounted for almost 90 per cent of all entries in the database of this study; this being a reflection of both the relative ease of monitoring information on online platforms, and, in part at least, the financial support given to fact-checkers to verify misinformation on such spaces.[32] This might be considered merited given the potential of such platforms for large-scale reach. To consider just one example among the more than two hundred examined, a false claim that South African telecoms provider MTN was giving away gifts to people who followed them online was shared hundreds of thousands of times, with tens of thousands of people responding to the scam promoted (Case 2.1). Other content appeared not as one-off claims but repeated in similar or different versions on multiple platforms, developing or reinforcing strong false narratives about topics from vaccines to the activities of foreign countries.

Though more difficult to monitor than claims appearing on open social media platforms, false claims that spread in group emails and in audio messages sent direct to people's phones can also reach wide audiences, to great potential effect. After platforms including Meta's Facebook and Instagram, and later TikTok, stepped up measures to counter the spread of information seen as potentially harmful after 2016, many who promote contested information switched to using group emails and audio notes to avoid unwanted scrutiny. A false claim examined for this study that promoted a dangerously ineffective form of stroke treatment was an early example of the practice, circulating via email for decades in

Asia before later spreading on social media (Case 2.2). Another claim – that an Ebola vaccine delivered in Eastern Congo contained a poison developed in Rwanda to kill Congolese – spread to mobile phone users as an anonymous voice note (Case 2.3).

Beyond social media, false information has long been studied in mainstream print, broadcast and online media, and found to have important effects. In 2020, researcher Yochai Benkler and colleagues at the Berkman Klein Center for the Internet and Society at Harvard University analysed over fifty-five thousand media stories, and millions of social media posts, and concluded that 'contrary to the focus of most contemporary work on disinformation', what they termed a 'highly effective disinformation campaign' about the risk of voter fraud in the US presidential elections had been driven by existing elements in mainstream broadcast media and the political elite. 'Social media played only a secondary and supportive role,' the researchers said. The findings were consistent with an earlier study which found that US political and media elites were 'far more influential in spreading false beliefs than Russian trolls or Facebook clickbait artists'.[33] Of the false claims examined in this book, numerous were carried in respected print and broadcast media, and shown by audience responses to have influence with politicians and policymakers (Case 2.4).

Much of the public discussion of false information post-2016 relates to false information appearing, first, not on major social media platforms or mainstream media but, first, and sometimes only, on websites with small, niche audiences – for satire, hyper-partisan and junk news, at one end of the content scale (Case 2.5), and institutional and corporate websites, at the other. A group of political scientists writing in *Nature* argued in 2024 that while false information spread to a 'narrow fringe' on niche hyper-partisan and junk news sites can have consequences – influencing behaviour among a motivated fringe – these consequences, if they occur, would be different to, and perhaps more limited than, those caused by information spread to a wider mainstream audience.[34]

For false information spread through hyper-partisan websites (Case 2.6), or via junk or fake news sites (Case 2.7), to cause or contribute to substantive consequences beyond the actions of a fringe often requires that the messages are picked up and amplified in large social media platforms, by political elites and mainstream media. While, other things being equal, information on institutional and corporate websites (Case 2.8) is more likely to be perceived as credible than information on hyper-partisan or junk news sites, it still needs amplification on other platforms to reach more than a niche audience and – in most cases – to contribute to a substantive consequence.

*

As the above discussion indicates, most research of misinformation in recent years has focused on whether false information affects the factual understanding and beliefs of the general public.[35] Less attention, by contrast, has been paid to the influence of false information on the understanding or opinion among decision and policymaking elites. As both history and examples in the database show, however, false information often spreads offline too, in parliaments and other political and policymaking settings where – depending on the topic, context and capacity of those whose understanding is affected to act – the false claim may affect the decisions of policymaking elites in ways that affect society as a whole.

In a case examined in the database, for example, South Africa's police minister falsely claimed during a parliamentary debate about police performance and the force's budget in 2019, that police numbers in South Africa were below the internationally recommended levels for a country of its size. Made in Parliament ahead of the vote on a higher budget, the claim had potential to have influenced lawmakers' judgement, voting through a new budget and not tackling underlying problems identified by others as affecting police performance (Case 2.9).

False claims appearing in academic journals and think-tank and conference reports also have potential influence on decision-making by policymakers, just like claims in parliamentary settings. False claims of a link between vaccines and autism were first published in *The Lancet*, and have influenced the decision-making of senior health officials in the second administration of US President Donald Trump.[36] The false claim that HIV does not cause AIDS that influenced health policy in South Africa a quarter of a century before that, first appeared in an academic journal too.[37] In 2012, an investigation by the Erasmus Medical School in the Netherlands found that one of its most eminent researchers had used 'fictitious data' and 'knowingly unreliable data' in formulating guidelines promoting the use of beta blockers for patients prior to certain types of surgery, affecting decisions by health practitioners and policymakers. This had deadly effects on a staggering scale.[38] Confidence in scientific publishing overall has been undermined in recent years by evidence of the failure to replicate numerous published studies.[39] And what is true in science and wider academic publishing, is even truer in the world of think-tanks and institutions; sometimes for reasons of bias but often due to errors in understanding. To consider a case from this study as an example, an official body in Kenya – the National Aids Control Council – published figures in 2018 on the populations most affected by HIV infections. The figures substantially over-estimated the prevalence of HIV among adolescents and understated spread among young adults (Case 2.10). Officials acting on the false data thus risked misdirecting support needed by young adults to adolescent populations.

Compared with information shared in online and offline media, or parliamentary settings, false information spread, peer-to-peer in offline community settings – from religious meetings and impromptu gatherings to taxi parks and marketplaces – is difficult or impossible to monitor efficiently and consistently and news of false claims spread in these settings often emerges only when reports of incidents appear later. In December 2019, for example, false claims spread peer-to-peer among the congregation of a church in a small Nigerian town that the church's pastor had been arrested and the body of a missing child had been discovered under the altar. Tension over the disappearance was running high and the false claims caused the crowd to attack the church, one of more than fifteen cases examined in the database which originated in an offline community setting, causing incidents of abuse, violence and, in one case, killings (Case 2.11).

In addition to claims spread by word-of-mouth, false claims about health and social topics from false job offers to miracle cures appear commonly on street posters, public signage and product labels all across Africa, and in many parts of the world. Appearing, as they do, in places and on products that consumers use to decide about jobs to apply for or medications to take up, such false claims have substantive potential functional effects. In 2023, UN agencies reported almost half a million deaths a year in Africa alone, due to mislabelled and substandard health treatments.[40] However, with rare exceptions, the false claims made on posters, signs and product labels have drawn little attention from fact-checkers and researchers of misinformation, in part, perhaps, because of the difficulty of monitoring such information compared to monitoring information online or in the media. An exception examined in the database is a claim, made both online and on a product label, for an ineffective health treatment promoted as an AIDS vaccine (Case 2.12).

Settings and Platforms Where False Claims Appear

Case 2.1 – Large social media and messaging platforms

Mayowa Tijani, 'This is a scam to get your details – MTN is not giving 122gb to customers in Nigeria', *AFPFactCheck*, 15 October 2019, https://factcheck.afp.com/scam-get-your-details-mtn-not-giving-122gb-customers-nigeria.

Case 2.2 – Chain emails

Mary Kulundu and Rachel Yan, 'Doctors warn against "dangerously misleading" posts claiming you can treat a stroke with a needle', *AFPFactCheck*, 7 August 2019, https://factcheck.afp.com/doctors-warn-against-dangerously-misleading-posts-claiming-you-can-treat-stroke-needle.

Case 2.3 – Audio notes

Rodriguez Katsuva, 'Faux, le vaccin contre Ebola n'est pas un poison mortel pour tuer les Congolais', *CongoCheck*, 27 July 2019, https://congocheck.net/faux-le-vaccin-contre-ebola-nest-pas-un-poison-mortel-pour-tuer-les-congolais/.

Case 2.4 – Mainstream print, broadcast and online media

Motunrayo Joel and David Ajikobi, 'What a waste: fact-checking four claims about Nigeria's garbage problem', *Africa Check*, 26 July 2019, https://africacheck.org/fact-checks/reports/what-waste-fact-checking-four-claims-about-nigerias-garbage-problem.

Case 2.5 – Satire sites

Mayowa Tijani, 'The tale of a Nigerian who hacked the US government to grant his friends citizenship? It started on a satirical site', *AFPFactCheck*, 20 December 2019, https://factcheck.afp.com/tale-nigerian-who-hacked-us-government-grant-his-friends-citizenship-it-started-satirical-site.

Case 2.6 – Hyper-partisan sites

Jennifer Ojugbeli, '"Biafran Airlines" plane? No, photo of Lufthansa Airbus', *Africa Check*, 23 October 2019, https://africacheck.org/fact-checks/meta-programme-fact-checks/biafran-airlines-plane-no-photo-lufthansa-airbus.

Case 2.7 – Junk news sites

Africa Check, 'South African police stations to close at 6pm to avoid criminals? No, fake quote from old fake news site', 13 September 2019, https://africacheck.org/fact-checks/meta-programme-fact-checks/south-african-police-stations-close-6pm-avoid-criminals-no.

Case 2.8 – Institutional or corporate websites

Allwell Okpi, 'No, malaria doesn't kill 300,000 people in Nigeria a year, as insurance seller claimed', *Africa Check*, 19 September 2019, https://africacheck.org/fact-checks/reports/no-malaria-doesnt-kill-300000-people-nigeria-year-insurance-seller-claimed.

Case 2.9 – Parliaments and other political or official settings

Cayley Clifford, 'South Africa's police recruitment drive based on dubious UN standard', *Africa Check*, 17 July 2019, https://africacheck.org/fact-checks/spotchecks/south-africas-police-recruitment-drive-based-dubious-un-standard.

Case 2.10 – Academic, think-tank reports

Vincent Ng'ethe, 'No, adolescents don't account for half of new HIV infections in Kenya', *Africa Check*, 29 August 2019, https://africacheck.org/fact-checks/reports/no-adolescents-dont-account-half-new-hiv-infections-kenya.

Case 2.11 – Offline community settings

Segun Olakoyenikan, 'Remains of a missing baby discovered under a church altar in Nigeria? No evidence yet', *AFPFactCheck*, December 6, 2021, https://factcheck.afp.com/remains-missing-baby-discovered-under-church-altar-nigeria-no-evidence-yet.

Case 2.12 – Product label or public sign

Charlotte Durand and Monique Ngo Mayag, 'Un médicament pour guérir du sida? Un faux, depuis interdit dans plusieurs pays', *AFPFactuel*, 6 July 2019, https://factuel.afp.com/un-medicament-pour-guerir-du-sida-un-faux-depuis-interdit-dans-plusieurs-pays.

*

The first lesson we should draw from this review of the tools, channels, settings and contexts used to spread false information – in Africa as elsewhere – is that false information emerges in many different formats, not only online but also offline. False information, the samples examined show, appears as doctored images spread online.[41] It spreads peer-to-peer as deadly rumours at the school gate.[42] It emerges as a simple error in a broadcast interview[43] and as a complex false claim set out in respected academic journals.[44] For all the necessary focus on false information spread on social media, almost half of the claims in the database and possibly more, appeared first in another channel or setting. And in many cases, subject to a variety of factors, it had potential to cause or contribute to substantive consequences for individuals or society.

Second, it is clear from cases studied in the database that some types and topics of false information are more likely to appear in some channels or settings than in others. Other things being equal, financial scams and hoaxes are more likely to appear on social media or in messaging apps or emails, than in print or broadcast media. And false information about arcane aspects of public policy, are more likely to appear first in a parliamentary debate, or a think-rank report, than in a community setting or on social media. These differences, of course, carry lessons for researchers, fact-checkers, policymakers and platforms seeking to understand and counter particular potential effects about where to focus their efforts.

Third, it is clear from the cases studied that where and when false information appears – and thus the topic, the audience and the context in which it is exposed, and the capacity of that audience to act on the understanding caused as a result – affects its potential to cause or contribute to substantive consequences. And, this being the case, if the aim of society is to counter negative consequences, it is necessary to understand and respond to the effects of false information in not only one, but all these different settings.

At the same time, it is also clear from examining cases in the database that public understanding is affected not only by the spread of false claims or narratives, but also by other aspects of information disorder, from the denial of easy access to clear, accurate information to the distorted focus, or partisan selection, of information to which the public and elites are exposed. This is the challenge I discuss next.

Chapter 3

RETHINKING THE NATURE AND DRIVERS OF INFORMATION DISORDER

When interest in false information surged in 2016, misinformation researchers Claire Wardle and Hossein Derakhshan identified the challenge faced as 'information disorder', defining the phenomenon as three forms of problematic information: 'misinformation', 'disinformation' and 'malinformation'.[1] The first two of these are the different forms of false or misleading information discussed in Chapter 1. Malinformation was defined as genuine but private information published to inflict harm on an individual or group. Forms of malinformation, they suggested, would include the nonconsensual sharing of sexual images and the public release of personal health information. Others would later argue that definitions of malinformation could include hate speech and malign behaviours such as trolling or doxing.

Sceptics of the concern expressed about information disorder since 2016 dispute these and other widely used definitions as 'too amorphous' and argue that those they identify as media elites and policymakers define information as true or false by arbitrary or subjective standards. Taking a narrow view of the real challenge of information disorder as limited to information that can be shown to be entirely false, they dismiss the fears expressed about misinformation and disinformation as a 'moral panic' about a limited problem.[2] Doing so, such critics fail to recognise the capacity of accurate information, seen out of context, and inaccurate information, whether wholly or only partially false, to cause a substantively false factual understanding and real world effects.

They also fail to acknowledge that what undermines public understanding is not only exposure to false or misleading information. Rather it is a three-fold disruption of the information system: the circulation of false and misleading information, the lack of access to and trust in accurate information, and the distorted focus in, or partisan selection of, information to which people are exposed. This understanding matters since, if accepted, it implies a response or responses focused not solely on restrictions of information but also on enabling greater access to accurate information, and greater plurality in the information to which society is exposed.

*

Since the term information disorder emerged in the field in 2017, it has been taken up widely, cited in academic papers and referred to in institutional and practitioner reports. According to Nirmal Kandel, an official at the World Health Organization in Geneva, the expression may be used to refer to a 'psycho-social syndrome' – the condition of sharing or developing false information – requiring counselling for 'sufferers'.[3] The term is today widely used but what constitutes information disorder is still 'vague and complex', a study of disinformation in the Global South noted in 2022.[4]

In regular public discourse, the term 'disorder' is most commonly applied to describe a state of confusion or disruption of the functioning of a complex system, as shown by the terms 'medical' or 'political' disorder. Using it in this sense, the term information disorder ought to apply not only to three forms of problematic information but to the broader disruption of the information system that causes the unwelcome condition: an undermining of public understanding.

What we mean when we talk of communication, and how individuals and society shape, use and are influenced by it divides academics. As the late communications theorist and professor of journalism James W. Carey noted in 1989, the role of communication in society can be seen through two distinctly different prisms which he called the 'transmission view of communication and a ritual view'. The former view, which Carey believed an 'exhausted … mechanical analysis', understands communication in terms of 'imparting … sending … or giving information to others'. The latter perspective, which Carey adopted, sees communication in terms of ritual and drama and 'linked to terms such as "sharing", "participation", "association", "fellowship", and "the possession of a common faith" '.

Communication, in this view, is less concerned with 'the act of imparting information' and more with 'the representation of shared beliefs'.[5]

Reviewing the communication examined in detail in the database, it is clear that we can and should see communication as both of these things: at times, the 'transmission of information' and, at times, an act of association or 'representation of shared beliefs', serving social ends. To do this, we need to recognise the distinction between what French philosopher Dan Sperber identifies as 'factual' and 'representational' beliefs.[6] This broad view of communication and belief can help cast a new light on how we understand information disorder, and the way people construct and apply different forms of belief.

The Effects of False and Misleading Information On Attitude and Understanding

Critical writers, philosophers and others have long argued that the effects of false information on public attitudes and opinions are exaggerated. Opinions, once formed, are slow to change, these sceptical thinkers suggest. For some, this is a result of individuals selecting information to confirm existing views. 'The human understanding when it has once adopted an opinion draws all things else to support and agree with it,' the English philosopher Francis Bacon declared in 1620.[7] For others, people are simply not as manipulable as some maintain. 'The psychological premise of human manipulability has become one of the chief wares that are sold on the market of common and learned opinion,' the writer Hannah Arendt argued fifty years ago.[8] French cognitive scientist Hugo Mercier agreed. 'We don't credulously accept whatever we're told … On the contrary, we are skilled at figuring out who to trust and what to believe,' he suggested.[9]

Attitudes and opinions are shaped more by our experiences and the attitudes or opinions of those we know and trust than by what we see or read in mass media, the American sociologist Paul Lazarsfeld and colleagues argued in 1948;[10] fellowship and shared beliefs playing a greater role than information in shaping opinions – communication serving as ritual as James W. Carey said. In his 1960 work *The Effects of Mass Communication*, the American communications theorist Joseph Klapper argued the primary effect of mass media on public opinion is the reinforcement of existing opinions and attitudes. 'Persuasive mass communication functions far more frequently as an agent of reinforcement than as an agent of change,' he maintained. Minor changes in understanding or in the intensity of an attitude or opinion also occur but less frequently. Mass media can be 'quite efficient in creating opinions among people who were not previously inclined one way or another,' he acknowledged, but major changes in attitude are possible but rare.[11]

What evidence is available today suggests such philosophers, cognitive scientists and communications theorists all correctly identify the limited effects that brief exposure to new information typically has on long and firmly held opinions. This finding is confirmed by multiple studies, from a famous investigation of the persistent false beliefs of a religious cult in the United States whose doomsday predictions in the 1950s failed to materialise,[12] to laboratory studies of the struggles of new information, true or false, to change persistent false beliefs more recently.[13] What such perspectives do not always reflect is evidence from other studies that show that false information may often influence individuals' factual understanding in other, consequential ways, such as misleading particular voters about the time at which polling ends in an election to misdirecting them about the best route to take for safety in a natural disaster.[14] Nor do such perspectives reflect evidence that information that is repeated or feeds into a broad narrative may shape and affect some individuals' attitudes and opinions over the long term.

*

Examining the effects on understanding of the false information in the database, I first reviewed indicators of their audience members' prior understanding of the topic from the readers' and viewers' profiles and comments. I then reviewed their responses to the claims, such as written comments and online reactions, the adoption of the false claim in subsequent communication and evidence of behaviour based on the false understanding caused.

And, as set out in more detail in Chapter 5, I found clear evidence of a range of effects. This ran from false claims having no observed substantive effect on factual understanding among most or all the audience in just over one-fifth of cases studied (Case 3.1), to claims causing a minor change in factual understanding, or intensity of attitude, in just under one-fifth of the cases examined (Case 3.2). In just under half the cases examined, I identified false claims as confirming or reinforcing an existing understanding (Case 3.3), and in more than half of cases I identified claims as causing or contributing to a specific new false factual understanding (Case 3.4). Many of the claims studied, of course, caused more than one effect on understanding, depending on the prior understanding and attitude of different audience members.

Claim Effects On Individuals' Factual Understanding

Case 3.1 – No substantive effect on factual understanding

Dancan Bwire, 'Weeping soldier from DRC, not Nigeria', *Africa Check*, 30 July 2019, https://africacheck.org/fact-checks/meta-programme-fact-checks/weeping-soldier-drc-not-nigeria.

Case 3.2 – A minor change in factual understanding, intensity of attitude

Monique Ngo Mayag, 'Non, le Tchad n'a pas les tarifs Internet les plus élevés au monde', *AFPFactuel*, 25 July 2019, https://factuel.afp.com/non-le-tchad-na-pas-les-tarifs-internet-les-plus-eleves-au-monde.

Case 3.3 – Reinforcing an existing factual understanding

Monique Ngo Mayag, 'Le corossol n'est pas un remède miracle contre le diabète', *AFPFactuel*, 12 November 2019, https://factuel.afp.com/le-corossol-nest-pas-un-remede-miracle-contre-le-diabete.

Case 3.4 – Causing a specific new false factual understanding

Tendai Dube, 'False kidnapping rumours spread during South Africa violence', *AFPFactCheck*, **9** September , https://factcheck.afp.com/false-kidnapping-rumours-spread-during-south-africa-violence.

See a longer discussion of the effects of these and other cases in Chapter 5.

Taken as a whole, the evidence from the cases examined for this book reinforces both of the findings of the existing studies cited: first, that long-held attitudes are typically slow to change and false information commonly has a reinforcing effect, and second, that false and misleading information may also – subject to multiple factors discussed below – have potential to influence the factual understanding and attitudes of at least some of the individuals exposed to it, in ways that have potential to cause or contribute to substantive negative consequences. And, on this basis, false or misleading information is or can be an important factor in information disorder – affecting public understanding and causing real world effects. In this, however, I argue it is not alone. Lack of access to and trust in accurate information is also a factor.

Effects of Lack of Access to and Trust in Accurate Information on Public Understanding

Our understanding of the world is shaped not only by what we know, or think we know, from information we receive, but also by what we do *not* know about events and situations. A lack of knowledge or an incomplete picture can cause an understanding of events that is not just partial but, often, wrong. Examining cases studied in the database shows that lack of access to, and trust in, accurate information can have just as adverse an effect on understanding as exposure to some types of inaccurate information. It does so both by denying individuals the information they require for a full and accurate understanding of events and also by enabling the creation and spread of false information.

Authorities around the world commonly fail to gather reliable information on important topics of public interest and, if this information *is* collected, they fail to provide the public easy access to it. Even in open information economies, with well-resourced data agencies and access to information laws that are enforced, studies show that a lack of public access to 'timely and verifiable information' during security incidents, natural disasters and health crises adversely affects public understanding and can be linked to negative outcomes.[15]

During a notorious terrorist attack in Norway in 2011, for example, it was lack of access to timely, reliable information about what was happening – more than exposure to false information – that denied those targeted by a far-right gunman an accurate understanding of where and when they would be safe to emerge. Many died as a result.[16] The same was true during similar security incidents in Paris and London in 2015 and 2017. 'The immediate problem for the authorities was that they had no way of being sure that the rampage was over,' one report found.[17]

During the Ebola outbreak in West Africa in 2014, lack of timely, accurate information on the causes and spread of the disease denied both authorities and the public a good understanding of how best to act, to limit deaths.[18] Six years later, a lack of timely, accurate information about the nature and characteristics of the SARS-CoV2 virus made it harder for authorities to bring the Covid-19 pandemic under control. Lack of timely access to accurate information also makes it harder for citizens, fact-checkers, platforms and others to identify and counter false information, as they do not have accurate information to check claims against.[19]

Even when accurate information *is* available, it is rare that it is universally trusted. Distrust in traditional media is widespread around the world.[20] While a regional study published in 2021 found no evidence of 'general mistrust of established news media' in six sub-Saharan countries,[21] qualitative research across the continent found trust in both media and official information to be lower in some communities than others.[22] And this lack of trust in accurate sources contributes to wider problems. In countries such as the United States, for example, lack of trust in mainstream media has been found to fuel consumption of false information.[23] And while accurate information about on the effects of vaccines and causes of climate change is easily available, worldwide, it is disregarded by many who believe, share and act on the basis of false claims as a result.[24]

Reviewing cases examined in the database, I found lack of access to and trust in information a clear contributory factor both in facilitating the creation and spread of false claims and in undermining public understanding. The credence given by millions of Nigerians to the false claim that their president, Muhammadu Buhari, had died in 2017 and had been replaced by a foreign lookalike,[25] was possible only because audiences believed that the Nigerian and international media – who continued to film, photograph and report his activities as normal – were either duped or part of a conspiracy; either way, an unreliable source of information (Case 3.5). Even where information might be believed, authorities often do not gather important data and this enables the spread of false claims. After the Minister for Women's Affairs in Nigeria made an unproven claim about the number of rapes each year for example, her officials blamed the fact that they had no data available to support her statement (Case 3.6). In other cases, authorities do have, but fail to release information in a suitable, timely way and this enables the spread of false or unproven claims. As the researcher Nechama Brodie noted in 2022, 'numbers and statistics are essential for understanding crime.' But in South Africa, critical data is often withheld, sowing distrust and facilitating the spread of false claims about rates, victims and perpetrators of crime (Case 3.7).

In other cases, claims circulate that are so unspecific in nature or relate to events that simply did not occur – such as a purported remark made at an unspecified time or a fabricated report of a military strike on an unspecified location – that they cannot be verified or disproved. With no specific data in the claim to check, statements such as these can often be near impossible to compelling disprove (Case 3.8).

How Lack of Access to, and Trust in, Accurate Information Undermines Understanding

Case 3.5 – Lack of trust in accurate media reports can fuel false claims

Mayowa Tijani, 'A separatist group said images of Buhari arriving in Japan were fake. But AFP photos show he did attend Yokohama summit', *AFPFactCheck*, 2 September 2019, https://factcheck.afp.com/separatist-group-said-images-buhari-arriving-japan-were-fake-afp-photos-show-he-did-attend-yokohama.

Case 3.6 – Failure to collect accurate data enables the spread of false claims

Kunle Adebajo, 'Are 2 million Nigerians raped every year? Here's what we know', *ICIR/FactHub*, 3 December 2019, www.icirnigeria.org/fact-check-are-2-million-nigerians-raped-every-year/.

Case 3.7 – Failure to release data that has been collected enables the spread of false claims

Nechama Brodie, 'How to read South Africa's quarterly crime statistics after the Covid pandemic', *Africa Check*, 30 November 2022, https://africacheck.org/fact-checks/blog/how-read-south-africas-quarterly-crime-statistics-after-covid-pandemic.

Case 3.8 – Lack of data for claims unspecific in nature or about events that did not occur

Anne-Sophie Faivre Le Cadre, 'L'armée frappe une base au Niger? Les autorités des deux pays démentent', *AFPFactuel*, 27 November 2019, https://factuel.afp.com/larmee-frappe-une-base-au-niger-les-autorites-des-deux-pays-dementent.

The Effects on Understanding of Distorted Focus of Information

If information is accurate on the specific details presented, the choice of information which audiences select or to which audiences are exposed may cause or contribute to a false understanding of scale or degree, nevertheless. Research conducted over many years in the second half of last century provides strong, supportive evidence that, at that time, traditional print and broadcast media played a role in setting the agenda of public debate, priming audiences to consider particular themes and framing those debates in particular ways, the American media effects scholar Elizabeth M. Perse argued in 2001.[26]

In this framing role, media do not directly distort what people think about an issue, providing false information about the topic, but focus on one aspect or perspective, causing or contributing to a false understanding of the scale or degree of a situation or circumstance faced. Research shows that public attitudes to the importance of issues often 'corresponds more closely to news coverage than to real-world indicators', Perse argued. The same can be said today, for what people see both online and offline. The amount of coverage devoted to an issue makes audiences receptive to particular themes, the American communications researcher Alice Marwick argued in 2018.[27]

In South Africa, media reports of crime have for many years played a role in focusing national and international attention[28] on the relatively rare killings of white farm owners, while less attention is paid to the more common killings of black women in rural and urban neighbourhoods, a study by media researcher Nechama Brodie found in 2019.[29] This focus in reporting correlates with false public perceptions of the prevalence of these different crimes. While the 2019 study found no evidence of *causal* links between the media coverage and public perceptions, studies such as those by psychologists Sara Tiegreen and Elana Newman in 2009[30] and communications researchers Claudia Paola Lagos Lira and Patsili Toledo five years later,[31] suggest the distorted focus of news coverage may have contributed. The same lessons apply to exposure to online content due to algorithmic biases today.

Examining cases in the database for this book, I found numerous false claims that – along with information viewed out of proportion to the reality of the situation described – fed one or more of the false narratives of the type discussed in Chapter 2: exaggerating the level of crime in South Africa,[32] the threat of inter-religious violence in Nigeria,[33] or distorting the role of French forces in West Africa.[34] The research cited above from Perse to Marwick and Brodie suggests that this false information may be seen by audiences as credible, in part, because of false understandings caused by the distorted focus in information to which audiences are exposed.

Together with exposure to false information and lack of access to and trust in accurate information, the range of information to which the public is exposed contributes to undermining public understanding around the world today.

How Different Forms of Communication Shape the Effects of False Information

In his 1989 work *Communication as Culture*, the theorist James W. Carey distinguished between two distinct views of communication: seen in one perspective as the 'transmission of information', and in another as a form of 'drama … the representation of shared beliefs'.[35] Based on the cases examined for this study, I argue both occur and these different forms of communication feed what the philosopher Dan Sperber identifies as, respectively, 'factual' and 'representational' beliefs. 'Subjectively, factual beliefs are just plan "knowledge", while representational beliefs would be called "convictions", "persuasions", "opinions", "beliefs" and the like,' Sperber wrote.[36] These different forms of communication and effects occur, at different times, through different processes and contexts.

In 2011, the psychologist Daniel Kahneman, winner of a Nobel Prize for his work on decision-making and judgement, proposed a distinction between two modes of thinking that might affect how different individuals respond to false and misleading information, in different circumstances. In *Thinking, Fast and Slow*, Kahneman distinguished between what he defined as a 'system 1' mode, which operates 'automatically and quickly with little or no effort and no sense of voluntary control', and a 'system 2' mode, which 'allocates attention to the effortful mental activities that demand it' and is thus slower, more deliberative and more logical.[37]

Reflecting this understanding, psychologists and cognitive scientists Gordon Pennycook and David G. Rand in 2019 published the results of a study of individuals' propensity to believe and share false political information online, arguing that susceptibility to false factual claims is 'driven more by lazy thinking than it is by partisan bias per se'[38] – a system 1-type process of inattention or unconcern for accuracy shaping the effect on individuals' factual beliefs.

To other researchers, this view fails to take account of the extent to which individuals' political and social worldview – their own or shared beliefs – makes them more susceptible to believing, and sharing, false claims that fit their existing views. In 2021, Danish political scientist Mathias Osmundsen and colleagues published the results of a different trial that came to a different conclusion. The driving factor was political motivation, not inattention, they argued. Politically partisan individuals are 'the most likely to share political fake news and selectively share content that is useful for derogating opponents', they proposed. System 2-style motivated reasoning drove responses, they suggested.[39] Responses were a representation of shared beliefs.

On average, of course, only a small minority of those who see information online or offline go on to 'like' or share or spread the content. Individuals do not respond to information uniformly. In a study published in 2021, my colleagues, University of Westminster psychologists Tom Buchanan and James Kempley, argued that – beyond issues of inattention and politically motivated reasoning – individual characteristics help shape audience propensity to believe and share false information. In the study, they identified cognitive-perceptual schizotypy, which is associated with jumping to conclusions and bias against disconfirmatory evidence, as having a direct effect, and sub-clinical psychopathy as having an indirect effect on the acceptance and sharing of false information.[40]

*

Reviewing both the above research, and the audience responses to the different cases of false information in the database of this study, I argue that all three elements – inattention, motivated reasoning, and individual characteristics – can and do play their part in making audience members more or less likely to identify any given examples of false information as either 'true' or 'essentially' true. This reflects a number of elements including the nature of the message, source, audience and context, and whether the communication process serves as the transmission of information or sharing of a symbolic or cultural belief.

Five Broad Factors that Shape the Perceived Credibility of Information

Within those three frames of inattention, bias, and the variability of individual reactions, research, set out below, identifies five broad factors that influence the likely level of scrutiny audiences give to the accuracy of unproven claims: (i) the perception among some or all of the audience that the claim is or may be plausible; (ii) the ease and speed with which the claim is processed; (iii) whether the claim is repeated and/or coherent with existing narratives; (iv) audience perceptions of the credibility of the source, and (v) the emotional effect or alignment of the message with all or some of the audience's existing or prior views.

And – after examining audiences' online and offline responses to the cases of false information studied for this book – it is clear that claims which, these responses showed, were perceived by all or some of the audience to both be potentially plausible, and to meet a majority of the other criteria, were more likely to be seen as 'factually' or 'essentially' true, than those that did not. And, of all these, audience perception that the claim was potentially plausible was the most significant element.

The Perceived Plausibility of the Claim

For a claim to be considered true, or likely to be true, it must first – in most cases – be considered plausible; that is, it must be considered to be both internally credible and within the realm of the possible according to external evidence. Numerous studies show that, to be seen as plausible, a claim must first be seen as consistent in its internal logic – numbers should add up, the timeframe should make sense, it should be coherent in style – and the content presented should be consistent with the claim made.[41] Where this does not occur, to take a case examined for this book as an example, a video claiming to show a Nigerian soldier grieving the death of an enemy fighter was quickly dismissed by audiences who instantly recognised that the language and uniforms shown were from the Democratic Republic of Congo, not Nigeria. The content presented was inconsistent with the claim (Case 3.9). Second, claims are also quickly dismissed when contradicted by readers' or viewers' existing knowledge. When a Kenyan man made a false claim about a foreign-owned supermarket, in another case examined in the database, for example, many readers provided evidence that showed the claim was false. Compelling contradictory evidence from other audience members led readers to dismiss the claim (Case 3.10).

By contrast, the claim – first discussed in Chapter 1 – that President Muhammadu Buhari of Nigeria had died in 2017 and been replaced by a foreign body-double was seen by many people outside Nigeria as clearly implausible[42] but viewed as plausible by many in Nigeria given their understanding of its recent history. Nigerians who believed the claim remembered the case of a previous president who died after months during which the government had hidden his health problems[43] and had also, reportedly, considered using a body-double to keep his ill-health secret. The apparent consistency of the false claim with precedent boosted its perceived plausibility (Case 3.11).

Consistency With Precedent and Existing Knowledge Affect Perceptions of Plausibility

Case 3.9 – When a claim is inconsistent with the material shown, it is likely to be dismissed

Dancan Bwire, 'Weeping soldier from DRC, not Nigeria', *Africa Check*, 30 July 2019, https://africacheck.org/fact-checks/meta-programme-fact-checks/weeping-soldier-drc-not-nigeria.

Case 3.10 – When audience members know that the claim is false, it is likely to be dismissed

Grace Gichuhi, 'No, Carrefour not selling half-price maize after toxin ban', *Africa Check*, 19 November 2019, https://africacheck.org/fact-checks/meta-programme-fact-checks/no-carrefour-kenya-not-selling-half-price-maize-after-toxin.

Case 3.11 – When a claim is consistent with past precedents, it is more likely to be accepted

Temilade Onilede, 'Picture on Buhari's Death Is False!' *Dubawa*, 26 August 2019, https://dubawa.org/picture-on-buharis-death-is-false/.

The Ease With Which the Claim Is Processed

If a claim is considered plausible, readers are more likely – studies show – to believe and share it if the claim is easily processed – clicked and share without real thought or attention. The greater the ease of processing – the simpler the language, the larger the font, and the greater the use of familiar visual images[44] – the more quickly and superficially the claim is likely to be assessed, and the more likely it is to be seen as true. Examining audience responses to cases studied in the database, claims that were easily and superficially processed were more likely to be seen as true by those responding than convoluted claims that asked a cognitive effort of its audience and were not widely believed (Case 3.12).

The Repetition of the Claim and Coherence With an Existing Narrative

If a claim is considered plausible, but is not easy to process, it is more likely to be considered true, nevertheless, if frequently repeated. Numerous studies, from laboratory experiments carried out on responses to rumours during the Second World War,[45] to naturalistic trials of the effects of repetition today,[46] have long shown the strongest effects of media on public attitudes the strongest effects of media on public attitudes to be reinforcing, not changing, existing attitudes and understandings. In the database, audience members frequently reported having heard a claim previously as reason to believe it to be true. 'It is already known. It is no longer news,' was how one reader responded to the frequently repeated claim that the Nigerian president had died two years earlier. Responded to the latest false report (Case 3.13).

The Claim Has Emotional Effect and/or Aligns With an Audience's Existing Attitudes

Claims that arouse strong emotional responses, such as fear or anger, or align with pre-existing attitudes and opinions, or do both,[47] are also more likely to be processed quickly and superficially, and thus more likely to be believed, than claims that present less emotive information not aligned with any particular existing views, studies show.

When a rumour emerged in South Africa that gangs of foreign nationals were kidnapping children from schools near Johannesburg, parents reacted in fear to an emotive false claim, rushing to the school gates to collect their children. The susceptibility of audiences to affective and partisan information is well known and exploited by many who spread false claims on both partisan and emotive issues (Case 3.14).

The Perceived Credibility of the Source

Other studies show the perceived credibility of the source also affects whether a claim is seen as likely to be true. Which sources may be perceived as credible varies, of course, with the audience, topic, culture and context, but can be an important influence on perception of credibility where the credibility of a claim may be in doubt.[48] Health information published by reputable figures in medical journals is more likely, for example, to be seen as credible by most of those who trust medical journals. Less so among those sceptical of mainstream medicine.[49] All things being equal, false claims are more likely to be seen as true by in-group members than out-group members, be they members of traditional community networks, communities of specialist knowledge, or political or religious in-groups. The fact that a claim examined in the database, suggesting wrongdoing by members of a Christian community in Nigeria came from leaders of the country's Muslim community, for example, was taken by many Christians as reason to dismiss it as untrue (Case 3.15).

Ease of Process, Repetition, Emotional Effect and Source Credibility Affect Credibility

Case 3.12 – A convoluted claim requiring cognitive effort was less likely to be seen as true

Taryn Willows, 'No, 1939 Cancer Act does not stop health professionals from finding a cure', Africa Check, 2 August 2019, https://africacheck.org/fact-checks/meta-programme-fact-checks/no-1939-cancer-act-does-not-stop-health-professionals.

Case 3.13 – A frequently repeated claim is more likely to be considered true

Temilade Onilede, 'Picture on Buhari's Death Is False!' *Dubawa*, 26 August 2019, https://dubawa.org/picture-on-buharis-death-is-false/.

Case 3.14 – A claim that arouses strong emotions more likely to be processed quickly and seen as true

Tendai Dube, 'False kidnapping rumours spread during South Africa violence', *AFPFactCheck*, 9 September 2019, https://factcheck.afp.com/false-kidnapping-rumours-spread-during-south-africa-violence.

Case 3.15 – A claim from a source seen as biased less likely to be accepted than from neutral source

Allwell Okpi, 'No evidence nine Nigerian kids kidnapped to convert them to Christianity', 1 November 2019, https://africacheck.org/fact-checks/meta-programme-fact-checks/no-evidence-nine-nigerian-kids-kidnapped-convert-them.

*

What Drives Information Disorder: From False Information to Lack of Access

If information disorder, and the harm it causes to public understanding, does cause or contribute to behaviour with negative consequences for society – from disrupting democracies,[50] to harming public health[51] – it is important to consider what factors drive its different aspects, starting with false information.

Drivers of False Information – Political Processes and Mechanisms

Since interest in the problems caused by false information rose in 2016, much attention has focused on the individual psychological processes that drive its circulation online. Less attention has been paid to the processes and mechanisms that drive and enable the spread of political misinformation and disinformation online, in print and broadcast media, and in the inner workings of government.

'The truth is that all governments are engaged to some extent in propaganda as part of their ordinary peace-time functions,' the political scientist Harold Lasswell noted in 1927.[52] Then and since, disinformation operations run by and for politicians and political parties have been exposed on numerous occasions around the world. A study by researchers at Oxford University found in 2017 that the governments of twenty-eight countries had already, by then, engaged in some form of 'social media manipulation' to promote a political agenda.[53] In December 2018, Facebook and X, then known as Twitter, took down politically linked accounts in Bangladesh for misleading voters ahead of elections.[54] In 2019, Facebook and Instagram removed two hundred inauthentic accounts run by pro-government activists in the Philippines.[55] In South Africa, politicians, or their backers, hired a UK-based PR firm, Bell Pottinger, to spread known false information for political purposes.[56] In 2013 and 2015, politicians in Kenya[57] and Nigeria[58] hired British communications consultancy Cambridge Analytica to spread false information aimed at swaying the result of upcoming elections.

Reviewing cases in the database of this study, more than one-fifth of the claims examined were created or spread, or both, by domestic politicians and activists – using false information in an effort to strengthen support for particular candidates,[59] suppress voting in opposition electoral wards,[60] or deceive the public about the outcome of an election.[61] Yet, while legislators around the world have introduced and amended dozens of laws and regulations since 2016 to counter the spread of false information online, and in traditional media, the processes and mechanisms that enable and incentivise the spread of false information by politicians and policymakers have been largely ignored or taken for granted.

As a start, consider the political process. The competitive nature and mechanisms of politics – from parliamentary debates to routine media appearances – provide politicians with strong incentives to fabricate and mislead. In a limited number of countries, such as the United Kingdom and Kenya, parliamentary rules require that legislators correct the record if or when found to have misled parliament. However, even in those countries where these rules exist, they are not always enforced. And in many countries, there is nothing to stop the spread of false information within government's walls.

Then there is international competition. In 2020, the US Senate Intelligence Committee published a 966-page report which concluded Russia had attempted to influence the 2016 election's outcome by spreading divisive false claims and narratives.[62] In 2020, the European Commission accused both Russia and China of spreading false information related to the Covid-19 pandemic.[63] In the same year, Saudi Arabian disinformation networks were found to have impersonated and spread false information in the name of key Qatari political figures.[64] The United States, itself, has of course a long history of overt and covert attempts to influence elections in other countries, including in Russia in 1996.[65] Britain's use of disinformation in and about Northern Ireland is a matter of public record. In most cases, both the extent and the effects of foreign-sponsored political disinformation campaigns appear overstated, but where motivation and mechanisms exist to fund, support and organise them, they may have more powerful consequences, as indicated in recent events in Ukraine.[66] The same is true of domestic political disinformation campaigns.

The Role of Business in Spreading False News – From Traders to Tech

While the public in many countries commonly blame politicians, media and each other, for the circulation of false news, business has long been a major cause, with its own incentives, mechanisms and processes to spread false information, both to the public and within the business world itself. Since the earliest days of commerce, falsehoods have been told by sales people and companies about themselves, their products, their rivals and the markets in which they work. False claims about services and markets spread along the Silk Road, and across the American West, where the false claims of nineteenth-century 'snake oil' salesmen duped hundreds of thousands into buying ineffective treatments for dangerous health conditions.

Tobacco companies spread deliberate falsehoods, denying evidence of their products' carcinogenic qualities,[67] and energy companies have told falsehoods in more recent years, denying evidence of harm caused to the climate by their activities.[68] Fraudsters have manipulated financial trading markets, from using false information to provoke a sudden price surge on a product to sparking a run on a bank.[69] Companies have attacked and been attacked by their rivals. 'Brands both fuel fake news and are burned by it,' professors of marketing Pierre Berthon and Leyland Pitt summarised, neatly, in 2018.[70] False information has fuelled economic booms and crashes which have enriched some and impoverished more, from the eighteenth-century South Sea Bubble to the subprime crash of 2008.

Business, like politics, is competitive in nature and on trading floors, in shareholder meetings and in company boardrooms; the incentives and mechanisms to rein in the falsehoods are often weak, as the collapse of firms such as Enron[71] and crypto exchange FTX[72] have shown. Not only do traders, shareholders and board members often fail to question false claims that benefit them, in the short term at least; accounting mechanisms often fail to do so too.

Business plays a role, of course, not only as victim and perpetrator of false information, but also through the role of major commercial platforms, and their incentivisation and distribution of false information about the wider world. Companies including Alphabet (Google and YouTube) and Meta (Facebook, Instagram, Threads and WhatsApp), have over the past two decades drained advertising revenue that would previously have gone to traditional media organisations – many operating to some form of editorial codes – and instead have incentivised low-cost, and often false or misleading content.[73]

The spread of false information online is due not only to this financial incentivisation but also the way these companies operate, with design mechanisms promoting the spread of engaging, divisive and often false or misleading content over more measured, accurate and balanced information.[74] While some major platforms responded after 2016 by announcing programmes to reduce the spread of harmful false information, many companies made no such efforts or rolled them back. In 2025, Meta ended its fact-checking programme in the United States and suggested a similar retreat in other countries.[75]

The Roles of Traditional Media Structures and Practices: Community Networks

The structure and practices of traditional print and broadcast media also play an important role in the creation and spread of false information. While most responses to false information since 2016 have focused on misinformation spread on social media networks, many studies, such as one about mail-in ballots and electoral fraud in the 2020 US presidential election, have found the false narrative was driven primarily by partisan broadcast media and political elites, not social media. 'Social media played only a secondary and supportive role,' the researchers found.[76] The same year, a meta-review of misinformation studies found that, around the world, mainstream media 'play a significant and important role in the dissemination of fake news' – either originating false claims or reporting or broadcasting false claims by others.[77]

Media structures – from ownership to reach – and traditional newsroom practices such as broadcasting the speeches of politicians live without verifying claims first are an important factor in these effects. Across the world, print and broadcast media have long been politically and commercially influenced. In many media organisations, owners pressure journalists to take particular political or commercial lines, even if this means reporting information the journalists know or believe to be false or misleading.[78] And while the share of audiences receiving news and information from online platforms continues to grow around the world,[79] politically and commercially influenced media that create and share false or misleading information still reach vast audiences in many countries.

False information does not, of course, spread only via elite-run structures such as political settings, or traditional media, but also offline in grassroots settings and community networks. During the Ebola crisis in West Africa in 2014, false claims about the virus spread peer-to-peer, in offline community settings, such as marketplaces and transport parks, exacerbating the health crisis in the three countries most affected.[80] In Nigeria, false information from a traditional ruler about ways to ward off the haemorrhagic virus was spread in in-person meetings and the media and taken up by thousands of his followers.[81] Across the continent, researchers have found similar evidence of community networks and religious organisations having a substantial role in creating and spreading false information in countries from Sierra Leone,[82] in the west, to Malawi in the south.[83] This means of spreading false information is not particular to Africa. During the Covid-19 pandemic, researchers identified false information spread peer-to-peer through faith communities as playing a major role in the spread of the pandemic in countries from South Korea to the United States.[84]

What Drives Lack of Access to And Trust in Information: Distortion in Focus

In many countries, political parties, politicians and political structures play a major role not only in creating and spreading false information, but also in the lack of public access to, and trust in, official information the public requires. In many of these countries, the lack of access to timely, accurate information results from the inability, reluctance, or failure of governing authorities to gather and release accurate official data and information on matters of public concern in a reliable and timely manner.

In many countries, underfunding of statistics bodies, unreliable methods of data collection, political pressures on public bodies not to release information that authorities might find embarrassing and a lack of verification processes in data-collection centres have all undermined the range and quality of information available over many years. Across Africa, authorities who wish to do so 'are not able to make informed decisions because existing data are too weak or the data they need do not exist', development economist Morten Jerven argued in *Poor Numbers*,[85] a review of statistics agencies on the continent in 2013.

The number of countries across Africa, and around the world, with freedom of information laws in place has risen in the past decade but application of the laws requiring easy public access to information remains poor in many countries.[86] And even when information is available at normal times, governments in many countries across Africa, South and Central Asia and the Middle East often cut access to the Internet during times of unrest or around elections. These are times citizens need access to information most to stay safe or follow what is happening at the polls.[87]

Where information is available, but not widely trusted, this lack of trust undermines public understanding. This occurs for many reasons, including social and cultural norms and authorities seeking to exert significant influence over the media and sources of official information. Here, again, the problem is structural. Given the role that governments play in some countries in shaping state-run media, and in most countries in overseeing the rules for media ownership and gathering and publication of official data, authorities have clear responsibility for both the lack of access to and lack of trust in information available to the public from these sources.

Recognising and Responding to a Wider Information Disorder

I proposed in the Introduction that it is important to recognise information disorder as a wider phenomenon than the circulation of false and misleading information, and to acknowledge the role of lack of access to trusted, and balanced information in undermining the factual understanding of both the public and elite. Responses to alarm about information disorder have focused primarily since 2016 on countering the spread and effects of false information. The effects of false information of course matter, but failing to tackle the other causes will – just as failing to tackle the reservoirs of a rare virus helps to keep it alive – ensure such responses do not achieve what they might. Although misinformation research has proliferated, 'there has been no organizing framework guiding its study,' communications scholar Michelle Amazeen argued in 2023, proposing a new research model.[88] I agree such a framework is needed and propose it should encompass these broader challenges too. I would argue this is what is known today as 'information integrity'.[89]

In this, the first part of the book, I have proposed what I believe are clear, coherent definitions of the terms fake news, misinformation and disinformation, grounded both in existing thinking and evidence from the case studies. I identify fake news as fabricated news presented in a 'pseudo-journalistic' format and distinguish between misinformation and disinformation by intent to deceive. At the same time, I have suggested that, like the phrase fake news, the terms misinformation and disinformation fail to require users to explain the way in which information is said to mislead. And I have argued for the wider use of more specific terms ranging from unproven to mislabeled to conflated that do not simply declare information false, but explain the way in which information is untrue or misleading.

I have proposed a broader definition of information disorder than that most widely used today, as the disruption, or dysfunction of the information system that undermines understanding of the world around us – not just misinformation and disinformation, but also the lack of access to, and trust in, accurate information and the distorted focus in information to which people are exposed. I have proposed that to understand and counter the causes and consequences of undermining of public understanding, fact-checkers, researchers, policymakers and platforms need to understand and counter all elements of this disorder by promoting information integrity.

I have made a case that the story of false information is both older and more complex than is widely appreciated, and that – depending on the topic and context – false information that directly affects understanding among political, business and social elites has or may have potential to cause or contribute to consequences as powerful or more powerful than information which influences public opinion. To consider this last point more fully, though, it is necessary now to consider the nature of the communication we are concerned with and what we know and do not know of its effects on audiences' factual understandings and symbolic beliefs, and the consequences, or harms, these effects do and do not cause.

Part 2 – What's the Harm?

If information disorder were to cause no consequences for individuals or society, the debate about the phenomenon might be of purely theoretical interest. Since 2016, however, laws and regulations have been amended in dozens of countries around the world, enabling authorities to penalise publication and order the removal of information said to be false or misleading.[1] At the same time, the European Union and United Kingdom have introduced legislation that requires the largest online platforms to put in place policies that counter disinformation, among other presumed causes of harm.[2]

Under political pressure, and at risk of significant fines if they fail to comply, several of the largest social media and messaging platforms, for a period at least, adopted policies to curb the potential for false information to cause or contribute to negative consequences. Between 2016 and 2025, Meta used external fact-checkers to identify information that is false or misleading and either add warning labels or curb the content's circulation.[3] In 2025, Meta ended its fact-checking programme in the United States and suggested other countries would follow. X, formerly Twitter, enables users to add warning labels to content they consider false.[4] Meta announced it will adopt a similar system. TikTok has both partnered with fact-checkers and, like other platforms, used AI tools to remove content it says violates its community guidelines.[5]

While the laws and regulations passed in the EU and UK recognise, at least in principle, the need to protect freedom of speech, a report by misinformation and online harms think-tank the Center for News, Technology and Innovation in 2024 found the majority of 'fake news' laws passed between 2020 and 2023 show little regard for freedom of expression. The effect of most such laws has been to 'lessen the protection of an independent press and risk the public's open access to a plurality of fact-based news', the body found.[6]

At the same time as new laws and regulations have been come into force, media literacy programmes have been launched or proposed by educators and officials in countries from Finland to the United States. And the number of fact-checking initiatives operating around the world – not only publishing reports, but seeking corrections and advocating for better access to accurate information – more than doubled from 188 in 2016 to almost 440 in 2024.[7]

All these actions have been premised on the notion that false information causes, or has potential to cause or contribute to, substantive negative consequences for individuals and society. And yet, not only do laws and regulations drawn up since 2016 'often struggle to properly define categories of "harmful content" they seek to regulate', as the disinformation researcher Camille François noted in 2019.[8] The wider community responding to the challenge – fact-checkers, researchers, educators, policymakers and platforms – lack both a clear and coherent framework for understanding the potential of false and misleading information to cause or contribute to the sort of harms they fear and for understanding the impact of measures to counter it.

In his 2022 work *Free Speech: A Global History from Socrates to Social Media*, Danish free speech advocate, Jacob Mchangama acknowledges that 'It is true that freedom of speech can be used to amplify division, sow distrust, and inflict serious harm.' However, he adds, 'The view that the deep challenges to dignity, trust, democracy and institutions of our splintered age can be overcome by rolling back free speech rests on shaky grounds.'[9] This is, at least in part, because of lack of agreement about what is meant by free speech, the processes by which information does and does not have effects, and distinctions between false beliefs, harm and offence.

The very notion of media, or communication, effects has been a matter of serious scholarly debate and argument going back more than a hundred years and, as concern about the consequences of false information surged over the past decade, many serious communications researchers expressed concern that past lessons have been ignored. 'We perhaps risk rehashing mid-20th century debates about strong and weak media effects in the 21st century, when we ought to be finding new analytical categories and paradigms,' communications researcher C. W. Anderson, then at University of Leeds, argued in 2021.[10]

Certainly, I would acknowledge, the debate today has similarities with the debate that took place last century, as two clashing multiple-author articles published in *Nature* in 2024, about the consequences of misinformation, demonstrate.[11] However, I would argue these disagreements, then and now, spring, at least in part, from the different forms and contexts of information considered by the different researchers, different understandings of the nature of communication and information, and different understandings of the mechanisms by which consequences may thus occur.

While familiar ground for media researchers, the history of media effects theory is less well-known among fact-checkers, policymakers and platforms and, I start Chapter 4, therefore, with a brief account of the twentieth-century debates about the effects of the then-new 'mass media' on individuals and society. This is followed by a review of recent research into the consequences of false and misleading information felt in different, specific fields, forms and contexts, from politics and international relations to health and climate change.

I then explore, in Chapter 5, the main different perspectives taken – discussed briefly in Chapter 3 – on how we understand communication and how exposure to information does and does not change individuals' factual understanding and shared beliefs. And finally, in Chapter 6, I set out evidence of a dozen examples of false or misleading information, examined in the database of this study, which evidence shows caused or contributed to specific consequences, from the killings of health researchers in Ethiopia to a reduction in resources for residents of the largest city in Nigeria. And I consider the factors common to these cases, and those common to similar examples that caused or contributed to no such effects, and how that may have influenced the nature of the different outcomes.

Chapter 4

MEDIA THEORY AND EVIDENCE OF FALSE INFORMATION CONSEQUENCES

A decade after the United States entered the First World War in 2017, following a concerted mass media campaign run by British authorities, political scientist Harold Lasswell, then just 25, published a seminal book on the power of the media to influence public attitudes and behaviour. In *Propaganda Technique in the World War*, Lasswell identified the new mass media as a powerful tool used by governing elites in countries such as Britain and the United States to sway public opinion. Like those concerned that 'fake news' played a role in the outcome of elections around the world nearly a century later,[1] Lasswell argued that mass media during the First World War had moulded US public opinion to the will of foreign and domestic propagandists. Americans now understood and were 'uneasy or vexed at the unknown cunning which seems to have duped and degraded them', the political scientist wrote: 'They writhe in the knowledge that they were the blind pawns in plans which they did not incubate.'[2] The British argument for the United States to enter the war had been effective 'for American public opinion has often been a cockleshell, floating helplessly and unconsciously in the wake of the British man-of-war,' he lamented,[3] referring to a notoriously directionless type of boat of the time.

Lasswell was an early proponent of what became known as the school of 'powerful media effects'. And once this notion was established, financial support flowed from US corporations and the US government for researchers to study the phenomenon in more depth. The argument that media offer an effective means of persuasion laid the foundations of the modern advertising industry and shaped government propaganda efforts. For years, early practitioners of public relations such as Edward Bernays – author of works such as *Propaganda* (1928) and *Public Relations* (1945) – promoted the notion that mass media had the power to sway an impressionable public, whether to support entry into a war or buy the latest soap brand. The process they proposed was straightforward and linear: exposure to messages has direct effects on individual and social attitudes and behaviour.

As compelling as this idea was for those in advertising and public relations who promoted it, it alternately excited and alarmed political and military leaders on all sides when the Second World War broke out in 1939; causing officials both to set up media and communication teams to spout their own messages, and to worry about the potential of enemy propaganda to undermine public morale and support for the war. In the United Kingdom, concern extended beyond the effects of enemy propaganda to fears of other forms of unhelpful information after a Home Office study found many Britons took newspaper columns by astrologers sufficiently seriously to change their behaviour during an air raid. If newspaper readers would change their activity based on the predictions of astrologers, how much easier would they be for enemy propagandists to influence, officials feared.[4]

The challenge for the researchers and scholars who followed Lasswell was that proof of such effects was harder to obtain than they first imagined. After many years of research efforts, all that was clear, behavioural scientist Bernard Berelson wryly suggested, in 1948 was that 'Some kinds of communication, on some kinds of issues, brought to the attention of some kinds of people, under some kinds of conditions, have some kinds of effects.'[5] The paradox, the eminent British communications theorist Denis McQuail wrote four decades later, was that while there is 'a widespread belief, nearing on certainty, that the mass media are a powerful instrument of influence on opinion and of effects on behaviour', at the same time, 'there is great difficulty in predicting effects, engineering them by design or in proving that they have happened after the event.'[6]

One of those Berelson worked with on this challenge was Paul Lazarsfeld, a prominent Austrian-American sociologist. In 1940,

Lazarsfeld, Berelson and Hazel Gaudet set up the first large-scale panel survey, interviewing 3,000 voters in Erie Country, Iowa, either side of the 1940 presidential election campaign. After asking voters what shaped their views and studying the responses, the researchers concluded that individuals were far more likely to be affected by the views and opinions of their family, friends, or colleagues than by what they read or saw in the media. 'Personal contacts appear to have been more effective than the mass media in influencing voting decisions,' Lazarsfeld and colleagues argued: putting forward what became known as the *two-step flow theory* of communication.[7] Concern about the power of mass media to influence public opinion had been overplayed. Supporters of this new school of 'limited effects', such as the communications theorist Joseph Klapper, acknowledged that mass media could cause or contribute to changes in public attitudes but 'more frequently as an agent of reinforcement than as an agent of change'. This was because of a process he called 'selective exposure', 'selective perception' and 'selective retention' of information. Audiences choose media to follow that aligns with their existing views, and interpret and retain the information in ways that reinforces these attitudes, he wrote.[8]

From the 1970s onward, however, new generations of scholars looked again at these questions and came to different conclusions. The sociologist Todd Gitlin, for example, identified earlier researchers as having sought to find evidence of immediate changes in attitude and behaviour, an approach that he argued failed to recognise media's potential for longitudinal effects such as agenda-setting and framing. Klapper, for example, had leaned for evidence of media's 'limited effects' on the failure of a one-week promotional campaign in Missouri to change long-set attitudes to the oil industry in the state. Another study that Klapper cited assessed the effects on voter intentions of a one-off political telecast. What was needed was a whole new paradigm, to understanding of effects, Gitlin and others suggested. 'Most current research', no longer questions whether some sort of effects occur, American media scholar Elizabeth Perse argued in 2001, but seeks 'to improve our understanding of media effects by refining our theoretical explanations of the processes by which media effects occur'.[9]

How What We Study Shapes the Debate About Misinformation Consequences

As the communications researcher C. W. Anderson feared, much of the public and policy discussion since 2016 has, indeed, involved replaying much of the mid-twentieth-century debate about whether information effects are 'weak' or 'strong'.[10] As some of those participating in the public and policy discussion acknowledged in 2024, the different conclusions reached often hinge, at least in part, on differences in the form and context of information that is examined and consequences that arise. These differences include the nature of the communication, the type of understandings formed, by whom and the mechanisms or processes by which consequences may or may not then occur.

The debate began as the last ballots were being counted in the 2016 US presidential election and media commentators provided a snap explanation for a result most had not predicted. 'Donald Trump won because of Facebook' ran one headline on the day after the vote. 'The most obvious way in which Facebook enabled a Trump victory has been its inability (or refusal) to address the problem of hoax or fake news,' journalist Max Read declared.[11] Many commentators agreed and, in 2018, the results of a study published by Ohio State University political scientists gave support to the claim. After interviewing voters who had switched allegiance from the Democrat Barack Obama in 2012 to the Republican Donald Trump in 2016, and discounting for confounding factors such as a negative attitude to female candidates, Richard Gunther, a professor of political science at Ohio State, and colleagues concluded that voters' exposure to a large number of fake pro-Trump reports 'most likely did have a substantial impact on the voting decisions of a strategically important set of voters … sufficient to deprive Hillary Clinton of a victory'.[12]

As the next election approached, this understanding prevailed in much liberal US media and commentary. 'Conventional wisdom now holds that without Facebook's help spreading misinformation, Trump probably would not be in office,' one prominent American media commentator wrote in 2020.[13] The public took seriously claims that false information spread on social media has potential for such effects. In a survey of 1,200 US adults in 2020, 81 per cent of respondents told pollsters they were either 'very' or 'somewhat' concerned that false information online would sway the next election against their candidate.[14]

The same phenomenon – blatantly false information spread on social media[15] – was identified as having affected the outcome of elections around the world, such as the 2016 presidential election in the Philippines[16] and the Brexit vote in the United Kingdom.[17] Most British voters did not have fixed attitudes to EU membership at the start of the campaign and, after the vote, one of the main groups campaigning for Britain to leave the European Union claimed it had swung the vote its way by targeting nine million voters identified as 'persuadables' with social media messages making three false or misleading claims in favour of leaving.[18]

Soon the belief that false information spread on social media during an election campaign can affect its outcome by persuading voters to switch party preference became widespread. In Africa, a 2020 study in Zimbabwe found politicians on all sides believed false information spread online had played a huge role in determining the results of the country's 2018 elections.[19] In Sierra Leone and Nigeria, researchers found politicians and activists were convinced that false information was having the same effect:[20] a new version of 'powerful media effects' theory had emerged.

Countering this view, research soon emerged however, reinforcing the earlier argument that exposure of voters to this particular type of false information during a typical, brief election campaign has limited effects. In 2017, a meta-analysis of forty-nine field experiments undertaken in the United States by political scientists Joshua Kalla and David Broockman found that the average effect of campaign contact during elections on US voters' choices was 'zero, or close to zero'.[21] The following year, a study by Princeton University political scientist Andrew Guess and colleagues assessed changes in voting behaviour in 2016 against exposure to false information on 'fake news' sites and concluded that such information had had 'limited effect' on voters' choices. Any effect that occurred would have been largely restricted to reinforcing, not changing, the views of a small subset of the population with a strong pre-disposition to the views the sites put forward, they suggested.[22] In 2020, a follow-up study found false claims on fake news sites had had 'limited effects beyond increasing beliefs in false claims' – not changing votes.[23] Other societal factors, including race and religion, play a far larger role in determining voter choices, political communication researchers Shannon McGregor and Daniel Kreiss added.[24]

Outside the United States, the claims made by British political consultancy Cambridge Analytica that its use of false information on social media had influenced voter choices in Kenya and Nigeria are not borne out by firm evidence. In 2013, Cambridge Analytica's parent company – Strategic Communication Laboratories – boasted about its effectiveness in 'election management', but evidence to support the claim was weak.[25] Research suggesting that false information influenced voter preferences in an election in Nigeria in 2015[26] and in Zimbabwe in 2018[27] were based more on perceptions than hard evidence. A consensus developed among a majority of communications scholars, in the United States at least, that – while not ruling out possible consequential effects in narrow elections where candidates or issues are new to voters – short-term exposure to blatantly false information spread on niche sites and social media has limited potential for direct effects on enough voters' preferences to affect the election outcome. Some researchers in other disciplines went much further. 'Most popular misconceptions … have few practical consequences,' cognitive scientist Hugo Mercier argued in 2020.[28]

Reviewing these arguments today, I suggest that the studies showing, correctly, the 'limited effects' that the sort of blatantly false information spread on niche fake news and hyper-partisan sites have on voter preference in certain political contexts, fail to address the consequences of this and other false or misleading that circulates online over time and that spreads to broader audiences via mainstream print and broadcast media. Nor do such studies address the consequences of false or misleading information set out in other forms, on other topics and contexts, affecting the factual understanding and decision-making of policymakers and members of the public.

At the same time, many of those works identifying exposure to any form of false information on social media as having direct effects on beliefs and behaviour reflect neither the different ways in which individuals and groups communicate – to transfer information and to represent shared beliefs – nor differences in the consequences that occur as a result. Instead, the studies set out below suggest the need for a more nuanced understanding of the challenge faced from false information, about how people use communication and the mechanisms or processes by which consequences, if any, may occur.

Consequences of Public and Elite Exposure to False Information in Ten Different Fields and Contexts

Research conducted in a broad range of fields over many years provides a useful means to identify different types of false information to which different audiences are exposed, in different contexts, the different understandings formed and the means by which different sorts of consequences may or may not take place. What this shows, I argue below and in Chapter 5, is that false or misleading information can indeed be used both to form and represent shared beliefs, and to transmit or impart particular false factual and functional understandings. The evidence I set out shows that audience responses differ not only at the individual level, but also are subject to a complex variety of factors including the nature of the message, source, audience and context. The mechanisms or processes by which any consequences do or do not occur vary, I argue, depending primarily on the topic of information, the effects the information has or does not have on audience factual understanding or attitude, and the capacity and motivation of the audience to act on the false understanding, if caused. To explain this theory, I first set out below evidence from a range of existing research across ten fields, from politics to health to the economy, identifying consequences caused or contributed to by exposure of, first, the public and, then, elites to different types of false and misleading information. And in Chapter 6, I set out evidence of such consequences or potential consequences in real cases from the database examined for this study.

Consequences for Election Participation and Results: Public Exposure to False Claims About Election Threats, Rigging and Process – Effects of Repetition on Attitudes

If, as suggested by political scientist Andrew Guess and others, blatantly false information that spreads on 'fake news' sites during a typical brief election campaign rarely persuades sufficient voters to switch party preference to change an election's outcome;[29] their research still suggests that an election result *may* be affected if the vote is close, many voters' attitudes are not firmly set beforehand, and the false messages are targeted and repeated.[30]

A more probable way for false political information – spread online or via print and broadcast media – to affect an election outcome is to influence whether or not sufficient voters participate in the poll in the first place. On election day in the United States in 1980, television networks called the election for Republican California Governor Ronald Reagan as polling stations closed on the East Coast, declaring the expected result a landslide. While Reagan would indeed go on to win, the reports from sources seen by millions that the race was effectively already over dampened turnout by Democrats in the western states, where voting was still taking place, a study by University of Michigan political scientist John Jackson concluded.[31] Studies show people participate in elections when the reasons for doing so outweigh the perceived costs.[32] And given the election was considered effectively over, the consequence of the broadcasts was to reduce participation in the general election and to affect the outcome of several state-level elections, Jackson found.

Among other sorts of information that may affect voter turnout are false factual claims boosting turnout by raising the fears or interests of particular voter groups, or dampening turnout by exaggerating the perceived risks of electoral violence and threats to election integrity. During election in Spain in July 2023, for example, unidentified actors set up a counterfeit version of the Madrid regional government's website to falsely warn terrorists planned an attack on named polling stations, dampening participation among those who saw the false claim.[33] In 2015, a study of election violence across Africa found that fears of pre-election violence are likely to influence both turnout in the upcoming poll – motivating some and demotivating others – and stated willingness to vote in future elections.[34] Meanwhile, the perception that the elections are likely to be rigged has been found to reduce both current and intended future participation. Expectation of electoral integrity 'fosters participation in elections, whereas (expectation of) electoral malpractice reduces it', one study found.[35]

Evidence from media and election monitors, meanwhile, suggests that exposure of the public to false information about practical elements of the voting process – misdirecting voters about matters the date or timing of the polls, the location of polling stations, or the participation or exclusion of their preferred candidates – may also influence election participation. In Britain, false information about the voting hours for the leadership of a key committee governing one of the main political parties effectively disenfranchised a number of senior MPs from voting, contributing to them failing to turn up in time to take part, party officials reported.[36]

Beyond the potential of false information about immediate, practical matters – threats of violence, or the hours of voting – to affect voter participation on the day, numerous studies from 1945 to today have found that the more a claim, true or false, is repeated, the more likely it is to affect its audience's factual understanding and even attitude. While longitudinal studies of the effects of media on political and social thinking are notoriously difficult to run, behavioural political scientists Florian Foos and Daniel Bischof published one such study in 2021 that suggested long-term exposure to a particular news source can indeed, influence social and political attitudes over time, for at least part of its audience. In the study, the two researchers examined changes over a thirty-year period in political and social attitudes in Liverpool, England, and surrounding districts, and found statistically significant differences between those areas exposed to the source and those not.

In 1989, residents of Liverpool, a city of almost 500,000 people, began a more than three-decade boycott of a popular newspaper, *The Sun*, over its coverage of a local event. In the study, Foos and Bischof compared attitudes to British membership of the European Union between residents of Liverpool and people living in a number of socio-economically and politically comparable surrounding areas, which were not part of the boycott and continued to receive the newspaper. Changes in attitude to Europe were significantly weaker among residents of the city, who had not been exposed to three decades of anti-European messaging from *The Sun*, than among people in the surrounding areas who had received the paper, the study found.[37] Repeated exposure, or lack of exposure, to a strong narrative, true or false, may have potential to affect long-term political and social attitudes in ways that have potential to contribute to behaviour change, the researchers concluded.

Consequences for International Relations and Conflicts: Public Exposure to False Information About the Actions, History or Capabilities of Other Countries

International relations and conflicts are not, in general, decided by a public vote. There are exceptions, such as the referenda held in a number of European Union countries on international treaties, or elections in which foreign affairs play a major role, such as the 2015 and 2019 votes in the United Kingdom. In such cases, studies such as that of Foos and Bischof, cited above, and reports of persuasive effects of false claims targeting millions of 'persuadable' voters in the final days of the Brexit referendum,[38] suggest false information spread over time or in particularly close votes have potential to influence outcomes.

While evidence of such influence of false information on foreign relations is relatively limited, the same is not true of effects on military events. 'The history of the War shows that modern war must be fought on three fronts: the military front, the economic front and the propaganda front,' the American political scientist Harold Lasswell wrote in 1927, looking back at the events of the First World War. Even when governments fail to consult the public or national assembly on the decision to launch a conflict, propaganda can have practical effects in fields such as recruiting volunteers and support for a war effort from business, Lasswell argued.[39] In the years since his book was published, subsequent research since has identified a greater potential for information campaigns to affect public understanding of foreign and military affairs than to influence understanding and attitudes to domestic issues.

Lacking the more detailed knowledge they have of events at home, the public in the United States are often more dependent on and susceptible to media and political narratives on international and military affairs than on domestic issues, communications scholars Matthew Baum, of Harvard, and Tim Groeling, of University of California, argued in 2010. On foreign and military policy, 'citizens are highly responsive to what they see and hear from political elites – more so than in most areas of domestic policy,' their study of the influence of media and political narratives on US attitudes to the 2003 war on Iraq found.[40]

All conflicts take place, of course, in what is a home theatre for some of those involved, and even here, public exposure to false information may influence the occurrence and outcome of certain types of conflicts.

The Democratic Republic of the Congo has long been a scene of conflict, for example, and became host in 1999 to the world's largest UN peacekeeping mission (MONUSCO). While many valid criticisms were made to be of the operation, MONUSCO was also the subject of false claims that may have contributed to some of the domestic opposition to the operation, UN reports found. In July 2022, for example, false rumours spread in the community that MONUSCO troops, already resented over valid criticisms, had colluded with a brutal rebel group, the Allied Democratic Forces (ADF) in a massacre that left many dead in Nord-Kivu Province. Acting on this false understanding, residents attacked the UN base in the town of Butembo, killing three peacekeepers and wounding a fourth. Diplomats reported that these and similar attacks on the UN force contributed to the UN Security Council's decision in December 2023 to reduce and ultimately withdraw the operation.[41]

Consequences for Individual and Public Health: Public Exposure to False Information About Causes and Effects of Health Conditions and Treatments, Actions of Health Workers

The potential for false or misleading health claims to influence individual health decisions and behaviours in ways that harm their' and others' health has been well studied in recent years. False information spread, both online and offline, was identified as a major public health risk by the World Health Organization in 2020[42] and, in 2022, a systematic review of studies of public health effects of false health information found evidence of effects, from 'distorting the interpretation of scientific evidence' to 'misallocation of resources' for health services and treatments.[43]

To start with, numerous studies and reports provide evidence that, subject to factors including health awareness and access to regular health services, false information may affect public health by persuading individuals to use treatments and products that cause them direct medical harm. Over three months in 2020, for example, more than seven hundred Iranians died, and more than a thousand were hospitalised, after false claims circulated online that drinking neat alcohol would prevent infection with Covid-19. The thousands of alcohol poisonings and seven hundred deaths registered by Iranian authorities over three months represented an eleven-fold increase over the same period in previous years.[44] And, in West Africa, records from optometrists show that hundreds of citizens have in recent years suffered either short-term or permanent damage to their eyesight as a result of acting on a false claim, spread in community networks for years, that breast milk, urine or, in the most extreme cases, diluted battery acid can be used to treat conjunctivitis, known in Nigeria as 'pink eye'.[45] Many of those who take up the harmful treatment in the hope that it will be effective, are on a low income and less able to afford medical consultation and treatment fees, medical records show.

Studies have also proven that, if individuals are convinced by a false claim to use alternative treatments that are ineffective but cheaper than regular medication, the use of more effective treatments may be reduced. In 2014, for example, a study found that the use of anti-retroviral (ARV) treatments by people living with HIV in northern Tanzania, dropped precipitously after the group accepted the false claims of a faith healer that he was able to provide a 'cure' for HIV at a fraction of the cost of ARVs.[46] In 2021, one Kenyan patient, Doreen Moraa Moracha, gave journalists an example, recalling that, born with HIV, she had been taken in 2005 by her mother for treatment by a faith healer operating in Tanzania. The mother and daughter drank the herbal medicine, and returned home, and, believing that they were now HIV-negative, stopped taking the anti-retroviral medicine. This sent their viral load soaring and would have killed them had they not returned to treatment, Moracha said.[47]

Exposure to false information may also, subject to factors including sometimes legitimate reasons to distrust public services in general, be found to harm public health by persuading individuals that safe and effective treatments are dangerous and the health workers who provide them are not to be trusted. While almost all medical interventions carry some risk, false information about vaccines, for instance, has long exaggerated the risks of side-effects, reducing the take-up of an intervention crucial to public health.[48] False claims about the combined vaccine for measles, mumps and rubella by a now-disbarred British medical practitioner have been shown, for example, to have contributed to a rise in cases in several countries for over twenty years.[49] And false understandings caused by inaccurate claims about the so-called MMR vaccine contributed to reducing the take-up of vaccine treatments during the Covid-19 pandemic, studies have shown.

At the same time, false claims about health and medical staff may also, in certain contexts, cause or contribute both to attacks on health personnel and a reduced take-up of medication and adherence with medical guidelines. During the West African Ebola crisis in 2014, for example, false claims that health workers were the ones causing the outbreak contributed to crowds attacking, and in some cases killing, public health workers, not only affecting them and their families directly but also weakening efforts to curb the spread of the disease.[50] During the Covid-19 pandemic, health workers in countries from the United States and Mexico to India and Australia, suffered attacks for the same reason.[51]

Consequences for Individuals' Mental Health: Publication of False Information About the Character and Actions of Particular Individuals

It has been widely recognised that, subject to the characteristics and circumstances of those involved, putting individuals into the public spotlight, unwanted, or falsely accusing them of wrongdoing may cause them serious negative mental health effects as a result. In a case discussed in more detail in Chapter 6, the appearance online of false information misidentifying a Zambian man who had been subject to an earlier, traumatic assault, severely retraumatised the man by resurfacing the memory of the earlier incident.

False accusations of wrongdoing have also been shown to cause serious mental health effects,[52] and, in rare cases, may even contribute to acts of self-harm, up to and including suicide. In 2019, false accusations spread in the media and online were found to have contributed to the suicide of the co-founder of a disaster response organisation, operating in Syria; the man concerned was found to have taken his own life due to severe distress to which the false accusations contributed.[53]

Consequences of Discrimination and Abuse, Vigilantism and Unrest: Public Exposure to False Information About the Character, Actions, or Threat Posed by Individuals and Groups

Numerous academic studies and media reports show that, where false or misleading information concerns the character, actions, or threat posed by particular individuals, groups or communities, this may cause or contribute to acts of discrimination, abuse, vigilantism and unrest, subject to a range of factors, including pre-existing political and social attitudes and trust in authorities to respond effectively to the perceived threat or wrongdoing.

At one end of the scale, false allegations that particular mid- and low-ranking election officials were involved in tampering with election results in the US presidential election of 2020 led to officials and their families being targeted with vicious online and in-person abuse and death threats.[54] In other contexts, the effects are not limited to verbal abuse and intimidation. In India, more than a hundred lynchings and other acts of communal violence were caused between 2015 and 2019, in part at least, by false messages spread on social media, provoking fear and anger toward particular individuals or types of individuals.

In April 2018, for example, hundreds of messages spread on WhatsApp in India claiming that gangs from particular, marginalised communities were infiltrating named rural areas and kidnapping children to harvest their organs or exploit them in other ways. The messages primed a sense of threat that was triggered when people saw unfamiliar individuals or groups in the district, and, over a few weeks, more than two dozen people were killed in attacks on marginalised individuals and groups. The oldest killed was 65; the youngest were children. One study that examined the messages found the false claims exhorted those who saw them to take action to 'keep our children safe', and played on a lack of public trust in the police to protect the community. The social context of distrust in the authorities played a major role in the consequences that followed.[55]

In some circumstances, false information has been used to stoke violence on a larger, more organised scale, as seen in events from Rwanda in 1994 to Myanmar less than a decade ago. In 2003, the International Criminal Tribunal for Rwanda (ICTR) found directors of the notorious *Radio-Télévision Libre des Milles Collines* radio station guilty of using a combination of disinformation and hate speech to build public support for the genocide that occurred in 1994.[56] The international court found false claims were used over time to both foster hostility toward the minority Tutsi population, and to trigger particular acts of violence. In Myanmar, the military, known as the Tatmadaw, worked with militant anti-Muslim groups to spread false reports of attacks on Burmese Buddhists by Burmese Rohingya Muslims. While many factors play their part in any such violence, United Nations researchers concluded the combination of long-term false narratives and specific false claims that triggered violence played a critical role in the killings.[57]

Consequences for the Justice System: Public Exposure to False Information About Particular Court Cases, Court Authorities and the Workings of the Justice System

Research by forensic psychologists, carried out over many years, has identified four important ways in which false and misleading information has the potential to influence public engagement with and outcomes in the justice system.

First, when cases come to court, false information spread online, in print, or broadcast media can cause eyewitnesses to change their evidence and report witnessing events they never saw or experienced. One UK study, for example, found that when asked whether they had seen the video footage of a bus exploding during terrorist attacks in London in 2005, 40 per cent of respondents confirmed they had done so despite the fact that no such video exists.[58] Known in the justice system as 'the misinformation effect', the phenomenon 'refers to the impairment in memory for the past that arises after exposure to misleading information' and may influence the course and outcome of particular cases, forensic psychologist Elizabeth F. Loftus wrote in 2005.[59]

Second, false information about the outcome of particular cases or types of cases has been found to affect public engagement with the system, such as dissuading women from reporting sexual assaults, or persuading individuals to pursue vigilante responses to alleged crimes or threat of crimes.

Third, public exposure to false information about the perpetrators and victims of crime can, subject to a variety of factors, contribute to discrimination in the justice system for or against those seen as responsible for or victims of crimes, based on false stereotypes.

Fourth, false information spread about particular judges or the judiciary has been found to undermine public faith in the judiciary and the perceived credibility of rulings they make.[60]

Consequences for Business And The Wider Economy: Public Exposure to False Information About the Actions, Effects of Business or State of the Economy and Market

Since the earliest days of human commerce, the public has been regularly exposed to false information about the performance of businesses, business products and the state of particular markets or the wider economy. Inflated claims about the prospects of a British joint-stock firm, the South Sea Company, led thousands of investors to financial ruin when its stock price burst in 1720. The exaggerated claims of wealth available from gold mining ruined thousands more during the California Gold Rush in the United States in the 1850s. Companies, before and since, have been both purveyors and victims of false information, from tobacco firms denying the harms to health caused by cigarettes,[61] to companies whose reputations have been falsely tarnished, suffering a drop in sales, in some cases, and a ruinous collapse in investor confidence in others.[62]

False information has been used to manipulate markets and, with the advent of online disinformation, the already considerable potential for false information to affect companies and markets is growing. At the macro-economic level, false information about the underpinnings of the economy has potential to distort whole economies, as seen in studies of the 2008 global financial crash.[63] The uncertainty caused to both the public and business by false information and lack of access to accurate information about basic issues, from demographic to spending data, hinders economic growth in many markets.

Consequences for Climate Change and the Environment: Public Exposure to False Information About Causes, Consequences of Climate Change, Environmental Effects

Millions of people around the world today believe that the effects of climate change identified by scientists are either overstated, or a sham and, if climate change *is* real, human activity is not responsible. Numerous studies show this false understanding can be attributed, at least in part, to public exposure to false and misleading information spread over decades by political and business elites connected with or supportive of the energy sector.[64] This false public understanding has, in turn, been shown to have contributed to private behaviour and public policy that undermines efforts to reduce carbon emissions and mitigate the worst effects of changes in the climate.[65]

Research also shows false information on wider environmental topics – from river pollution to the state of wildlife – has potential, subject to a variety of factors, to influence behaviour that affects the natural environment. False claims, widespread in East and South East Asia about the supposed medicinal properties of rhino horn, for example, drive demand for the product and thus, in turn, the sharp reduction in the world's rhino populations seen in recent decades.[66]

Consequences of Financial and ID Loss, Digital and Other Practical Harms: Public Exposure to Scams, Clickbait Including Viruses and False Safety Information

If public exposure to false information about conflict or the climate has potential for consequences at a global scale, the consequences of exposure to scams, clickbait and false safety information has the potential to take effect, primarily, at an individual level – in ways that can be devastating for those concerned. Hoaxes such as fake job advertisements are used in many low-employment economies to persuade job-seeking individuals to make payments they may ill afford and/or provide personal data to be used later, to defraud them out of their savings. And clickbait reports that use false information to attract readers can also be used to spread links to harmful malware or computer viruses, with effects felt at an individual or business level.

Negative consequences for individuals also follow when the public is exposed to flawed instructions or guidance during security incidents and natural disasters. One study of the consequences of false information during security incidents and disasters in Europe in 2009–18 found this sort of false information caused or contributed to harms for individuals and groups ranging from unnecessary home evacuations during earthquakes in Italy, to avoidable deaths for those sheltering in place during a terrorist attack in Norway and told, prematurely, that they were safe to come out from their hiding places.[67]

*

The Social Consequences of Direct Exposure of Political and Governing Elites to False and Misleading Information

In 2003, Robert Entman, an eminent professor of media and public affairs at George Washington University, described the process by which he suggested political ideas spread and have effect in society; a concept he termed 'cascading activation'. Political ideas, he argued, generally flow 'downhill', like a cascade, from the highest level of politics to other elites, through the media and finally to the public. Political ideas cascade due to the powerful framing mechanisms at the elite's disposal. Ideas, he suggested, may flow uphill if notions from the public, picked up by the media, are adopted by elites. However, ideas, like water, flow less easily uphill due to the great power of elites. 'The ability to promote the spread of frames is highly stratified, both across and within each level,' Entman argued.[68]

Observing the consequences that occur when the factual understanding of policymakers is influenced by factually false information – a false claim about the link between HIV and AIDS in South Africa in 2000,[69] the risks of polio vaccination in Nigeria in 2002,[70] or the powers of a herbal tonic to prevent infection with the SARS-CoV2 virus in Madagascar in 2020[71] – it is clear that in such cases the consequences of this false understanding also cascade 'downhill', and, if or when they do so, occur on a greater scale than those of false understandings held by hundreds or thousands of members of the public due to the greater powers of the policymaking elite to mandate outcomes to the public.

The power, or capacity, of elites and members of the public to act in a way that affects others varies with the topic and context. Individual members of the public, for example, may have capacity to act on a false factual understanding about a matter of private behaviour or conscience. But if the false understanding concerns public resources that should be allocated to particular health treatments, public officials have the power to act, consequentially, in a way members of the public do not.

The same is true in other fields too. In the fifth century BCE, the Chinese military strategist Sun Tzu argued that military and political leaders should use a tactic of 'leaking information which is actually false' to secret agents who, when captured by the enemy commanders, 'report this false information … [so that] … the enemy will believe it and make preparations accordingly'.[72] The consequences occur when enemy commanders whose understanding is affected act on that false understanding, he suggested. And when British and American forces sought to turn the course of the Second World War in 1944, they applied this lesson, spreading false information to deceive the opposing commanders, not foot soldiers, about plans for Allied D-Day landings in Europe.[73] Looking back twenty years after the end of the US war on

Vietnam in 1975, the then US Defense Secretary Robert McNamara blamed Washington's exposure to 'very inaccurate information' received behind closed doors – not decisions taken by the American public – for the 'very poor decisions' that shaped the outcome of the war.[74] In a similar way, when Russian forces invaded Ukraine in 2022, the foot soldiers were unprepared for the scale of resistance they encountered due to a failure in understanding not on the part of the soldiers but of their political and military commanders, misinformed in the weeks and months before the invasion by false information about the scale of opposition to be expected.[75]

Around the world, political, social and business elites make decisions every day that affect individuals and society in a wide range of fields from public health and education to the functioning of the justice system and urban planning. Where those decisions are made based on a false factual understanding, or framed by an attitude shaped over time by false factual information, they can cause or contribute to substantive, real-world consequences for individuals and society. In Kenya in 2019, health officials may – in a case from this study, discussed in more detail in Chapter 2 – misassigned, or may have misassigned, resources for HIV/AIDS treatments based on false information about the communities affected.[76] In Nigeria, the central government in Abuja misassigned resources due to the city of Lagos, based on the use of a false figure for the size of the city's population.[77]

These effects reflect not the persuasive, attitudinal effects of false information but the functional consequences of false information taken, wrongly, as the basis for practical decisions. In 2012, the Erasmus Medical School in the Netherlands found, in a shocking investigation, that one of its most eminent researchers, Don Poldermans, had used 'fictitious data' and 'knowingly unreliable data' in formulating European guidelines for the use of beta blockers to protect the heart in treatment of patients prior to surgery. The inquiry found that the use of beta blockers prior to surgery made it 27 per cent more likely that a patient would die within thirty days of their surgery. Some researchers believe the guidelines may have resulted in hundreds of thousands of excess deaths before the guidelines were withdrawn.[78]

Reviewing both the studies mentioned above, and the cases of false information examined for this study, it is clear that the potential for false or misleading information to cause or contribute to substantive negative consequences for individuals or society depends on a broad range of factors including among them, the type of message, source, audience and context. Of these, I argue that the capacity and motivation of those whose factual understanding or attitude is affected to then take action based on that false understanding or belief is a key element. I consider in the next chapter what is known of how different forms of information make these changes to factual understanding and attitude and shape the potential for effects.

Chapter 5

HOW CHANGES IN FACTUAL UNDERSTANDING MAY CAUSE OR CONTRIBUTE TO THESE CONSEQUENCES

For much of the twentieth century, funding from government and the corporate sector oriented media research toward the effects of mass media exposure on public attitudes and opinions. As discussed in Chapter 5, many of the resulting studies focused on the effects of one-off or brief exposure to mass media campaigns, what the 1960s communications theorist Joseph Klapper termed 'short-term opinion and attitude effects'.[1] Less attention was paid to long-term effects on attitude or to short-term or long-term effects on factual understanding.

Writing *Communication as Culture* in 1989, the communications theorist James W. Carey argued that this effect on attitude and opinion was critical: 'Under the sway of realism, we ordinarily assume there is an order to existence that the human mind through some faculty may discover and describe. I am suggesting that reality is not there to discover in any significant detail.'[2] Certainly, much communication – in mass media, on social media, and in political debate today – is still less concerned with the 'brute facts' of reality than it is with the sharing of opinions, attitudes and beliefs.

Nevertheless, many claims examined for this study do relate to matters of substantive, provable fact: a false claim of gunfire at an event where none occurred,[3] a false claim promoting a potentially deadly medication as a health treatment,[4] a false claim that a president died, when he had not.[5] And when individuals understand such false claims as 'true' – causing or reinforcing a specific false factual belief – the factual understanding formed or reinforced may, subject to a variety of factors, cause or contribute to actions that cause or contribute to specific substantive consequences for those involved or others. For while individuals exposed to new information are typically slow to change existing attitudes and opinions, they are both quicker and more likely to adopt new specific factual understandings.

This difference in the likelihood and nature of the consequences that follow, is explained, in part, by the difference between factual information that, on its own or by repetition, forms or reinforces what the philosopher Sperber calls 'factual beliefs' and what he identifies as 'representational' or 'symbolic' beliefs, or attitudes. The former helps to explain many of the proven consequences observed in cases examined for this study, discussed in the next chapter, and the latter, the potential for contribution to future effects.

*

It is, of course, possible for false information to have consequences for individuals or society without needing to affect the factual understanding of those who see the claim. As discussed in more detail in the next chapter, cases examined for this study prove that certain types of information such as false accusations, may, affect the mental health of those concerned, whether or not they believe the claim to be true. And clickbait reports that use false information to attract readers may cause practical harms of another sort, exposing readers to a malware or computer virus, whether or not they affect understanding.

A broader consequence occurs when the prevalence of false claims in society undermines public trust in media and other sources of information in general, without necessarily creating a false understanding about a specific subject. This effect is not new. In 1971, the administration of US President Richard Nixon planned a disinformation campaign to 'destroy the credibility of the press' before the 1972 presidential election, using false claims and innuendo to undermine faith in the media in general.[6] In 2016, Rodrigo Duterte, candidate for president in the Philippines, waged a similar campaign for similar reasons.[7] The same year and throughout his first term in office, then US presidential candidate Donald Trump repeatedly labelled journalists whose reports he did not like as producing 'fake news', for the same reason.[8]

Beyond these ad hominem attacks on the media, another tactic elites use to undermine trust without needing to cause a specific false understanding, is to flood a space or network with both true and false information and thus sow uncertainty about information in general. 'Propagandists often don't care whether everyone, or even most people, really believe the specific things they are selling … They just have to get you confused enough so that you don't know what is true,' the American philosopher Michael P. Lynch argued in 2016.[9] Multiple studies show that the tactic is effective.[10]

Certainly, evidence discussed in more detail in the next chapter shows that certain types of false information may still contribute to specific consequences without needing to create specific false understandings. However, the evidence in the study also shows that most false information has potential to cause or contribute to specific substantive consequences only when it causes, changes or reinforces a specific false understanding that individuals or organisations then act on.

To identify changes in audience members' factual understanding or attitudes, for this study, I first determined whether the information related to a topic that is sufficiently new that any specific understanding, true or false, is automatically a new one. Where the topic was not new, I looked for evidence of audience members' original understanding or attitudes from evidence in the fact-checks. In some cases, written online statements and comments provided evidence of audience understanding. In other cases, audience attitudes to the information could be deduced from other online reactions. A much-cited paper published in 2013 by Stanford organisational behaviourist Michal Kosinski and colleagues found written statements and online reactions such as likes and emojis to be an accurate indicator of attitudes and understanding.[11] In other cases, it was also possible to identify evidence of effects from information in the fact-checks of specific audience behaviours caused or contributed to by a false new understanding. Examples I studied included individuals taking up a particular false health treatment,[12] or assaulting people falsely accused of wrongdoing.[13]

In the vast majority of cases studied, audience responses varied, often considerably, with at least some in the audience showing they believed the claim even when most did not. Many factors contributed to this including differences in individuals' prior knowledge or understanding – giving some and not others reason to dismiss a false claim – their prior attitude to the topic, and the contexts in which they were exposed to the claim – from a heated argument in a community setting to a sober policy debate in Parliament. There were, in summary, many reasons for individuals to show different responses to the claims examined in the database. However, I argue that if a substantive consequence can follow if just one individual acts on a false understanding, the fact that most people dismiss it will not be enough to prevent the consequence from happening.

Reviewing the cases examined for this study, I applied the same scale of changes established by communications theorist Joseph Klapper for changes in attitude to change in factual understanding, from reinforcement to minor change, major change, and the creation of an entirely new factual understanding.

Studying the claim and evidence from the fact-check of prior and new understandings, I identified slightly under one-fifth of all entries in the database as having created no meaningful change in or reinforcement of a factual understanding among a substantive number of readers or viewers, compared with what would have been created by entirely accurate information. In just under half the cases, I identified entries as having reinforced an existing factual understanding on a false basis. In around one-fifth of cases, I identified the claim as having caused or contributed to a minor change of degree in either an existing understanding or in the intensity of an existing attitude or opinion. And in almost two-thirds of cases in the database, I identified the claim as having caused at least a substantive number of those exposed to the claim to have a new specific false factual understanding.

Claims examined in the study that caused no meaningful change in, or reinforcement of, a false understanding among the audience, did so for a number of reasons. This was due, in some cases, to the claim's failure to convince a meaningful number of readers that the claim made was true. When a man in Kenya made a false claim about a foreign-owned supermarket, and called for a boycott of its stores, for example, the claim was promptly dismissed as false by a clear majority of those who responded, many of them providing photos and links as evidence that the claim was false. Even if a modest number believed and acted on the claim, the number would be insufficient for the putative boycott to have a meaningful effect on the company's bottom line (Case 5.1).

False Claims That Created No Meaningful Change or Reinforcement of a Factual Understanding

Case 5.1 – Reader responses show the message was inconsistent with the existing audience knowledge

Grace Gichuhi, 'No, Carrefour not selling half-price maize after toxin ban', *Africa Check*, 19 November 2019, https://africacheck.org/fact-checks/meta-programme-fact-checks/no-carrefour-kenya-not-selling-half-price-maize-after-toxin.

Case 5.2 – The message was only narrowly inaccurate & did not create a substantively false understanding

Monique Ngo Mayag and Ange Kasongo, 'Non, cette vidéo ne montre pas des ministres gabonais arrêtés pour détournement de fonds publics', *AFPFactuel*, 13 December 2019, https://factuel.afp.com/non-cette-video-ne-montre-pas-des-ministres-gabonais-arretes-pour-detournement-de-fonds-publics.

In other cases, the claim was only narrowly inaccurate and the understanding created was thus not substantively different to the understanding that would have been created by wholly accurate information. When a video of former lawmakers in Democratic Republic of Congo staging a sit-down protest spread online, for example, it was wrongly captioned in Gabon as showing ministers and officials recently arrested there for corruption. The caption on the video was wrong but – given that senior ministers and officials in Gabon had just been arrested on corruption charges, and detained in similar circumstances – the substantive understanding created or reinforced that top officials had been detained in Gabon over corruption was correct. Any action taken based on the understanding caused by the video would have been broadly similar to action taken, had the video properly explained it showed scenes from Democratic Republic of Congo, similar to those that had recently occurred in Gabon (Case 5.2).

False Claims That Reinforced an Existing Factual Understanding on a False Basis

Case 5.3 – Reader responses show the claim confirmed an existing false specific understanding

Temilade Onilede, 'Picture on Buhari's Death Is False!' *Dubawa*, 26 August 2019, https://dubawa.org/picture-on-buharis-death-is-false/.

Case 5.4 – Reader responses show the claim confirmed an existing related false understanding

Monique Ngo Mayag, 'Le corossol n'est pas un remède miracle contre le diabète', *AFPFactuel*, 12 November 2019, https://factuel.afp.com/le-corossol-nest-pas-un-remede-miracle-contre-le-diabete.

By contrast, evidence in the fact-checks showed that just under half the entries were substantively false and reinforced an existing false factual understanding among a substantive number of readers. Many of the readers who responded to a false claim, circulating in Nigeria in 2019, that President Muhammadu Buhari had died two years previously, for example, made clear that the post reaffirmed an existing understanding (Case 5.3). When an article was published online in Cameroon claiming, falsely, that seeds of the soursop fruit are an effective cure for diabetes, hundreds made written online comments that the false claim reinforced their prior belief that the fruit was a health cure, and natural treatments are always the most effective (Case 5.4).

Examining the claims in the database, evidence in the fact-checks showed that another substantial body of entries caused or contributed to a minor change of degree or intensity in an existing understanding or an existing attitude or opinion. In these cases, the evidence in the fact-check showed the false claim did not change the substance of the existing understanding but changed it on a minor aspect or to a minor degree. For example, a claim examined in the database, which was widely believed in Chad, suggested the cost of accessing the Internet there was the highest, when it was only among the highest, in the world. Reader responses showed that this caused only a minor change in degree of understanding compared to the understanding that would be caused by wholly accurate information; a change so minor as to have no substantive potential for consequences (Case 5.5). Meanwhile, responses showed that a false claim that foreign nationals had been responsible for a fire in a historic building in Johannesburg in 2019 did not cause most of those who believed it to be true a wholly new opinion of foreign nationals. Rather, the false understanding caused a minor intensification in an existing attitude (Case 5.6).

False Claims That Caused a Minor Change of Degree in Understanding or Intensity of Attitude

Case 5.5 – Reader responses show the claim caused a minor change of degree in factual understanding

Monique Ngo Mayag, 'Non, le Tchad n'a pas les tarifs Internet les plus élevés au monde', *AFPFactuel*, 25 July 2019, https://factuel.afp.com/non-le-tchad-na-pas-les-tarifs-internet-les-plus-eleves-au-monde.

Case 5.6 – Reader responses show the claim caused a minor intensification of an existing negative attitude

Tendai Dube, 'Johannesburg emergency services say this week's fire had "nothing to do with foreign nationals"', *AFPFactCheck*, 8 August 2019, https://factcheck.afp.com/johannesburg-emergency-services-say-weeks-fire-had-nothing-do-foreign-nationals.

Unlike Joseph Klapper's findings on the effects of mass media on public attitudes, the largest single effect I identified from the sample of factually false information was the creation of a new specific false factual understanding among a substantive number of those exposed to the claim. I refer to a specific false factual understanding in the narrow, but important, sense of a specific piece of knowledge about a particular event or circumstance – not a broad belief, conviction, or persuasion.

There was, for example, no evidence of a change in overall attitude among those exposed to a video, circulated online in Nigeria in 2019, that was said to show a Nigerian man being stoned to death amid violence in South Africa. Audiences expressed a range of emotional responses but no change in attitude to the violent events. The audience reactions did show, however, that the video caused a false factual understanding about one specific killing: the incident shown in the video (Case 5.7). In a similar way, when a false claim spread in South Africa in 2019 that groups of foreign nationals were kidnapping children from a specific group of schools near Johannesburg, the rumour caused a new, specific false understanding among hundreds of parents, who rushed to the schools to collect their children. There is no evidence the claim caused a substantive change in overall attitude to foreign nationals in South Africa – amid a much larger series of violent events ongoing at the time – but it did cause a specific false understanding (Case 5.8).

False Claims That Caused a New Specific False Factual Understanding

Case 5.7 – A claim caused a false understanding about when the man died and why he was killed

Tendai Dube, 'South Africa unrest: video of a man being pelted with stones is a month old', *AFPFactCheck*, 5 September 2019, https://factcheck.afp.com/south-africa-unrest-video-man-being-pelted-stones-month-old.

Case 5.8 – A claim caused a false understanding foreigners were kidnapping children from schools

Tendai Dube, 'False kidnapping rumours spread during South Africa violence', *AFPFactCheck*, 9 September 2019, https://factcheck.afp.com/false-kidnapping-rumours-spread-during-south-africa-violence.

While, in many cases, there is no evidence that these specific false factual understandings caused or contributed to any specific, substantive consequences, that is not evidence that they did not do so. In other cases examined in the database, such changes to factual understanding can be shown to have caused an individual or group to take consequential action. What matters for both protecting individuals and society from harm and protecting freedom of speech is identifying the distinction – as I seek to do in the next chapter – between a claim that has a substantive potential to cause substantive consequences, and one that does not.

*

In *Mass Communication Theory*, which first appeared in 1983, British communications theorist Denis McQuail acknowledged the 'great difficulty' of predicting the consequences of exposure to mass media for public attitudes, opinions, or behaviour. At the same time, he recognised the influence that basic factual information has, or may have, on a wide range of quotidian activity. He acknowledged:

> 'Everyday experience provides countless, if minor, examples of influence. We dress for the weather as forecast, buy something because of an advertisement … Good or bad economic news clearly affects business and consumer confidence … significant changes in behaviour, sometimes with large economic impact.[14]

The challenge for those seeking to predict such effects is that – as recognised more than sixty years ago by Joseph Klapper and others – the way such information affects behaviour 'obviously depends on numerous extra-communication factors',[15] from differences in individual psychological characteristics and existing knowledge and attitude to differences in context and in the capacity and motivation of those whose understanding is affected to act on the understanding formed.

Hundreds or thousands of people might see and believe the same information, but not all will react in the same way, to the same effect.[16] Some motorists who receive a report, true or false, of a traffic jam ahead will decide to change route. Others will doubt the claim. Others may have no choice but to stay on the original road. When individuals do act on the basis of a false understanding, the capacity they have to act in a manner that affects not only themselves but others also varies. When a member of the public refuses an effective medical treatment, the consequences will be felt by them and their family. When a politician or official believes the same false claim about the treatment and changes public health policy, the decision may affect tens or hundreds of thousands of people, or more, as shown in the cases discussed earlier, from Nigeria[17] to South Africa[18] to the United States,[19] Madagascar,[20] and across Europe.[21]

In all such scenarios, the false understanding caused is – in most cases – a necessary but not the determining factor in what follows. The question I seek to answer in the coming chapters is what factors influence the potential of a false factual information to cause or contribute not to a specific false understanding, or change in attitude, but to specific substantive consequences.

Chapter 6

THE SPECIFIC SUBSTANTIVE CONSEQUENCES OF FALSE INFORMATION EXAMINED FOR THIS STUDY

Since interest in false information surged in 2016, the vast majority of research has focused on its effects on beliefs and attitudes, and not its 'real world' consequences. After analysing more than 550 research articles published between 2016 and 2022 on misinformation and disinformation, psychologist Gillian Murphy and colleagues at University College Cork and University College Dublin made a striking point: 'While many researchers identified behavioural consequences of misinformation exposure as a pressing concern, we observed a lack of research directly investigating behaviour change,' they reported.[1]

In this chapter, I identify a dozen cases drawn from the database that clear evidence shows caused or contributed to specific substantive consequences for individuals or society – from influencing public policy in Nigeria, to causing, or contributing to, a vigilante killing in Ethiopia. I set out evidence – drawn from both the 250 cases in the database and a broad range of research literature – of a set of factors that govern the potential of individual false claims to affect not only elite and public factual understandings but also their behaviour in ways that have potential to cause or contribute to specific substantive consequences. Reviewing evidence about the nature and source of these claims, the context in which they emerged, proof of their reach and repetition, the characteristics the audience and their capacity to act on the understanding caused, I identify factors common to the cases that lead to specific consequences. And I compare these with the factors common to similar claims that caused no such substantive effects.

As discussed in the Introduction, I suggest that the different forms of cases examined in the database, while not exhaustive, provide a range of different types of false information to examine, from claims spread by the public online, on messaging apps or in offline community settings, to statements spread by political, social and business elites to other such elites in print media, academic journals, business reports and political settings.

The criteria I used to assess the evidence for my findings in each of the thirty categories set out in the database on each claim are outlined in the database guidelines to be found in the Appendices. The findings explain why some were and others were not found to have caused or contributed to any specific consequences.

A Dozen False Claims That Caused, Contributed to Substantive Consequences

From a database of just 250 examples of false information, I identified a dozen false or misleading claims that caused or contributed to specific false factual understandings, that in turn caused or contributed to specific, substantive consequences for individuals, groups or society as a whole. The consequences identified ranged from acts of abuse and violence to harming the mental health of individuals, as well as financial and practical costs for individuals and the distortion of public policy.

Making these assessments, I identified a specific substantive consequence as an outcome with a meaningful material effect on the condition or well being of the subject. This measure includes, for example, notable effects on an individual's physical or mental health, substantive effects on the operation of a business or market, and meaningful effects on the integrity and outcome of political processes. It does not include minor or fleeting effects such as brief changes in emotion or a minor dent made in a firm's business operations from which it promptly recovers.

Making any such judgements, it is necessary to recognise that almost all individual or group behaviour occurs as a result not of one but of a combination of factors. For the purposes of this study, I identify false information as provably causing a consequence when credible evidence shows, beyond reasonable doubt, that the claim caused or contributed to a false factual understanding and this false understanding was an essential, if not the sole, factor in causing the outcome that followed. I identify false information as contributing to a consequence where, by force of repetition, it causes or reinforces an attitude or false understanding which, in time, is essential to behaviour with a consequential effect.

The principle of proving 'beyond reasonable doubt' is, as recognised in many legal systems, that after due investigation no other reasonable explanation exists that could plausibly explain the behaviour. The standard of judgement used to identify a substantive potential for a consequence to occur or have occurred is different and will be discussed later.

Three False Claims From 'Reputable' Sources That Influenced Policy Decisions

As noted above, false factual information from sources considered 'authoritative' can, and sometimes do, influence the decisions not only of members of the public but also of members of the political and governing elites. As described in Chapter 2, South African President Thabo Mbeki, in 2000 changed pubic policy on treatment for people living with AIDS based on a false factual understanding that the HIV virus does not cause the condition. The change made by Mbeki, and a small group of colleagues, had disastrous public health consequences, contributing to an estimated 330,000 excess deaths over five years.[2] In 2002, governors of half-a-dozen northern Nigerian states banned a World Health Organization polio vaccination campaign from operating in the region at the time, based on a false factual understanding that the vaccine contained carcinogenic and anti-fertility agents aimed at reducing the region's mainly Muslim population.[3] Meanwhile, research in Europe suggests that official medical guidelines recommending – based on 'fictitious data' – the use of beta blockers for patients prior to certain types of surgery may have led to hundreds of thousands of excess deaths in Europe in the early 2000s.[4]

Other leaders, at other times, acted, or are thought to have acted, at least partly, on the basis of false and misleading information in launching and running conflicts, from the United States' war in Vietnam from 1955–75,[5] to the full-scale Russian invasion of Ukraine fifty years later.[6]

Among the 250 cases examined for this study, I identified three examples of false information that, as shown by evidence in the fact-checks and corroboration provided to the author, were essential to policymakers in three countries applying or adopting policies, based on a false factual understanding the information caused, in ways that had substantive consequences for society in the countries concerned.

False Figures Distort Allocation of Public Funds and Services to the City of Lagos

Since military rule ended in Nigeria in 1999, government funds and services for cities such as the former capital Lagos have been misallocated, and services inefficiently planned, due, in part, to the use by officials of false or inaccurate figures for the population. In 2019, officials in Lagos, which is recognised as Nigeria's most populous city, declared that the state population had risen to 21 million. The number was an estimate that used as a starting figure the number of people recorded living there during the most recent census, whether or not they had been seen physically by enumerators. The figure was used as a basis on which to plan state-level services such as transport and sanitation.

While Lagos officials put the city population at 21 million, officials of the federal government, based in the capital, Abuja, declared Lagos' population to be 12.6 million, or only just over half the Lagos State figure. This was also an estimate, but one produced by the National Bureau of Statistics, using as a basis the number of people seen in person by enumerators during the census. This figure was used by central government to allocate federal funds under a funding formula set down in the constitution to plan federal services and determine how many members the state has in the lower chamber of the Nigerian Parliament.

Whichever figure was closer to the truth, at least one of the figures and quite possibly both – each of them used as the legal and political basis to determine public policy decisions – was substantively wrong. One and quite possibly both of the figures, appearing year after year, in official statements and policy documents were inaccurate and used to determine the planning and funding of services, as a functional effect of their publication (Case 6.1).

False Claim Contributes to Approval of Fake 'AIDS Vaccine' in Democratic Republic of Congo

In 2011, health authorities across Africa were alerted by the World Health Organization to false claims that a chemistry professor in Gabon had created a cheap and effective AIDS vaccine. A carefully controlled trial of a compound commonly known as DHEA, the main active element in the fake vaccine, had found the element had 'no beneficial antiviral … effects' for those living with HIV or AIDS, the global health body declared.[7]

When those promoting the treatment continued to declare it a scientifically proven AIDS vaccine, authorities in Gabon banned it from sale, but its promoters took their claims online, quoting findings from a French medical institute to suggest, falsely, that the drug was in advanced clinical trials in France and had been found to be safe and effective. The articles were widely shared online in Gabon and across neighbouring countries and, in 2016, health officials in Democratic Republic of Congo approved the treatment for sale.

Though the ban on sales in pharmacies was subsequently restored after news websites disproved the false claims, the treatment remained available online. In conversation with the author, public health officials from the Democratic Republic of Congo acknowledged that the false claims made in the articles shared online had played an essential role in convincing them to approve the medication for sale – causing or contributing to the policy change (Case 6.2).

False Claim on Food Security Used to Justify Change in Food Import Policy in Nigeria

A third case from the study of false information that caused or contributed to a change in public policy emerged in Nigeria, in August 2019, when Nigeria's President Muhammadu Buhari brought together ruling party state governors and announced a major change in his administration's economic policy. The country had 'achieved food security', the president told the meeting, and the attendant media. For this reason, Buhari said, he was ordering the Central Bank to halt support for food imports.

In reality, Nigeria was still a long way off achieving food security – defined by the United Nations as when all people have access at all times to the food needed to maintain an active, healthy life – ranking 96th out of 113 countries on the Global Food Security Index. The false claim was used to provide political justification for the policy, which Buhari wanted to bring in, of ending support for food imports. While the claim was not seen by officials as essential to causing the policy change, it was identified as contributing to it – enabling politically the controversial change to occur (Case 6.3).

Reviewing these three cases, and the others from outside the study period which I describe above, it is clear that where false information comes from seemingly reputable sources – be it outwardly authoritative

False Claims From 'Reputable' Sources That Directly Affected Public Policy Decisions

Case 6.1 – False figures about Lagos population contribute to misallocation of funds for city

Motunrayo Joel and David Ajikobi, 'What a waste: fact-checking four claims about Nigeria's garbage problem', *Africa Check*, 26 July 2019, https://africacheck.org/fact-checks/reports/what-waste-fact-checking-four-claims-about-nigerias-garbage-problem.

Case 6.2 – False claims about a fake AIDS vaccine convinced officials to approve sale in DR Congo

Charlotte Durand and Monique Ngo Mayag, 'Un médicament pour guérir du sida ? Un faux, depuis interdit dans plusieurs pays', *AFPFactuel*, 6 July 2019, https://factuel.afp.com/un-medicament-pour-guerir-du-sida-un-faux-depuis-interdit-dans-plusieurs-pays.

Case 6.3 – False claims about food security in Nigeria used to justify change in food important policy

Olugbenga Adanikin, 'Has Nigeria really achieved food security?' *ICIR/FactHub*, 19 August 2019, https://www.icirnigeria.org/fact-check-has-nigeria-really-achieved-food-security/.

scientists[8] or government agencies[9] or others – it has or may have potential to influence the decisions made by public policymakers that affect large parts of society, without any need to influence public understanding at all, in order to do so.

Three False Claims in Community That Caused, Contributed to Abuse, Violence

Three cases examined in the study also show evidence that certain false claims that spread peer-to-peer in the community have, or may have, potential to cause or contribute to consequences for individuals and groups ranging from abuse to vigilante violence and killings.

False Claims About Identity Led Group to Assault Subject of the Claims

In January 2011, a rumour spread among a group of political activists outside the Ivory Coast embassy in Paris that a passerby was a supporter of the country's ousted former president, Laurent Gbagbo. The idea enraged the partisan crowd who assaulted the man, beating and injuring him seriously. Eight years later, footage of the incident spread on social media along with a false claim that the man attacked was Laurent Gbagbo himself. Reviewing these two false claims, I identified no evidence that the online video caused or contributed to any fresh violence but participants and police who attended the 2011 incident confirmed it was triggered by the unfortunate false claim(Case 6.4).

False Claims Two Ailing Women Were Threat to Togolese Crowd Used to Justify Assault

In March 2017, the families of two elderly women from Lomé, the capital of Togo, brought them for assistance at a community event. The women suffered from diabetic encephalopathy, a medical condition which impairs cognitive and motor functions. During the session, the women went missing and, when found by police the next day, they had been stripped naked and beaten, and left sitting on the ground. Those who assaulted them justified their actions by falsely claiming that the women had taken part in occult rituals and, as such, were a threat to the community. Who genuinely believed the claims of occult behaviour, and who used the claims to escape punishment for a physical assault, is unclear. Either way, the claims played an essential role in the verbal and physical abuse. As in the case from Paris, mentioned above, I found no evidence in the fact-check or other online sources that the images, shared online two years after the assault, had caused or contributed to fresh abuse and violence (Case 6.5).

False Claims of Harm to Children That Led to Assault on a Church and Health Researchers

Two other cases examined in the database showed evidence that false claims – both of which related to supposed harm or threat of harm to children – caused or contributed to even more serious violence. One incident began when a young boy went missing as his mother attended church in south-west Nigeria in November 2019. Days later, a rumour spread that the boy's body had been found under the altar and the pastor had confessed to abducting the child. No child's body had been found and the pastor, though suspected by police, had not been arrested. Hearing the rumour, however, a crowd gathered, set the church on fire, and assaulted members of its staff (Case 6.6).

In another incident, the outcome of a false claim was fatal. In July 2018, two health researchers travelled to a remote town in Ethiopia's northern Amhara State to research the effects of its poor water quality on children's health. As they collected samples at a school, a false rumour spread that several children had become ill and died. Both angry and fearful of the threat that more children might be affected, a crowd went to the school, dragged the researchers into the street and beat them to death. A lab technician working with the men was maimed. While all such behaviours have many contributory factors, testimony from both police and participants gave the false rumour as the trigger for the assault (Case 6.7).

False Claims Spread Offline in Crowds That Caused or Contributed to Violence

Case 6.4 – False rumour spread in crowd caused violent assault; no similar evidence after claims online

Mayowa Tijani, 'No, this video does not show Ivory Coast's ex-president Laurent Gbagbo being beaten by a mob', *AFPFactCheck*, 13 November 2019, https://factcheck.afp.com/no-video-does-not-show-ivory-coasts-ex-president-laurent-gbagbo-being-beaten-mob.

Case 6.5 – False claims two ailing women were a threat to crowd used to justify abuse, assault

Anne-Sophie Faivre Le Cadre, 'Deux "oiseaux-sorcières" tombés du ciel au Congo? Non, des femmes atteintes d'encéphalopathie au Togo', *AFPFactuel*, 7 August 2019, https://factuel.afp.com/deux-oiseaux-sorcieres-tombes-du-ciel-au-congo-non-des-femmes-atteintes-dencephalopathie-au-togo.

Case 6.6 – False claims missing baby discovered caused crowd attack on accused church

Segun Olakoyenikan, 'Remains of a missing baby discovered under a church altar in Nigeria? No evidence yet', *AFPFactCheck*, 6 December 2021, https://factcheck.afp.com/remains-missing-baby-discovered-under-church-altar-nigeria-no-evidence-yet.

Case 6.7 – False claims health research made children ill, die, caused deadly assault in Ethiopia

Dawit Endeshaw, 'Mob action costs two researchers' lives', *The Reporter Ethiopia*, 27 October 2018, https://www.thereporterethiopia.com/6682/.

In each of the cases examined, from the assault in Paris to the beating and killings in Ethiopia, evidence in the fact-check, and corroborated in other reports, showed the false claims either caused or contributed to a false factual understanding that – coming in a particular social and cultural context – was essential to provoking anger and fear, or justification, and thus contributed to what took place. In each of the cases where consequences occurred, those whose understanding was affected were in close proximity to the subjects of the claims, thus had capacity to act on the emotions and false understanding caused. Where they were not in proximity, when images of these incidents circulated later online, I found no evidence this caused or contributed to similar violence at that later stage. For the consequence to occur, the combination of false understanding, capacity and motivation was critical.

Four False Claims That Caused or Contributed to Harms to Mental Health

Two Recurrent False Claims That Contributed to Measurable Distress, Depression

Mental and physical health experts have long recognised that repeated or chronic exposure to stress or fear, whether caused by circumstances or by information, have or may have the potential to harm individuals' long-term mental and physical health in ways going far beyond the effects of fleeting negative emotions. 'Both acute and chronic distress have measurable physiologic effects,' on top of 'particular effects for long-term mental health', a recent guide by medical practitioners found.[10] The effects that chronic fear and stress can have include depression and post-traumatic stress disorder, effects on cognition and the immune system, and susceptibility to gastrointestinal diseases and heart conditions.

Soon after Cameroon national football coach Rigobert Song suffered a stroke and was hospitalised in 2016, for example, a false rumour emerged online that the former sportsman was either seriously ill or had died. At first, Song and family brushed off the false reports, but when the claims were repeated, over time, they found recurrent exposure to the false claims more deeply unsettling. 'It is very distressing to have to repeatedly respond to this sort of rumour,' the former footballer noted in 2019. The repeated use of private photos and videos from a traumatic event in which he nearly died compounded the negative effects of the false claims, affecting his mental health (Case 6.8).

In 2014, South Africa's national team goalkeeper Senzo Meyiwa was murdered by robbers who broke into his home during a party. In subsequent media and online reports, Longwe Twala, the son of a well-known South African musician, who had been present at the event was falsely accused of involvement in the killing. Though he was not considered by police as a suspect, the false accusation was repeated frequently online and in traditional media for years, contributing to his well-documented problems with depression and drug addiction, the family doctors reported (Case 6.9).

Two False Claims Linked to Past Traumas That Contributed to Severe Distress

In another case examined in the database, a celebrity photographer in Nigeria, traumatised by an alleged rape by a prominent Nigerian pastor, was falsely accused online of having apologised for, and withdrawn, her report of rape. The woman was so distressed by the false claims that she required medical treatment and support. The effects of the false accusation compounded the trauma of the original incident, evidence in the fact-check showed (Case 6.10).

In Zambia, a farmer who was badly beaten by political activists during an incident in 2017, was retraumatised after being misidentified in a photo shared widely online two years later as a victim of a bout of violence in South Africa in 2019. The man, still recovering, physically and mentally, from the original attack, was severely affected, evidence in the fact-check found, by being made to 'relive the events of the day', negatively affecting his mental health (Case 6.11).

False Claims That Affected the Subjects' Mental Health

Case 6.8 – Recurrent false claim famous sportsman had died caused chronic distress

Monique Ngo Mayag, 'Non, le footballeur Rigobert Song n'est pas décédé', *AFPFactuel*, 17 July 2019, https://factuel.afp.com/non-le-footballeur-rigobert-song-nest-pas-decede.

Case 6.9 – Repeated false accusation of involvement in murder contributed to depression, addition

Tendai Dube, 'South African police deny claims that Longwe Twala was arrested for the murder of Senzo Meyiwa', *AFPFactCheck*, 22 November 2019, https://factcheck.afp.com/south-african-police-deny-claims-longwe-twala-was-arrested-murder-senzo-meyiwa.

Case 6.10 – False claims of wrongdoing contributed to chronic distress linked to rape trauma

Mayowa Tijani, 'No, Busola Dakolo did not apologise to the pastor she accuses of raping her', *AFPFactCheck*, 23 July 2019, https://factcheck.afp.com/no-busola-dakolo-did-not-apologise-pastor-she-accuses-raping-her.

Case 6.11 – False claim focusing attention on traumatic event re-traumatised a victim of violence

Mary Kulundu, 'Zambian farmer "greatly distressed" by posts falsely identifying him as victim of South African violence', *AFPFactCheck*, 13 September 2019, https://factcheck.afp.com/zambian-farmer-greatly-distressed-posts-falsely-identifying-him-victim-south-african-violence.

In all four cases studied, those affected knew the claims were untrue but were traumatised, to a lesser or greater degree, either by the unwelcome resurfacing of an earlier trauma, or by the perception that the public believed the claim to be true. In all four cases, the false claims made about them had negative consequences for their mental health.

Four False Claims That Caused Material Losses to Individuals and Organisations

While some false information causes material consequences at a global scale, many false claims have, or may have, potential to cause material losses for individuals and organisations – from loss of property to harm to their career.

To consider a case discussed earlier, when a crowd was incensed by false rumours that a church pastor in Nigeria was responsible for the death of a child, it not only caused violence against individuals, but also caused a direct material loss to the organisation: the building was burned down. A range of complex social factors, of course, play an important role in incidents such as the attack on the church, including strong sense of community among those who carried out the attack and a lack of trust in the police and courts to bring the alleged perpetrator to justice. But, according to police reports, the false factual understanding that spread that the pastor had been found to have abducted and killed the child was an essential factor in triggering what happened and causing both the violence against church workers and the burning down of the building (Case 6.12).

The same was true in another case in Kenya in 2019. An American woman working in the country with a religious group opposed to female genital mutilation was falsely accused by media of having undergone the process during her own wedding ceremony. Roundly criticised online and in the media, she was so affected that she left her role, the false accusations having a negative, material effect on her career. Again, other complex factors played a role in the effects of the false claim. Latent suspicion of outsiders, and the fact that the woman depended for her work on public acceptance of her credibility when arguing against the practice made her particularly vulnerable to the effects of the false accusation, but the false claim was the trigger (Case 6.13).

Alongside false accusations, false online claims promoting non-existent job or financial opportunities also have, or may have, potential to affect individuals or groups in practical ways. One of several such hoaxes examined in the database, for example, used false information to convince hundreds of job-seekers in Kenya to pay a fee of Ksh300

($2) to apply for work which did not exist. Often those who respond to such hoaxes are required to provide detailed personal and financial information too, which is then used impersonate them, or defraud them financially on a larger scale in future. Those targeted by such cases are typically in need of work and financially vulnerable (Case 6.14).

Clickbait reports that use false information to attract readers may also, in certain circumstances, expose them, and in some cases, their friends or colleagues, to a computer virus or malware, with the potential to sow practical harms, from identify theft to blackmail and operational difficulties. Those affected do not need to believe the claim to be true to suffer harm, but merely to find the claim sufficiently interesting, or entertaining, to click on the link they read. The clickbait headline of a report examined in the database, for example, suggested falsely that a popular Kenyan singer had died and been found 'in a wheelie bin'. Many of those who clicked on the report claimed they did not believe it to be true, but, nevertheless, their action exposed them to a computer virus (Case 6.15).

False Claims That Caused Material Losses for Individuals or Groups

Case 6.12 – False claims that caused crowd attack on church caused major damage to property

Segun Olakoyenikan, 'Remains of a missing baby discovered under a church altar in Nigeria? No evidence yet', *AFPFactCheck*, 6 December 2021, https://factcheck.afp.com/remains-missing-baby-discovered-under-church-altar-nigeria-no-evidence-yet.

Case 6.13 – False claims of wrongdoing caused harm to individual's career

Mary Kulundu, 'False reports claim US missionary underwent FGM in Kenya', *AFPFactCheck*, 30 July 2019, https://factcheck.afp.com/false-reports-claim-us-missionary-underwent-fgm-kenya.

Case 6.14 – False claims of hoax convinced unemployed to pay to apply for non-existent jobs

Grace Gichuhi, 'Job Scam! Kenya's Fresha Dairy doesn't charge for recruitment', *Africa Check*, 14 November 2019, https://africacheck.org/fact-checks/meta-programme-fact-checks/job-scam-kenyas-fresha-dairy-doesnt-charge-recruitment.

Case 6.15 – False claim that attracted readers to click on report exposing them to computer virus

Grace Gichuhi, 'Kenyan gospel music star Ringtone Apoke is alive and well', *Africa Check*, 12 July 2019, https://africacheck.org/fact-checks/meta-programme-fact-checks/kenyan-gospel-music-star-ringtone-apoko-alive-and-well.

Factors That Distinguish Claims That Cause No or Limited Effects

In contrast to the dozen cases described above that evidence shows, caused or contributed to the outcomes discussed, many outwardly similar claims examined in the study caused or contributed to no particular direct consequences beyond a false understanding, a fleeting impact on the emotions of those who saw the claim or a negative effect on public trust with no specific, substantive outcome for individuals or society. And many claims had even less effect than that – with evidence showing they had no substantive effect on understanding at all. Reviewing the different types of claim, audiences, sources and contexts in which claims appeared, I identified a variety of factors common to those that caused no or limited effects.

False Accusations and Fleeting Threats With No Substantive Mental Health Effects

To start with claims that made false accusations about the behaviour or character of named individuals, numerous cases studied in the database caused fleeting negative emotions for those falsely accused or misidentified online, but had no identifiable substantive effects on their subjects' mental health. In some cases, the subjects – such as a politician in Nigeria (Case 6.16), or another in South Africa (Case 6.17) – were reportedly inured to such criticisms, and not subject to prior trauma, and the false claims had no reported consequences on the subjects' mental health.

In other cases, claims provoked fleeting fear or anger – such as the fear that children at particular schools in South Africa were being kidnapped by foreign nationals (Case 6.18) – the emotional effects were real but fleeting and dissipated quickly when the claims turned out to be untrue. Fleeting emotions such as anger or fear may give rise to consequential behaviours but are not identified by mental health professionals as a substantive mental health effect in themselves.[11]

False Accusations and Fleeting Threats With No Substantive Mental Health Effects

Case 6.16 – A politician in Nigeria falsely accused of violent behaviour inured to criticism

Mayowa Tijani, 'This is not a video of Remi Tinubu fighting in the Nigerian national assembly', *AFPFactCheck*, 11 July 2019, https://factcheck.afp.com/not-video-remi-tinubu-fighting-nigerian-national-assembly.

Case 6.17 – A politician in South Africa, not subject to known prior trauma, unaffected by criticism

Tendai Dube, 'South African minister Pravin Gordhan has been facing questions over his pharmacy degree. Two institutions confirm that he graduated', *AFPFactCheck*, 10 July 2019, https://factcheck.afp.com/south-african-minister-pravin-gordhan-has-been-facing-questions-over-his-pharmacy-degree-two.

Case 6.18 – A claim that caused fleeing fear, no known long-term consequences

Tendai Dube, 'False kidnapping rumours spread during South Africa violence', *AFPFactCheck*, 9 September 2019, https://factcheck.afp.com/false-kidnapping-rumours-spread-during-south-africa-violence.

Reviewing the effects of these and other claims, I argue that, among many factors affecting individuals' vulnerability to false accusations about their behaviour or character are whether the claims are repeated, over time or by many sources, and whether the subjects have been through prior trauma. Claims that cause emotions such as fleeting stress, fear or anger may trigger severe consequences but only affect mental health where the stress, fear or anger are lasting. These effects on mental health may occur whether or not the claim is seen as true by the subject or the audience.

Substantively False Claims May Cause Substantive Effects; the Effects of Inaccurate Claims That Are 'Broadly True' Are Not Due to Misinformation

By contrast, the false claims studied in the database that caused or contributed to the abuse of two women in Togo (Case 6.19) and the killing of two health researchers in Ethiopia (Case 6.20) did all require audiences to believe claims that were substantively false. They created, or reinforced, an understanding of events that completely contradicted the known facts – that the women were engaged in an occult practice and that the health researchers had harmed children. The action taken based on the false understanding was substantively different from action taken that would be taken based on an accurate understanding. By contrast, while all entries in the database were in some way inaccurate, many were only narrowly inaccurate and, as shown by evidence in the fact-check, caused no substantive consequence. The key distinction, in such cases, was that the factual understanding caused was broadly true.

False Claims That Cause Misinformation Effects, Inaccurate Claims That Do Not

Case 6.19 – A substantively false claim that contributed to a substantive consequence; an assault

Anne-Sophie Faivre Le Cadre, 'Deux "oiseaux-sorcières" tombés du ciel au Congo? Non, des femmes atteintes d'encéphalopathie au Togo', *AFPFactuel*, 7 August 2019, https://factuel.afp.com/deux-oiseaux-sorcieres-tombes-du-ciel-au-congo-non-des-femmes-atteintes-dencephalopathie-au-togo.

Case 6.20 – A substantively false claim that contributed to a substantive consequence; a killing

Dawit Endeshaw, 'Mob action costs two researchers' lives', *The Reporter Ethiopia*, 27 October 2018, https://www.thereporterethiopia.com/6682/.

Case 6.21 – A narrowly inaccurate claim – no substantive effect on understanding, behaviour

Monique Ngo Mayag, 'Non, cette photo n'a pas été prise dans une maternité au Cameroun', *AFPFactuel*, 20 August 2019, https://factuel.afp.com/non-cette-photo-na-pas-ete-prise-dans-une-maternite-au-cameroun.

Case 6.22 – A narrowly inaccurate claim – no substantive effect on understanding, behaviour

Mayowa Tijani, 'This is an old picture that does not show a reprisal for recent xenophobic violence in South Africa', *AFPFactCheck*, 4 September 2019, https://factcheck.afp.com/old-picture-does-not-show-reprisal-recent-xenophobic-violence-south-africa.

Take, for example, a photo circulated online of shocking conditions in a maternity ward in Uganda. The image was falsely captioned as showing a maternity ward in Cameroon, leading people to a false factual understanding about the location. However, while the label was wrong, evidence in the fact-check showed the conditions shown were typical of conditions in maternity hospitals in Cameroon.[12] The calls for action the photo provoked were based on an understanding that was inaccurate in terms of the location of the image, but broadly true of conditions in hospitals in Cameroon. Any behaviour that followed, based on the claim, would be essentially similar to behaviour caused by entirely accurate information (Case 6.21).

In a similar way, when protests against South African-owned firms broke out in Nigeria in 2019 – following reports of attacks on Nigerians living there – a Lagos-based journalist circulated a photo of an earlier incident and mislabelled it as showing an attack on a South African business in Lagos that day. The photo was, in fact, from an unrelated event four years earlier, but the scene shown was broadly similar to what had, in fact, taken place in Lagos that day. Again, any action taken on the basis of the understanding the photo formed would have been essentially similar to action taken on the basis of entirely accurate information on events that day (Case 6.22).

Reviewing the effects of these and other claims examined in the database, I argue that, in most cases, for false claims to cause or contribute to substantive consequences, the key premise of the claim must be substantively false, and contradicted by the facts. And where the understanding caused is only narrowly inaccurate, any actions taken are not a misinformation effect.

False Claims That Convinced or Failed to Convince Sufficient People to Cause a Consequence

Examining entries in the database, I identified a series of claims which were superficially similar to the false claims – discussed earlier in the book – which came from seemingly authoritative sources and persuaded authorities to change public health policy in South Africa,[13] Madagascar,[14] or Brazil.[15] Like those cases, these entries presented a semblance of scientific evidence for the claim. Unlike those examples, however, these entries persuaded some members of the public but were insufficient to convince authorities to approve or promote the products for sale.

False claims examined in the database, for example, that apricot seeds 'kill cancer cells' (Case 6.23), or that a tisane made from the plant artemisia could cure malaria (Case 6.24), had an apparent basis in science to support them. Apricot seeds contain a substance called amygdalin which breaks down in the body to produce hydrogen cyanide. Hydrogen cyanide was used to treat different forms of cancer in Russia in the nineteenth century and in the United States up to the 1920s. Meanwhile the compound artemisinin, found in the artemisia plant native to the Chinese-Vietnam border region, is used in anti-malarial treatments worldwide and earned its discoverer, the scientist Tu Youyou, the Nobel Prize for medicine in 2015.[16]

In both cases, this seeming scientific evidence was sufficient to persuade many members of the public, who responded positively to the false claims, indicating intention to take the ineffective products as a treatment. The evidence was, however, insufficient to convince authorities to change policy and approve the products for sale. In fact, clinical trials show amygdalin has no beneficial effect against cancer and, taken in quantity, can lead to cyanide poisoning and death. And medical research has shown that artemisinin, while effective in tablet form, has no anti-malarial effect when diluted in a tisane.

False Claims That Convinced or Failed to Convince Sufficient, Necessary People

Case 6.23 – A false claim that convinced members of the public to take a health treatment

Taryn Khourie, 'Apricot seeds don't kill cancer cells, can have deadly side effects', *Africa Check*, 25 October 2019, https://africacheck.org/fact-checks/meta-programme-fact-checks/apricot-seeds-dont-kill-cancer-cells-can-have-deadly-side.

Case 6.24 – A false claim that failed to convince health authorities to approve a health treatment

Anne-Sophie Faivre Le Cadre, 'Non, la tisane à l'artémisia et la noix de cola ne guérissent pas le paludisme', *AFPFactCheck*, 8 July 2019, https://factuel.afp.com/non-la-tisane-lartemisia-et-la-noix-de-cola-ne-guerissent-pas-le-paludisme.

Case 6.25 – A false claim that convinced health authorities and was then proven false

Olivier Hertel, 'Suite à notre enquête, le faux médicament Immunorex a été suspendu en Afrique', *Sciences et Avenir*, 20 January 2017, https://www.sciencesetavenir.fr/sante/exclusif-suite-a-notre-enquete-le-faux-medicament-immunorex-a-ete-suspendu-en-afrique_109932.

Case 6.26 – A false claim that did not convince sufficient people to launch an effective boycott

Grace Gichuhi, 'No, Carrefour not selling half-price maize after toxin ban', *Africa Check*, 19 November 2019, https://africacheck.org/fact-checks/meta-programme-fact-checks/no-carrefour-kenya-not-selling-half-price-maize-after-toxin.

In another case examined in the database, health officials in Democratic Republic of Congo were convinced by false information from a seemingly reputable source – the France-based *Institut International pour le Soutien à la Recherche Scientifique Innovante* – and false claims of support from world leading AIDS scientists to approve the sale of a fake AIDS vaccine; a change in health policy liable to reduce the take-up of effective treatments. The false claims were sufficient to persuade the health officials to endorse the product for sale (Case 6.25).

Reviewing these and other entries to the database, a second key difference between essentially similar claims that did and did not cause or contribute to a consequence is whether or not the claim was seen as true, or sufficiently likely to be true to act on, to cause the consequence concerned.

In the case of easily available supposed health treatments for a common condition – such as apricot seeds as a treatment for cancer, or an artemisia tisane as a cure for malaria – it may require only one member of the public to take up the ineffective treatment, to cause or contribute to the consequence. If the decision-making process is more rigorous – as it sometimes is the case for public policy decisions – more people may need to be convinced and the evidence produced to back up the claim may need to be more rigorous too.

By contrast, for some effects to occur, it is not enough for just one or two people to believe a false claim. For a call by a man in Kenya in 2019 for a boycott of a foreign supermarket chain to have had a substantive effect on the firm's operations, it would have had to have been heeded not by a handful of fellow shoppers, but by thousands (Case 6.26). Some consequences would require action based on a false understanding to be taken by thousands or hundreds of thousands of people to have effect.

False Claims That Cause False Factual Understanding With No Effect; the Capacity and Motivation of the Audience to Take Effective Action

Examining cases in the database, many similar claims were substantively false and seen as true by sufficient people to cause a specific consequence, but not all did so. The key difference in such cases was the capacity and motivation of those whose understanding was affected to take consequential action.

When a crowd in Togo stripped two women and assaulted them, justifying their actions on a false rumour of occult practices, they had capacity and motivation to do so. The women were right there, in front of them, and vulnerable. When images of that incident appeared on social media two years later, many readers made statements calling for action against any occult behaviour, but there is no evidence any violent incidents followed. The difference was in the capacity and motivation of the offline and online audiences to take consequential action (Case 6.27).

Two years later, South African lawmakers listening to a debate in Parliament about police numbers, heard a minister falsely claim South

Africa had fewer police than prescribed by the United Nations for its size of population. No such UN target figure exists, and security experts argue it would make no sense if it did – the ideal police-to-population ratio varies depending on context – but lawmakers believed the claim. While members of the public listening to the debate had no meaningful power to act on the false understanding the false claim caused, however, politicians attending the event did, and voted through the budget the minister demanded. The capacity of the politicians to act was key (Case 6.28).

False Claims – The Capacity and Motivation of the Audience to Act

Case 6.27 – False claim in the community on which an offline crowd had capacity and motivation to act

Anne-Sophie Faivre Le Cadre, 'Deux "oiseaux-sorcières" tombés du ciel au Congo? Non, des femmes atteintes d'encéphalopathie au Togo', *AFPFactuel*, 7 August 2019, https://factuel.afp.com/deux-oiseaux-sorcieres-tombes-du-ciel-au-congo-non-des-femmes-atteintes-dencephalopathie-au-togo.

Case 6.28 – False claim in parliament on which politicians had capacity and motivation to act

Cayley Clifford, 'South Africa's police recruitment drive based on dubious UN standard', *Africa Check*, 17 July 2019, https://africacheck.org/fact-checks/spotchecks/south-africas-police-recruitment-drive-based-dubious-un-standard.

Determining the Potential of False Information to Cause or Contribute to Specific, Substantive Effects

If false information has no meaningful potential to cause or contribute to substantive consequences, there is little reason, beyond an abstract, theoretical interest in 'the truth', to support the many initiatives launched since 2016 to counter its spread. Fact-checking and media literacy have grown, and, in Europe, major online platforms are now required by law to have clear processes in place to counter 'harmful misinformation'. However, these and most other legal frameworks set up to counter false information fail to set out how fact-checkers, policymakers, or platforms should decide what is harmful or potentially harmful information and what is inaccurate but harmless speech.

In the first part of the book, I proposed what I believe are clear and coherent definitions of the different aspects of information disorder and argued that, to counter the effects of information disorder, we need to take account of all these elements – and promote information integrity. I showed that, to have effect, we need to understand that false information spreads not only online, but also in print and broadcast media, in official communications, business meetings and communications, and in offline community and political settings too.

In this second part, after briefly reviewing both the history of media effects theory and the post-2016 debate over the consequences of false information,[17] I have argued that these disagreements arise, at least in part, from differences in the forms, topics and contexts of information studied, different understandings of the nature of beliefs formed, different understandings of the nature of communication – as the transmission of information, or as a sharing of symbolic beliefs – and different understandings of the mechanisms by which consequences may or may not then occur.

And, while much communication is today, as it always has been, less concerned with provable factual reality than it is with the sharing of views and opinions, many of the claims examined for this study do relate to specific provable facts, to audiences, and in contexts, that mean they have or may have the potential to cause or contribute to specific substantive consequences for individuals and groups.

Comparing entries from the database which evidence in the fact-checks shows caused or contributed to consequences with similar false claims which caused no such outcomes, I have identified in this section three broad factors as shaping the potential of claims to have such effects. I identify these three broad factors as: (i) whether the claim is substantively, or only narrowly, inaccurate, and thus, if believed, causes or reinforces a substantively false factual understanding; (ii) whether the claim, if substantively false, is seen to be true or sufficiently likely to be true by sufficient people for action they might take based on that understanding to cause or contribute to a specific substantive consequence, and (iii) whether those who believe the false claim to be true have the capacity and potential motivation to act in ways that might cause a meaningful consequence, then or later, based on the false understanding caused.

Clearly, the vast amounts of false information circulating online and offline today have or may have other broader effects than those specific to a particular false understanding. But, I argue that understanding the mechanism by which these three factors shape the impact of specific false claims matters. This includes not only analysis of the content but of the nature of audience responses to the information, the context in which the information spread, and the means by which consequential decisions are or may be made.

It is also true that, if we are both to protect society from the harms that false information may cause or contribute to, and to preserve wider freedom of speech while doing so, it is essential to differentiate between false information that does and does not have a real potential to cause harm. And in Part 3 of the book and the Conclusion, I propose a model to do so and the theory that lies behind it. I also discuss the nature and outcome of a trial of the model conducted by three leading fact-checking organisations, and reviewed by independent researchers, in 2024.

Part 3 – Predicting the Weather. Predicting Harm?

'All models are wrong, but some are useful,' the eminent British statistician George Box wrote in the mid-1970s. It would be remarkable if any system 'existing in the real world could be exactly represented by any simple model,' Box acknowledged. However, he added, well-chosen and 'parsimonious' models often do provide 'remarkably useful approximations'. The question is not whether the model is perfect but is the model 'illuminating and useful?'[1]

In a field as complex as misinformation, it would indeed be wise to take a cautious approach and be clear about the limits on what we can and cannot usefully predict about the potential consequences of false information. It is necessary to take account of many elements required for the outcome to occur. It is important, nevertheless, to recognise that, if it is possible to predict the potential of false information to cause, or not to cause, or contribute to substantive consequences, to some useful degree, then this is of great potential significance for the work of fact-checkers, researchers, policymakers and platforms interested in both countering the consequences of false information and defending freedom of speech.

Every day, at the timing of writing, some or all of the more than four hundred fact-checking organisations operating around the world[2] decide what claims to check based on a range of factors, from whether it amounts to a claim of fact or opinion, to the feasibility of finding evidence, the perceived interest of their audience and a more-or-less educated guess of the potential of the claim, if false, to cause or contribute to consequences. To make their selection, these generally small organisations can use a growing array of AI tools to identify potential claims to check, and a mixture of professional expertise and opinion to determine which are most suitable.[3] At the same time, online platforms used by billions of people for daily communication and as a source of information about the world, make increasing use of AI systems to identify content their systems have been trained to detect for potentially contravening their policies on 'offence' and 'harm'. Where they find such content, firms then either leave the content untouched, provide additional information in the form of fact-checks or warning labels, reduce the content's circulation, or remove it from their platform entirely; either way, important decisions are made about the information the world sees, and all done with a limited theoretical framework for how to judge potential to cause harm.

Regulatory systems, in general, are worse. In total, between 2016 and 2022, at least ninety-one laws were introduced or amended around the world, in ways intended, according to their proponents to reduce the harm caused by false information.[4] But while the new laws in the United Kingdom and European Union were aimed, ostensibly at least, at making online platforms more accountable for information they carry or publish, many around the world simply enable authorities to penalise publication of specific pieces of content they deem false, regardless of whether or not the content could be shown to have caused or be likely to cause harm.[5]

Supporters of freedom of speech, such as Danish human rights lawyer Jacob Mchangama, recognise that freedom of speech can be abused to 'amplify division, sow distrust, and inflict serious harm'.[6] However, he and many others view the often arbitrary ways that judgements are made by regulators and others today, about the potential of information to cause harm as a greater cause of concern for society.

*

In Part 3 of the book, I argue that having a carefully developed, widely accepted model that enables fact-checkers, researchers and platforms to identify information that does, and does not, have a substantive potential to cause substantive consequences for society, would meet the standard of being 'useful'. It would better enable fact-checkers, researchers and platforms to focus their attention on information considered to be potentially significant and enable platforms to resist pressure from authoritarian governments to remove content those authorities find disagreeable. It would also enable defenders of freedom of speech to hold platforms to account where they do not resist pressure from authorities, and provide researchers with examples of false information to research in more depth to assess the consequences that do and do not follow.

To assess the practicality of this model for fact-checkers, it was trialled over several months in 2024 by researchers at three leading fact-checking organisations – Africa Check, AFPFactCheck and Full Fact. For the trial, I developed two simple online tools: one to help fact-checkers decide which claims to check, and a second tool to use once a fact-check has been completed, to assess the potential of the claim to cause or contribute to specific substantive consequences. The tools consist of a prescribed set of questions, answers and criteria to be used to come to evidence-based conclusions.

The process and outcomes of the trial were studied by two doctoral researchers supervised by Professor Lucas Graves of the University of Wisconsin Madison. In a report in October 2024, the researchers identified the need for training for the fact-checkers and iteration of the tools, in order for the model to be effective, but that, if integrated successfully into their workflows, the tools would assist in focusing the fact-checkers' efforts on the most potentially impactful claims, and enable them to generate both case studies and aggregate data on misinformation with the potential to cause effects. These findings could then be assessed for 'real world' validity by independent researchers.

The model the fact-checkers used in the trial used, set out in outline in Chapters 7 and 8 of this book, draws on lessons from both the 250 cases of false or misleading information examined in detail in the database, shown in the Appendices, and the evidence from earlier studies of information effects in different fields and contexts, discussed throughout the book. While the model has limitations, which I discuss below, if it achieves what it promises, it might indeed be 'illuminating and useful' for all who are concerned by both the harm that misinformation and disinformation may cause or contribute to, and the need to protect free speech.

Chapter 7

A MODEL FOR IDENTIFYING THE POTENTIAL OF FALSE INFORMATION TO CAUSE OR CONTRIBUTE TO SPECIFIC CONSEQUENCES

British media theorist Denis McQuail noted four decades ago the 'widespread belief' in society that mass media influences public attitudes and behaviour and yet 'great difficulty' in predicting these effects and in attributing events to them later.[1] Had he chosen to do so, McQuail might have drawn on lessons from meteorology to explain the conundrum.

In a dynamic system, such as meteorology, many small events contribute over time to major outcomes in ways that are almost impossible to predict, the mathematician Edward N. Lorenz reasoned in 1972.[2] The analogy that the father of chaos theory used in a talk that year was that, in a chain of many small events, the flap of a butterfly's wings in Brazil might cause a tornado in Texas – a notion soon known as 'the butterfly effect'.[3] Fearing that the proposition could seem 'frivolous', Lorenz noted he was not suggesting this was inevitable. 'If the flap of a butterfly's wings can be instrumental in generating a tornado, it can equally well be instrumental in preventing a tornado,' he went on. His argument was the potential in a dynamic system for 'perturbations of small amplitude' to affect the predictability of subsequent events.[4]

Assessing the potential for one small event – the flap of a butterfly's wing or spread of a specific false claim – to cause or contribute to a larger one, such as a Texan tornado or a distorted election outcome, requires both evidence and understanding. And even in a field such as relatively well understood as meteorology, we lack the data needed to forecast storms far into the future. 'We do not know how many butterflies there are, nor where they are all located, let alone which ones are flapping their wings at any instant,' Lorenz pointed out.[5] Nevertheless, while our ability to forecast future storms remains limited, what meteorologists call our 'useful forecast skill' has improved by around one day for each decade of meteorological research over the past five decades.[6] And, while misinformation effects are less well understood and are affected by a wider range of variables, I argue that with the right model and evidence, it may be possible – knowing what we do know – to judge the potential of specific examples of false information, shared to a given audience, in a given context, to cause or contribute to specific consequences – not the exact timing and location of future storms, but whether such a potential exists.

How the Three Broad Factors Shape the Potential for Consequences

As noted earlier, most misinformation research since 2016 has focused on the influence of false information on individuals' factual understandings or beliefs. Less attention has been paid to whether and how such changes affect those individuals' behaviour.[7] The debate about influence on beliefs and behaviour, such as it is, has been muddied, as discussed in Chapter 5, by different understandings of the nature of the communication, the type of understandings people hold and the mechanisms by which specific and broader consequences may or may not occur.

False information that causes or contributes to specific and broader consequences can come in the form of the false official population figures which, as a function of the law in Nigeria, influence financial resources and political representation for the population concerned.[8] It can come in the form of a false claim made in an academic paper that helps distort a South African president's understanding about the role of HIV in causing AIDS – with disastrous consequences for society.[9] It can appear as a rumour spread in a crowd in a small town in Ethiopia that triggers a killing.[10] It can take the form of false accusations of wrongdoing that harm the mental health of the subject of the claims.[11]

These different forms of information – cognitive, procedural, and legal and affective – are part of the different forms of communication – the transmission of information of sharing of opinion or belief – identified by theorists such as James Carey. They play a role in shaping different forms of perception from factual understandings to symbolic beliefs. Understanding of these distinctions helps explain some of the major areas of disagreement in the field.

At the same time, I believe it is necessary to understand the mechanism or process by which substantive consequences do and do not occur as a result of these effects on understanding. First, I argue, for a claim to cause or contribute to consequences that can be attributed to misinformation, the message must be substantively, not narrowly, inaccurate, and cause or support a factual understanding that is substantively false. Second, sufficient individuals to cause or contribute to the consequence that action based on this false understanding might cause must believe the claim to be 'true', or 'sufficiently likely to be true' to act on the basis of the false understanding formed. Third, those whose understanding is affected must have both capacity and motivation to act on the false understanding in a way that causes or contributes to a substantive consequence.

How a Claim's Degree of Falsity Shapes the Potential for Specific Consequences

The Consequences of Accurate or Only Narrowly Inaccurate Claims

The model, set out below in Figure 7.1, starts with the possibly unremarkable premise that information that is accurate, and presented in proper context, cannot be reasonably identified as causing a misinformation effect. It suggests that the same is true of information that is factually inaccurate but so narrowly that, even if believed, it does not cause or contribute to a substantively false factual understanding or change in attitude on a false factual basis.

Reviewing the cases in the database by this standard, all of which were in some way flawed, more than one in ten were only narrowly inaccurate – such as a mislabelled image or a statistic that was either only

Figure 7.1: How three broad factors shape potential for substantive consequences

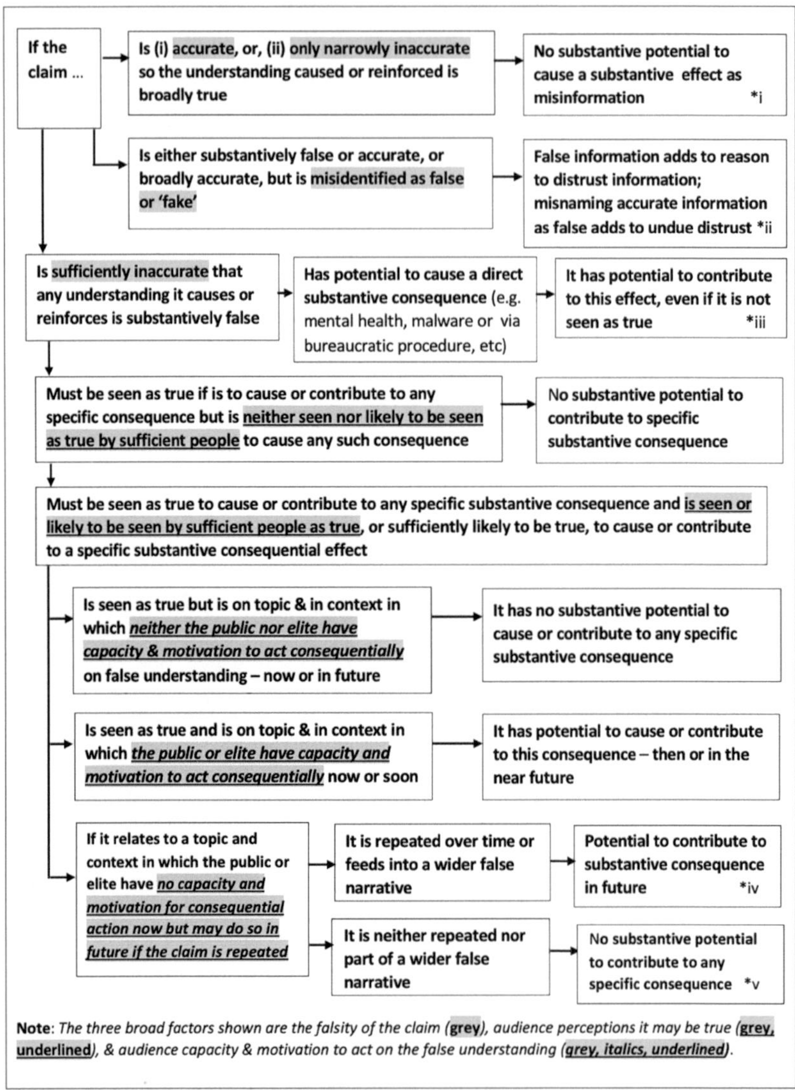

Note: *The three broad factors shown are the falsity of the claim (grey), audience perceptions it may be true (grey, underlined), & audience capacity & motivation to act on the false understanding (grey, italics, underlined).*

marginally wrong or was wrong in a way immaterial to the understanding formed. Evidence, available in the fact-checks, of audience responses to these claims shows that for most, if not all, this information caused or reinforced an understanding that was only narrowly inaccurate, on a detail, but reflected the broad reality concerned.

When prominent Senegalese opposition leader Ousmane Sonko used a photo of a prison in Malawi to illustrate a blog post about crowded prison conditions in his own country, for example, the unlabelled image created a false understanding about where the photo had been taken. Most readers assumed the photo was from a prison in Senegal. However, evidence in the fact-check from prison visitors showed the image and text broadly reflected the reality of prison conditions in Senegal, and audience responses showed that understanding. Any action that an individual – whether policymaker or private citizen – would take, based on the understanding caused, was no different to that which might have been taken had Sonko labelled his photo entirely correctly as 'scenes similar to those to be found in prisons in Senegal' (Case 7.1).

The same was true of images of scenes in a Ugandan maternity hospital,[12] or unrest in Nigeria, discussed earlier,[13] which were inaccurately labelled but nevertheless reflected the situation they described. This was also the case with textual claims, examined in the study, that were narrowly wrong, such as an error in the name of a company involved in a rail infrastructure deal in Democratic Republic of Congo,[14] or a claim that marginally overstated the cost of Internet access in Chad compared to the cost elsewhere in the world (Case 7.2). Here, too, action that policymakers or others might take based on the claim was no different to action they might take on an entirely accurate claim.

Degrees of Falsity – the Limited Effects of a Narrowly Inaccurate Claim

Case 7.1 – Audiences misled on photo, but the broad understanding caused reflected prisons reality

Anne-Sophie Faivre Le-Cadre, 'Ces photos ne montrent pas des détenus au Sénégal mais les conditions de détention y demeurent "extrêmement préoccupantes"', *AFPFactuel*, 6 September 2019, https://factuel.afp.com/ces-photos-ne-montrent-pas-des-detenus-au-senegal-mais-les-conditions-de-detention-y-demeurent.

Case 7.2 – Claim is inaccurate but broad understanding caused reflected reality of high prices

Monique Ngo Mayag, 'Non, le Tchad n'a pas les tarifs Internet les plus élevés au monde', *AFPFactuel*, 25 July 2019, https://factuel.afp.com/non-le-tchad-na-pas-les-tarifs-internet-les-plus-eleves-au-monde.

It is necessary to recognise, of course, that even if a claim that is so narrowly inaccurate that it has no potential to cause a substantive misinformation effect, attention to accuracy by private individuals and policymakers has clear social benefits. A culture that enables a lack of attention to the way claims and decisions are made has pernicious effects for society. This is a good reason to fact-check claims and one not related to countering the specific substantive consequences of a false claim; a fact recognised in point (i) of Figure 7.1, above.

The Consequences of Claims That Are Substantively False or Misidentify Accurate Information as 'Fake News'

By contrast with the claims described above, almost four-fifths of the cases in the databases created or contributed to a specific understanding that was either mostly or completely false or misleading. In a few further cases, the claim was unproven but evidence suggested it was likely to be false. In both scenarios, where action was taken based on a substantively false understanding, it was meaningfully different from the behaviour that would have followed based on an accurate or only narrowly inaccurate understanding.

When parents in townships east of Johannesburg, South Africa, heard false claims that foreign nationals were coming to named schools to kidnap the students, for example, dozens rushed to collect and bring their children to safety. While those who did not believe the false rumour stayed home until the normal hour, those who believed the claim acted in a way that was meaningfully different (Case 7.3). The same was true for action taken based on wholly false information promoting a dangerous health treatment in South Africa,[15] or misleading people about the time that polling closed in an internal party election in the United Kingdom.[16] Substantively false information had a substantive effect on behaviour.

While the consequences of such false claims emerge from the specific false understanding they caused, overexposure to false claims *in general*, and to false claims that accurate news is 'fake news' in particular, has potential to cause or contribute to consequences through an incremental level to distrust in public information. This effect occurs when a sphere is flooded with information of variable quality, spreading doubt about what information may and may not be trusted.[17] It also occurs when accurate information, or an accurate source, are dismissed as 'fake'. A four-country study published in 2020, for example, showed that the perception of 'being disinformed' was enough to increase individuals' distrust of public information.[18] In a case studied in the database, for example, reader responses showed that many followers of a separatist movement in Nigeria, accepted as true false claims that media reporting the activities of the president, Muhammadu Buhari, were 'fake news'. Evidence in the database shows the false understanding reinforced their distrust of the media (Case 7.4).

For this reason, the model set out above in Figure 7.1 identifies – in point (ii) – all cases of false or misleading information as reinforcing, at

Consequences of Claims That Are Substantively False; Mislabel Information as "Fake News"

Case 7.3 – Audiences acted on a substantively false understanding about supposed threat

Tendai Dube, "False kidnapping rumours spread during South Africa violence," *AFPFactCheck*, September 9, 2019, https://factcheck.afp.com/false-kidnapping-rumours-spread-during-south-africa-violence.

Case 7.4 – False claim accurate reports are "fake news" undermines trust in credible media

Mayowa Tijani, "A separatist group said images of Buhari arriving in Japan were fake. But AFP photos show he did attend Yokohama summit," *AFPFactCheck*, September 2, 2019.

a very minor incremental level, individuals' reason to distrust information, and false claims that accurate information is 'fake' as having potential to reinforce at a very minor incremental level individuals' undue distrust in accurate information.

To summarise these points, I argue that the degree to which inaccurate information is false or misleading varies greatly, from information that is narrowly inaccurate – wrong on a point, or to a degree, that is not material to the understanding caused – to information that is either mostly or completely false, or is accurate but taken out of context, and, either way, creates or reinforces a factually false understanding. Information that is substantively false has potential to cause or contribute to a false factual understanding, and, at the same time, reinforces, at a minor incremental level, individuals' reason to distrust information. And false claims that accurate information is false or 'fake news' have potential to reinforce, at a minor incremental level, their undue distrust in accurate information.

A key element of the model set out in Figure 7.1 is, thus, that information that is inaccurate but, only narrowly so, may have no substantive potential, if seen in context, to cause or contribute to specific, substantive consequences that would not have been caused by entirely accurate information. By contrast, substantively false information has or may have a potential to cause or contribute to substantive consequences, as shown in the cases discussed. This has important implications for understanding and responding to false information in ways that both address the risks that misinformation and disinformation pose to society and protect freedom of speech.

Whether Sufficient People's Factual Understanding or Attitude Is Affected to Cause or Contribute to Specific Consequences

False Information Can Contribute to Particular Consequences Even If It Does Not Affect Understanding

In some cases, it is possible for false information to cause or contribute to specific consequences – whether or not it is seen as 'true'. This occurs, at a broad level, through the disinformation effect described above – a barrage of claims not necessarily intended to be believed, but to cause or contribute to confusion. At the same time, certain types of specific false claims may have potential to cause or contribute to specific consequences whether or not seen as true.

One way this can happen is via audiences responding to clickbait containing links to computer viruses or malware, regardless of whether they believe the claims to be true, as a case from the database, discussed above, demonstrates. So where online reports that use false claims to engage attention contain a link to a computer virus or malware, they put readers at risk of exposure to digital harms without having to be believed to be true (Case 7.5).

I also argue that false claims about specific individuals may, subject to repetition and the individual's exposure to prior trauma, have consequences for the mental health of the subject of the claim, regardless of whether the claim is perceived to be true. In one case examined in the database, for example, mislabelling of a photo of a Zambian man who had suffered a traumatic physical attack two years earlier, caused severe distress for the man shown. The widespread sharing online of an old photograph of him online covered in blood from the earlier incident forced him to 'relive the events of the day', he explained (Case 7.6).

False Claims That Cause or Contribute to Consequences – Whether or Not Seen As 'True'

Case 7.5 – Clickbait false claim that attracted readers to article which included link to a virus

Grace Gichuhi, 'Kenyan gospel music star Ringtone Apoke is alive and well', *Africa Check*, 12 July 2019, https://africacheck.org/fact-checks/meta-programme-fact-checks/kenyan-gospel-music-star-ringtone-apoko-alive-and-well.

Case 7.6 – A false claim that – whether or not believed – retraumatised the subject of the claim

Mary Kulundu, 'Zambian farmer "greatly distressed" by posts falsely identifying him as victim of South African violence', *AFPFactCheck*, 13 September 2019, https://factcheck.afp.com/zambian-farmer-greatly-distressed-posts-falsely-identifying-him-victim-south-african-violence.

Case 7.7 – A false claim that had consequences for procedural, legal reasons

Motunrayo Joel and David Ajikobi, 'What a waste: fact-checking four claims about Nigeria's garbage problem', *Africa Check*, 26 July 2019, https://africacheck.org/fact-checks/reports/what-waste-fact-checking-four-claims-about-nigerias-garbage-problem.

Other types of false information can also have consequences for society for entirely bureaucratic, or legal reasons – regardless of whether the claim is seen as true. This is the case with the false data discussed earlier, used by officials in Nigeria to determine resource allocation and planning decisions for cities such as Lagos. In this and other such cases, the consequences of the false information are mandated by law and practice, once it is made public, not whether officials judge the figures to be true (Case 7.7).

Taking these examples into account, it is clear that, as set out in point (iii) of Figure 7.1, several specific types of false information may cause or contribute to specific substantive consequences – from harming individuals' mental health or exposing them to digital viruses or malware, to being taken into account in a decision for entirely bureaucratic or procedural reasons – regardless of whether the claim is considered to be true.

Most False Information Needs to Affect Factual Understanding or Attitude to Cause or Contribute to a Consequence

Nevertheless, as evidence from the database shows, in most cases, false information needs to cause or reinforce a false factual understanding or an attitude or belief among sufficient people to cause or contribute to a specific substantive consequence. For example, when individuals in South Africa saw a false claim that apricot seeds are a cure for cancer, they decided to take up the treatment, not as a side-effect, but as a result of the false factual understanding the claim caused. While some were rightly sceptical, many asked only where to buy dangerously large amounts of apricot seeds (Case 7.8).

A False Factual Understanding Caused or Contributed to Particular Behaviour

Case 7.8 – Readers who responded by ingesting apricot seeds acted on a false understanding

Taryn Khourie, 'Apricot seeds don't kill cancer cells, can have deadly side effects', *Africa Check*, 25 October 2019, https://africacheck.org/fact-checks/meta-programme-fact-checks/apricot-seeds-dont-kill-cancer-cells-can-have-deadly-side.

Case 7.9 – Readers who bought new insurance product acted on a false factual understanding

Allwell Okpi, 'No, malaria doesn't kill 300,000 people in Nigeria a year, as insurance seller claimed', *Africa Check*, 19 September 2019, https://africacheck.org/fact-checks/reports/no-malaria-doesnt-kill-300000-people-nigeria-year-insurance-seller-claimed.

Case 7.10 – Readers who believed false claim of a Muslim threat in Nigeria urged a violent response

Allwell Okpi, 'No, daggers seized by police in Nigeria's Kano state not for "killing Christians"', *Africa Check*, 19 August 2019, https://africacheck.org/fact-checks/spotchecks/no-daggers-seized-police-nigerias-kano-state-not-killing-christians.

In the same way, when readers in Nigeria responded to an insurance firm's claim exaggerating the number of deaths caused by malaria, they asked how to buy its health insurance product due to a false factual understanding of the risk the disease posed. The false understanding was a necessary causal element in the behaviour (Case 7.9).

In other cases, false claims about topics closely linked to audiences' identity and community – such as relations between religious groups in Nigeria or racial disparities in South Africa – were often taken as both a reaffirmation of existing beliefs and a factual basis for action. In one case examined in the database, for example, the response of readers to a false claim that Muslims in northern Nigeria were acquiring large stocks of knives to prepare attacks on Christians was to recommit to the separatist cause – 'God give us Biafra' – and make a call for a practical response to an immediate threat: 'Every Christian should get prepared spiritually and physically,' one man responded. 'Wake up Christian soldiers, we must not be defeated', wrote another. 'All I need is a machine gun', wrote a third (Case 7.10). How many of the people whose attitudes were reaffirmed by such false claims were among those who took part in subsequent violence is not clear from evidence in the fact-check.

Like these cases from the database, the examples discussed earlier in the book of governments in South Africa and Nigeria setting health policies based on false information, show that policymakers also do not, in general, take such decisions based on information that they consider to be factually false. As his own subsequent account makes clear, for example, when the then-President Thabo Mbeki of South Africa changed policy on treatment for AIDS patients in 2000, he did so neither on a whim, nor for political advantage, but on the basis of a false factual understanding.[19] 'Today I would stand by everything,' the former president wrote more than a decade later.[20] And interviews show the same was true of the small group of Nigerian politicians who banned the WHO polio vaccination campaign in half a dozen northern Nigerian states in 2002. The disastrous decision was, University of Ibadan medical anthropologist Ayodele Jegede wrote, 'a genuine, albeit misplaced and ineffective, attempt by the local leadership to protect its people'.[21] In both these cases, and those from the database discussed above, the factual misunderstanding the false information caused was both genuine and an essential factor in the outcome that followed.

In all the cases discussed so far, it took just an individual, or small group of individuals, to believe and act on the false understanding caused, for a consequence to occur – for individuals to take a dangerous medication,[22] or take part in inter-religious violence.[23] In the cases cited from the database, this concerned the actions of private individuals. In the earlier cases from South Africa and Nigeria, it concerned the actions of leading politicians – a state president and state governors. However, for other types of consequences to occur – to affect the outcome of an election,[24] or cause a boycott powerful enough to substantively affect a major company's operations[25] – hundreds, thousands or tens of thousands of people need to take action for the consequence to occur. Without sufficient people acting on the false premise, this type of substantive consequence does not occur. And this also has important implications, for how we understand and respond to concern about false information and address the risks it poses.

*

How Differences In Audience Capacity and Motivation to Act On False Understandings Shape Potential to Cause, Contribute to Specific Consequences

For substantively false information to cause a specific consequence, a false understanding alone is not enough. Rather, those whose belief or factual understanding is affected – policymakers or members of the public – must, have both the capacity and motivation to act, then or in future, on the false understanding caused.

Predicting human behaviour is, of course, a notoriously hazardous exercise, and this is often taken as reason for scepticism about attempts to predict the potential for information to cause or contribute to particular consequences. As the anthropologist Manvir Singh noted in 2024, US researchers concerned by the risks posed by misinformation often cite the case of North Carolina man Edgar Maddison Welch as an example. Acting on a false rumour that a particular pizza restaurant in Washington, DC was at the centre of a paedophile sex trafficking operation, Welch drove to the city, armed with an assault rifle, entered, and shot up the building in December 2016.[26] But those who use the so-called 'Pizzagate' incident as evidence of misinformation effects are missing the point, Singh argued. Millions saw and believed the false claims about the restaurant, but only one man picked up a rifle and attacked the venue. 'What's really striking is how anomalous that act was,' Singh wrote.[27]

Certainly, the variability of the way people respond to information makes individual reactions difficult to predict. But if one person's actions can have major consequences – shooting up a building, in this case, or affecting the lives of thousands by changing health policies, in another – the fact that the more common responses are anodyne does not diminish the concern, as Singh suggests. And while determining a claim's potential to cause secondary or tertiary effects is beyond the predictive capacity of the evidence normally available, I suggest that it is often possible to reasonably judge an audience's capacity and potential motivation to take action, then or in future, in response to a false understanding. And I argue, below, that five factors shape this potential.

Five Factors That Shape Capacity and Motivation to Act, From Topic to Context to Audience Characteristics

As audience behaviour detailed in the database shows, the *topic of a claim* plays an important role shaping the field or type of consequence that misinformation may cause – whether it relates to public health in DR Congo,[28] the operations of a bank in London,[29] the threat to life posed by health researchers in Ethiopia,[30] or the outcome of an election in Nigeria.[31] For this reason, claims which cause or contribute to a false understanding about an entirely abstract or impracticable topic will – in most cases – provide no course of action that would directly cause or contribute to a substantive consequence, affecting the well-being of individuals or society.

Take, for example, the direct effects of the false understanding that a group of underwater sculptures sunk into the seabed in the Caribbean had been intended by the artist as a tribute to the lives lost in the transatlantic slave trade. While the claims provoked an interesting debate, that could in theory give rise in time to hard-to-predict secondary or tertiary effects, the false understanding gave the audience who believed it no cause, there and then, for direct action that would cause or contribute to specific substantive consequences. The only direct consequence was the discussion itself (Case 7.11). The same was true, to consider another example, of a false claim that a large rock – an artwork resting on a short pedestal in Saudi Arabia – was not on a pedestal but floating in mid-air in Jerusalem: proof of God's work. The only substantive outcome was the false understanding caused (Case 7.12). The topic of the claim was a

How Audience Capacity and Motivation to Act Shapes the Potential for Consequences

Case 7.11 – No course of consequential action for those mistaken about a sculptor's artistic intentions

Amanuel Neguede, 'These statues were not intended as a tribute to drowned slaves — but the artist is glad they are "stimulating debate"', *AFPFactCheck*, 19 December 2019, https://factcheck.afp.com/these-statues-were-not-intended-tribute-drowned-slaves-artist-glad-they-are-stimulating-debate.

Case 7.12 – No course of consequential action for those misled a rock had been found floating mid-air

Mayowa Tijani, 'A giant rock in Saudi Arabia is being falsely hailed as the site of a miracle in Jerusalem', *AFPFactCheck*, 26 July 2019, https://factcheck.afp.com/giant-rock-saudi-arabia-being-falsely-hailed-site-miracle-jerusalem.

key factor in shaping the capacity and motivation of the audience to act on the false understanding caused.

The second factor is the *motivational effect* of the false understanding on behaviour. As seen in the 'Pizzagate' case discussed above, many factors will shape whether individuals are motivated to act on any given false understanding, from the nature of the claim's cognitive, affective, or behavioural effect, to its alignment with the readers' or viewers' pre-existing views or attitudes, to the perceived costs of taking action and/or inaction. For most of those who saw and believed the false claim that a paedophile ring was operating from a DC restaurant, the cost of the action that one man took – shooting up the restaurant and going to jail[32] – was too high to contemplate. By contrast, for dozens of parents who rushed to collect their children from school in South Africa when they heard a false rumour that students were being kidnapped, the cost of taking action was an unnecessarily early pickup. If the rumour had been true and they failed to act, the cost could have been the loss of their children (Case 7.13).

How Audience Capacity and Motivation to Act Shapes the Potential for Consequences

Case 7.13 – Individuals compare the cost of action and inaction before deciding on a false claim

Tendai Dube, 'False kidnapping rumours spread during South Africa violence', *AFPFactCheck*, 9 September 2019, https://factcheck.afp.com/false-kidnapping-rumours-spread-during-south-africa-violence.

A third factor that shapes audience capacity and motivation to act is the *practical, political, or social context* in which the false understanding occurs. At times, the issue is practical logistics. When false accusations spread against a specified individual, those who believe them can engage in online abuse at a distance, but other actions require the audience to be in close proximity. In the cases, discussed earlier, of the physical abuse of two women in Togo[33] and killing of two men in Ethiopia,[34] the consequence required that the crowd was close by. When similar claims spread online, no evidence of any such outcome emerged.

How Audience Capacity and Motivation to Act Shapes the Potential for Consequences

Case 7.14 – Individuals convinced of a false claim from another country may have no capacity to act

Africa Check, 'Unravelling claim that Hillary Clinton sold 20% of US uranium to Russia', 18 July 2019, https://africacheck.org/fact-checks/meta-programme-fact-checks/unravelling-claim-hillary-clinton-sold-20-us-uranium-russia.

Case 7.15 – Politicians may have more capacity to act than members of the public

Cayley Clifford, 'South Africa's police recruitment drive based on dubious UN standard', *Africa Check*, 17 July 2019, https://africacheck.org/fact-checks/spotchecks/south-africas-police-recruitment-drive-based-dubious-un-standard.

With other types of claim, the key factors can be the political or social context. When a false claim, examined in the database, spread in the United States that the 2016 US presidential candidate Hillary Clinton had sold 20 per cent of US uranium to Russia in 2010, those who believed the claim had the capacity, if they wished, to vote for or against her, and the claim may have influenced the decision of a few to a minor degree. When the same claim spread online in South Africa in 2019, those who believed it had no direct means to act on the false understanding it caused. Clinton was no longer running for office, and, even if she had been, most who saw the claim in South Africa would have had no vote (Case 7.14). In another case, most South Africans who saw and believed a false claim, spread in Parliament, that the country was missing a UN target for the size of its police force, had no direct way to act on the claim. By contrast, politicians taking part in the police budget debate had the opportunity and could have been motivated by the false claim in their vote (Case 7.15). The practical, political context was key to the outcome.

A fourth factor is the *duration of the false understanding* caused – shaped by the topic, the inherent durability of the claim, and repetition or lack of repetition of the information and the audience's willingness to reconsider a false understanding. While some false understandings are likely to be long-lived because they relate to a topic on which the audience has a long-fixed conviction,[35] false understandings on other topics are likely to be short-lived – such as false understandings caused by fake death notices of famous people who are easily and quickly shown to be alive.[36]

How Audience Capacity and Motivation to Act Shapes the Potential for Consequences

Case 7.16 – Claims may need to create a long-lasting false understanding to affect policy decisions

Motunrayo Joel and David Ajikobi, 'What a waste: fact-checking four claims about Nigeria's garbage problem', *Africa Check*, 26 July 2019, https://africacheck.org/fact-checks/reports/what-waste-fact-checking-four-claims-about-nigerias-garbage-problem.

Case 7.17 – Short-lived claims may not have time to cause or contribute to a substantive consequence

Tendai Dube, 'Botswana's president wasn't in a helicopter crash, but the pilots did perform a precautionary landing', *AFPFactCheck*, 25 July 2019, https://factcheck.afp.com/botswanas-president-wasnt-helicopter-crash-pilots-did-perform-precautionary-landing.

The duration of the false understanding often plays a role in shaping the potential for consequences to occur. Officials in Nigeria have acted for many years on the basis of false figures, published repeatedly, about the population of Nigeria's largest city, for example (Case 7.16). By contrast, when a false report circulated briefly in Botswana, that the president's helicopter had crash landed, members of the public or policymakers who might have responded to the false news had little time to do so before the president appeared before the media to refute the claim. It being a Saturday, even the stock markets had no time for a reaction. The market was closed – and with it, the opportunity for market consequences to occur. (Case 7.17).

When the topic is one on which individuals could act consequentially, *sufficient people* must still be motivated to take action for the consequence to occur. If the consequence requires that just one individual – policymaker or member of the public – take action, the bar for consequences is low. It was enough for just one individual to be sufficiently motivated to shoot up a DC restaurant, due to false information, for that consequence to occur. (Case 7.18).

How Audience Capacity and Motivation to Act Shapes the Potential for Consequences

Case 7.18 – Only one individual had to respond violently to a false claim to cause a consequence

Matthew Haag and Maya Salam, 'Gunman in "Pizzagate" Shooting Is Sentenced to 4 Years in Prison', *The New York Times*, 22 June 2017, https://www.nytimes.com/2017/06/22/us/pizzagate-attack-sentence.html.

Case 7.19 – Dozens needed to take action to cause the death of two health researchers killed by mob

Dawit Endeshaw, 'Mob action costs two researchers' lives', *The Reporter Ethiopia*, 27 October 2018, https://www.thereporterethiopia.com/6682/.

Case 7.20 – Thousands needed to boycott South African Airways to dent the company's fortunes

Tendai Dube, 'This is an airport worker in Hawaii, not a South African Airways baggage handler', *AFPFactCheck*, 13 December 2019, https://factcheck.afp.com/airport-worker-hawaii-not-south-african-airways-baggage-handler.

Other types of consequence require action by a group. When the two health researchers were killed, and a laboratory technician maimed, in Ethiopia in 2018, dozens of people were required to take part in the assault to cause the injuries that followed (Case 7.19). And for a boycott of a South African airline, caused by false claims of wrongdoing by staff, to have had a substantive effect on the company's fortunes, thousands would have been required to act. As it was, only a few dozen people agreed to stop using the airline and effect was negligible (Case 7.20).

How Differences In the Capacity and Motivations of Policymakers and the Public to Act On False Claims Shape Potential to Cause Specific Consequences

In 2003, Robert Entman of George Washington University argued that, with some exceptions, political ideas typically cascade down from the highest level of politics, through middle-ranking policymakers to the public, due to the framing powers of the elite.[37] Observing the cases discussed earlier in this chapter from South Africa and Nigeria, I argue that the consequences for society when elites are misinformed can also cascade 'downhill' to the public, due to the elite's power to make policy for individuals and society. However, the capacity and motivation of policymakers and the public to act on false information in a way that affects others also varies greatly with the topic and context concerned.

How Capacity and Motivation of Policymakers and the Public to Act On False Claims Varies

Case 7.21 – The public had capacity to decide whether to accept fake 'army rules' for their behaviour

Mayowa Tijani, 'Nigeria's army has been stepping up ID checks and troop deployments but says you should ignore this "fake" security alert', *AFPFactCheck*, 30 October 2019, https://factcheck.afp.com/nigerias-army-has-been-stepping-id-checks-and-troop-deployments-says-you-should-ignore-fake-security.

Case 7.22 – The public had capacity to decide whether to vote after fake warnings of election violence

Kunle Adebayo, 'Photos from 2015 polls, xenophobic attacks shared in connection to Kogi, Bayelsa elections', *ICIR/FactHub*, 16 November 2019, https://www.icirnigeria.org/fact-check-photos-from-2015-polls-xenophobic-attacks-shared-in-connection-to-kogi-bayelsa-elections/.

Case 7.23 – Policymakers, business leaders had capacity to act on false figures on Nairobi economy

Alphonce Shiundu, 'Nairobi produces a fifth of Kenya's GDP – not 45%, as the Guardian claimed', *Africa Check*, 20 August 2019, https://africacheck.org/fact-checks/reports/nairobi-produces-fifth-kenyas-gdp-not-45-guardian-claimed.

Case 7.24 – Politicians influenced by false claim on police numbers had capacity to vote police budget

Cayley Clifford, 'South Africa's police recruitment drive based on dubious UN standard', *Africa Check*, 17 July 2019, https://africacheck.org/fact-checks/spotchecks/south-africas-police-recruitment-drive-based-dubious-un-standard.

Members of the public, for example, have capacity, and may have motivation, to act consequentially in numerous aspects of their private and civic life. This was true for South Africans choosing whether to take up an easily available supposed treatment for cancer, discussed earlier in this chapter,[38] and for Nigerians choosing whether to follow rules for public behaviour, said falsely to have been issued by the army (Case 7.21). It was also the case for people choosing whether to vote in an election, despite false claims that violence was taking place around their polling stations (Case 7.22).

In other cases, where false claims related to particular organisational or public policy decisions, members of the public often have more limited capacity to take consequential action on the false understanding a false claim may cause. For example, official figures in Kenya have long overstated the share of the economy generated by the capital, Nairobi. While policymakers and businesses who believed the exaggerated figure had capacity to direct resources to or away from Nairobi on this basis, members of the public have had limited power for consequential action (Case 7.23). And members of the public who heard false claims on TV or social media about the number of police required in South Africa had limited direct capacity to act in ways that would affect the size of the police force, but lawmakers who heard the false claim in a parliamentary debate had an opportunity to vote on the police budget (Case 7.24).

How Capacity and Motivation of Policymakers and the Public to Act On False Claims Varies

Case 7.25 – Politicians had no capacity to act consequentially on false understanding on family matter

Mayowa Tijani, 'Social media abuzz in Nigeria over supposed presidential wedding. Here is what we know', *AFPFactCheck*, 15 October 2019, https://factcheck.afp.com/social-media-abuzz-nigeria-over-supposed-presidential-wedding-here-what-we-know.

Case 7.26 – No course of consequential action for those misled a rock had been found floating mid-air

Mayowa Tijani, 'A giant rock in Saudi Arabia is being falsely hailed as the site of a miracle in Jerusalem', *AFPFactCheck*, 26 July 2019, https://factcheck.afp.com/giant-rock-saudi-arabia-being-falsely-hailed-site-miracle-jerusalem.

By contrast, when false claims touch on matters outside the scope of public policy, elites may have similarly limited capacity to intervene. Nigerian officials, for example, criticised false claims spread in 2019 that the Nigerian president had secretly taken a second wife, but had no power or capacity, if they believed the claim to be true, to act on what would be essentially a family matter (Case 7.25). And, just like members of the public, if policymakers believed a false claim, discussed above, that a large rock had been found floating mid-air in Jerusalem, there was no course of consequential action for them to take based on the false belief (Case 7.26).

When judging whether any individual – policymaker or member of the public – has or may have the capacity and motivation to take consequential action, it is, of course, important to consider the context in which such consequences might occur. In November 2019, for example, supporters of one of the contenders in state elections falsely claimed that their candidate had won the vote. Election authorities had, in fact, declared the results inconclusive and ordered a new round of voting. Falling between the two rounds of voting, the false understanding the claim caused disillusioned many of the politician's supporters who stayed away from the second round of polls.[39] The decision to stage a new round of voting provided the context for the effect (Case 7.27).

Whether Context Exists, Then or In Future, For Consequences of False Understanding to Occur

Case 7.27 – False claim spread in Nigeria between rounds of voting – context for direct consequence

Jennifer Ojugbeli, 'No, Nigerian politician Melaye hasn't won Kogi West senator's seat – election declared inconclusive', 20 November 2019, https://africacheck.org/fact-checks/meta-programme-fact-checks/no-nigerian-politician-melaye-hasnt-won-kogi-west-senators.

Case 7.28 – False claim in Kenya three years before polls – no direct consequence without repetition

Mary Kulundu, 'Ignore these "polling figures" on the popularity of Kenya's possible presidential contenders — they didn't really come from IPSO,' *AFPFactCheck*, 3 July 2019, https://factcheck.afp.com/ignore-these-polling-figures-popularity-kenyas-possible-presidential-contenders-they-didnt-really.

A few month earlier in Kenya, supporters of a group of leading politicians spread a false claim that exaggerated popular backing for politicians they supported to run in the next polls. The difference was that the Kenyan polls were not due until 2022. Any false understanding formed in 2019 would have had little impact on perceptions three years later, unless the claims were repeated and reinforced over time. The context in which the false claim first emerged did not create an opportunity for direct, substantive consequences at the time (Case 7.28).

Taking all these points into consideration, I argue that where information is substantively false and affects the factual understanding of sufficient people to cause a consequence, but those influenced have no capacity and motivation for consequential action, then or in future, the claim – as shown in Figure 7.1 – has no substantive potential to cause or contribute to a specific substantive consequence. Where the information affects the factual understanding of people with the capacity and potential motivation to act consequentially there and then, consequences have potential to occur in the near term. And where such action is only possible in the future, the claim likely has the potential to cause a consequence only if the false claim is repeated or feeds into a broad false narrative, and the context allows, as set out in point (iv) of Figure 7.1. Where this does not happen, the claim is identified, as seen in point (v) of Figure 7.1, as having no substantive potential for specific consequences.

*

Criteria For Whether Claims Have a Substantive Potential to Cause Effects

The advances that have come in weather forecasting over the more than five decades since Edward Lorenz's talk on predicting storms have been the result, meteorologists say, of improvements in data gathering, understanding of the science involved and computational capacity.[40] A greater quantity and quality of data has been gathered on the complex conditions that contribute to major weather events and meteorologists have developed a better understanding of, and ability to compute, the interaction of the different factors.

By comparison, society's ability to predict the potential for particular false claims to cause or contribute to political, social, economic, or health consequences is still very limited due to both the lack of reliable, good quality data on the factors that shape effects and our poorer understanding of the processes involved.

While we cannot, today, predict the precise likelihood of particular consequences from the exposure of the public or policymakers to particular false information, I argue we can, however, make a reasonable judgement of whether a substantive potential for consequences to occur exists, based on careful judgements of the three broad factors set out in the model, above. We can, of course, only do this if clear and credible criteria are used for determining how these factors may be assessed in ways that are as objective and consistent as possible. As the misinformation researchers Ullrich Ecker and colleagues argued in *Nature* in 2024, 'Standards exist for domains outside science in which knowledge can be accumulated.' Why not this one, too.[41]

Criteria: Assessing Whether a Claim Is Accurate or Only Narrowly Inaccurate, or Is Substantively False or Misleading

Fact-checking organisations such as those whose work is used as a source of evidence for this study are assessed annually or bi-annually, by independent assessors drawn from academia and the media for adherence to agreed standards covering the non-partisanship, transparency and quality of their methodology and sources.[42] In this study, I have used evidence provided in these fact-checks to assess the falsity of the claims and their effects on the audience's factual understanding or attitudes.

Assessing the accuracy of claims, I first distinguish between claims that are wholly accurate or only narrowly inaccurate, on the one hand, and claims that are substantively false or misleading, on the other. For this model, claims are assessed as accurate, or only narrowly inaccurate, if credible evidence set out in the fact-check, shows that (i) all key elements of the claim are accurate and presented in context, or (ii) any elements that are inaccurate or out of context are either only marginally inaccurate or immaterial to the understanding created.

Claims that Are Wholly or Narrowly Inaccurate Vs Substantively False or Misleading

Case 7.29 – Error in the name of firm in a rail contract was immaterial to understanding caused

Ange Kasongo, 'Non, la RDC n'a pas signé un accord avec la firme russe Russell', *AFPFactuel*, 29 October 2019, https://factuel.afp.com/non-la-rdc-na-pas-signe-un-accord-avec-la-firme-russe-russell.

Case 7.30 – Obasanjo spoke to media but did not make claimed remarks – understanding was false

Jennifer Ojugbeli, 'Obasanjo did not say there will be a second war in Nigeria', *Africa Check*, 5 July 2019, https://africacheck.org/fact-checks/meta-programme-fact-checks/obasanjo-did-not-say-there-will-be-second-war-nigeria.

Case 7.31 – Video was real but not related to the violence – effect on understanding was misleading

Mayowa Tijani and Tendai Dube, 'This video of a South African minister blasting immigration was filmed in 2017 and he's since been replaced', *AFPFactCheck*, 4 September 2019, https://factcheck.afp.com/video-south-african-minister-blasting-immigration-was-filmed-2017-and-hes-been-replaced.

By contrast, claims are assessed as substantively false or misleading when credible evidence, presented in the fact-check, shows that (i) material elements of the claim are inaccurate, or accurate but distorted, taken out of context, or conflated with others in a way that is misleading and (ii) any elements of the claim that are accurate are immaterial to the understanding caused. In such a case, I argue the broad factual understanding the claim causes or reinforces is substantively false, or misleading.

When an official in Democratic Republic of Congo made an error, misnaming a Russian company involved in a rail infrastructure contract in 2019, for example, the aspect that was wrong was immaterial to the understanding caused. The firm concerned was misidentified, but the broad understanding the report caused – that the government had signed an agreement with a Russian firm to build a major piece of transport infrastructure – was correct (Case 7.29). By contrast, when separatists in Nigeria claimed that former President Olusegun Obasanjo had warned in an interview that a new civil war in the country was looming, the understanding created was false. It was true that Obasanjo had spoken to the media, but this was immaterial to the understanding caused.

He had made no statement about a coming civil war and was known to believe the opposite (Case 7.30).

When a video of a former South African minister making hostile remarks about foreign nationals circulated during a wave of xenophobic violence in the country, the claim made about it was misleading. The video was genuine, and the remarks made were material, but the recording dated from two years previously and the minister had since been dismissed. His views had been repudiated and did not represent the view of the authorities, as the video claimed. The effect of the claim on the audience's understanding was misleading (Case 7.31).

Reviewing the examples in the database, it is clear that it is possible, through content analysis of the claim and evidence of both the situation described, and audience responses, to distinguish between claims that are accurate or broadly accurate, and cause a factual understanding that is essentially accurate on the one hand, and those that are substantively false or misleading, and cause or reinforce a factual understanding that is broadly false, on the other.

Criteria: Assessing Whether a Claim Is or May Be Seen as Sufficiently Credible by Sufficient People to Cause or Contribute to a Specific Consequence

Reviewing cases in the database, it is also clear it is possible, in many cases, to develop good understanding of a claim's reach, based on evidence of (i) the type of channel or setting in which the claim was seen or heard and data on channel reach and audience responses, such as shares, and (ii) whether or not the claim has been or is likely to be repeated over time. It was already evident in 2019, for example, that the conditions existed for the false claim, discussed earlier, that spread in Kenya exaggerating support for particular politicians to continue to spread then and over the coming years, extending the reach to a large audience (Case 7.32). Having assessed the known and potential reach, it can then be possible to assess whether some or any of the audience believe the claim to be true by reviewing evidence in the fact-checks of (i) the actions and (ii) the statements and comments of the audience in response.

Assessing Whether a Claim Is Seen as Credible by Sufficient People to Cause a Consequence

Case 7.32 – Claims repeated or feeding into a narrative can have greater reach than single claims

Dancan Bwire, 'Huge crowd greeting Kenya's deputy president? No, fans at 1973 rock concert in US', *Africa Check*, 17 July 2019, https://africacheck.org/fact-checks/meta-programme-fact-checks/huge-crowd-greeting-kenyas-deputy-president-no-fans-1973.

Case 7.33 – Offline behaviour can provide evidence an audience perceives a claim to be true

Tendai Dube, 'False kidnapping rumours spread during South Africa violence', *AFPFactCheck*, 9 September 2019, https://factcheck.afp.com/false-kidnapping-rumours-spread-during-south-africa-violence.

Case 7.34 – Online comments and responses can provide evidence of audience perceptions

Charlotte Mason, 'This photograph shows Eritrean torture victims in Egypt, not slaves in Libya', *AFPFactcheck*, 20 December 2019, https://factcheck.afp.com/photograph-shows-eritrean-torture-victims-egypt-not-slaves-libya.

Sometimes the effects of false claims on understanding can be assessed from evidence of behaviour for which the false understanding created is the only plausible explanation. When a false claim, discussed earlier in the chapter, spread in South Africa suggesting that foreign nationals were kidnapping children, parents rushed to collect their children early. The only reason they had to do so was fear that the claim was or could be true (Case 7.33). In other cases, audience members' statements in person, in print or broadcast media, or via online reactions such as 'likes' and 'emojis',[43] can provide useful indications of audience member perceptions of the claim (Case 7.34).

If evidence of audience responses is not available, the model uses content analysis and the five criteria discussed in Chapter 3 to assess whether the claim could be seen by sufficient numbers of people as potentially plausible,[44] and is easy to understand and process,[45] emotionally affecting,[46] aligns with some of the audience's views,[47] comes from a source some of the audience would see as credible,[48] and conditions exist for the claim or similar claims to be repeated.[49]

To judge a claim's potential to cause or contribute to a particular consequence, it is, of course, necessary to assess not only the reach of the claim, and how many believe it to be true, but how many must do so in order for the claim to have a substantive potential to cause or contribute to any potential outcome or outcomes envisaged: an individual or larger group and the capacity they must have to act in ways that affect them or others.

Assessing whether or not a claim is or may be seen as sufficiently credible, by sufficient people, to have a substantive potential to cause or contribute to a consequence, the model thus first considers the number required to act to cause the consequence, then evidence in the fact-check of the online and offline spread of the claim, and whether the claim has been or may be repeated. If evidence is available in the fact-check of audience statements and actions, the model then assesses whether the number identified as finding the claim credible would exceed the minimum number required to cause, or contribute, to the consequence.

If no such evidence is available, the model works on the basis that, if a claim is or may be considered plausible by at least some of the audience, and meets a majority of the other above criteria, it is likely to be considered true by at least some of the audience, and assesses whether the number who would likely see the claim as true may exceed the minimum needed.

Of course, while the studies referenced above show that these five factors are, or may be, a useful means for understanding whether people are more or less likely to see claims as credible, the model recognises that audience responses vary depending on the topic, the audience and context, and that caution is required in coming to any findings on how different audiences may respond to information. If a claim circulates in a context such as a courtroom, or committee hearing where claims are likely to be debated and challenged, these factors of language and presentation may have less influence than if the claim is spread in a crowd or online setting that is more subject to groupthink than to debate. The model also takes account of what may be at stake for the audience in assessing the accuracy of a claim – and the jeopardy of getting it wrong.

Criteria: Assessing Audience Capacity, Motivation For Consequential Action

As noted at the beginning of this chapter, different forms of false information play a part in different processes of communication, some of which do and some of which do not depend on audience members acting on a false understanding caused.

Assessing potential consequences that don't require action

To establish whether or not a message contained a computer virus or malware that could cause consequences for those who receive it, the model relies on either digital forensics, or audience reports, or a combination of both. Determining the potential for a false claim or claims to cause or contribute to substantive consequences for the mental health of its subjects is or can be more of a challenge, depending as it does on information about the individuals concerned that is typically less readily available. For this reason, the model identifies a claim or claims as having potential to have a substantive consequence on a subject's mental health where the claims (i) are negative in nature and relate to the behaviour, character, or circumstances of an individual or group known to have been subject to prior trauma or poor mental health, and (ii) are repeated over time. Establishing the potential of false official figures to cause consequences by the way they are applied in decision-making, as happened in the case in Nigeria discussed earlier, the model relies on evidence of the country's laws and official procedures.

Assessing capacity, motivation to act on a false understanding

In most cases, consequences occur from individuals' decision-making and actions – a field of behaviour notoriously difficult to predict.

Assessing the capacity and motivation of audiences to act on a false understanding, the model first divides audiences into policymakers and members of the public, recognising the differences, discussed at more length in Chapter 6, in the capacity and motivation they have to take consequential decisions on different topics.

The model then considers a combination of factors: (i) the topic of the claim; (ii) its observed or potential motivational effect; (iii) the practical, social or political context in which the claim has spread; (iv) the duration or likely duration of the false understanding caused, and (v) the number of those whose understanding was needed to cause the effect.

The model identifies the topic of the claim by a process of content analysis. Depending on the topic and context, members of the public, may have capacity to engage in attacks on vulnerable individuals or groups, in person or online, but have less capacity than elites to set public policies related to them. Members of the public may have capacity to take up or reject the use of an effective or ineffective medication, such as some of those discussed earlier in the book.[50] And policymakers may have the capacity to authorise an ineffective medication or ban a safe and effective one, as happened in the catastrophic ban on polio vaccinations in northern Nigeria in 2002.[51]

To judge the motivational effect of the information, the model first assesses evidence of audience responses, such as of readers' actions, statements, or online responses. Where evidence of reactions is not available, the model uses content analysis to judge whether the claim is affective and includes a call to or means of action – such as calls to apply for a job, protect the community against a given threat, or take up use of a supposed medication.

Most consequences can only occur in a particular practical, social, or political context. For election-related misinformation to affect the outcome of a poll directly, an election must be due, and the voting must be sufficiently close that a change in behaviour of those affected would make a substantive difference to the outcome. For a crowd to engage in physical violence, as happened in the cases discussed earlier in Togo,[52] Ethiopia,[53] and India,[54] it is not enough that the audience see false claims about the individual or group named. They must also be close enough to the subject to carry out their assault. In all the cases mentioned above, distrust in authorities to protect the community was also an essential, contributory factor.

Timing is also part of context. Some claims that cause a fleeting false understanding may cause or contribute to a consequence if those exposed to it take consequential action immediately. They have less potential to do so if the false understanding dissipates before the consequences can occur. In July and August 2024, members of the public, far-right and anti-immigrant activists and others in the United Kingdom responded within hours to false reports that a young man arrested for the murder of three young girls that day, was an illegal immigrant and a Muslim. The false claims triggered a series of attacks on mosques and immigration centres before they could be disproved.[55] Where the false understanding is fleeting but does not lead directly to immediate substantive consequences, it is less likely to have significant long-term effects, as seen in incidents in South Africa discussed earlier.[56]

The model assesses the potential duration of the false understanding based on evidence in the fact-check of (i) the audience's initial perception of the claim's credibility, (ii) the repetition of the claim by a source or sources seen by the audience as credible, (iii) the availability of credible disconfirmatory evidence, and (iv) audience members' resistance or likely resistance to that disconfirmatory evidence.

*

As the statistician George Box said, 'all models are wrong but some are useful.' For each claim studied, the model outlined in this chapter has been used to produce a judgement of the potential of the claim to cause or contribute to a specific substantive consequence, and other wider effects, based on the evidence set out in the fact-check, using the criteria outlined above.

Where the evidence suggests a substantive potential for substantive consequences exists or may exist, the model assesses not only the field of potential consequence but also whether those consequences might occur by a direct effect or by repetition over time. Where the evidence suggests that no substantive potential for consequences exists, the model suggests reasons for this.

The problem in predicting the weather, as the meteorologist and mathematician Edward Lorenz argued in 1972, is that doing so requires both a good model and good data, and this is, or was, lacking: 'We do not know how many butterflies there are, nor where they are all located, let alone which ones are flapping their wings at any instant.'[57] Misinformation consequences are less well understood than meteorological ones. There is often disagreement, among fact-checkers, researchers, policymakers, platforms and others about the nature of the information we are discussing. Its consequences are subject to even more variables than the atmosphere and we often have access to only limited and poor quality data. Recognising the limits of what can be proven, I argue, nevertheless, that the model can help fact-checkers, researchers, policymakers and platforms advance useful knowledge of the types of false information that do and do not have substantive potential to cause or contribute to substantive consequences for society; not predicting the precise date or timing of the storms but establishing whether a meaningful potential for such events exists. To assess this in practice, the model was tested in a trial in 2024 by three leading fact-checking organisations. And a group of doctoral researchers at University of Wisconsin-Madison conducted an independent study of the trial. I set out their key findings in the conclusion.

Chapter 8

A MODEL FOR IDENTIFYING THE POTENTIAL FIELD AND WEIGHT OF FALSE INFORMATION CONSEQUENCES AND INFORMATION DISORDER

In 2020, a study of disinformation that spread on fake news sites ahead of the 2016 US presidential election, found the false claims had had 'limited effects beyond increasing beliefs in false claims'. Public exposure to the claims had not changed the voting intentions of a sufficient number of voters enough to substantively affect the outcome of the election, the researchers found.[1] Four years later, in 2024 and again in 2025, the World Economic Forum identified disinformation spread online as the 'gravest threat' to global stability facing the world over the next two years, exceeding the threat posed by climate change and the conflicts then taking place in countries from Ukraine to the Middle East.[2]

To respond effectively and proportionately to the challenges posed, it is necessary not only to assess, as the model outlined so far seeks to do, whether particular false claims and narratives have a substantive potential to cause or contribute to specific substantive consequences, but also who those consequences might affect, in what field, with what severity and duration: the overall weight of consequences that may be or may have been caused.

Topic Shapes the Field of Consequences

The model set out in Figure 7.1, in the previous chapter, shows the primary factor that shapes not just the potential for, but the type of, consequences false information may create, is the topic, and hence the field in which the false understanding is caused. Other things being equal, a claim that causes or contributes to a false factual understanding about the treatment for a medical condition such as cancer or diabetes, has potential to affect public health but limited potential to affect politics or international relations (Case 8.1). By contrast, a false claim about international relations has a potential to affect relations between various countries but limited potential, in most circumstances, to affect individual or public health (Case 8.2). When the Covid-19 virus emerged in 2020, some claims about the origins of and responses to the outbreak contributed, marginally, to strained relations between the United States and China. However, ostensibly related to the topic of health, the claims were primarily about the actions and responsibilities of governments, not medical science. The primary topic still shaped the primary consequences (Case 8.3).

The Field of False Understanding Is the Primary Factor Shaping the Field of Consequences

Case 8.1 – A false understanding about medication had potential consequences for public health

Monique Ngo Mayag, 'Le corossol n'est pas un remède miracle contre le diabète', *AFPFactuel*, 12 November 2019, https://factuel.afp.com/le-corossol-nest-pas-un-remede-miracle-contre-le-diabete.

Case 8.2 – A false understanding about countries' actions had potential effects for foreign relations

Mayowa Tijani, 'No, the presidents of Rwanda, DR Congo and Malawi did not boycott the World Economic Forum in South Africa over anti-foreigner attacks', *AFPFactCheck*, 12 September 2019, https://factcheck.afp.com/no-presidents-rwanda-dr-congo-and-malawi-did-not-boycott-world-economic-forum-south-africa-over-anti.

Case 8.3 – False claims about origin of the SARS-CoV2 virus affected international relations

The Economist, 'Relations between China and America are infected with coronavirus', 26 March 2020, https://www.economist.com/united-states/2020/03/26/relations-between-china-and-america-are-infected-with-coronavirus.

Many claims relate, of course, to more than one topic, and even with simple claims, may have a potential for effects beyond the field of understanding caused. The claim spread by tobacco companies in the 1960s, for example, that smoking was safe related specifically to health effects but had significant public health and economic and social effects The false claim contributed to the continued spread of smoking-related disease and sustaining the operations of the tobacco industry for years longer than would have happened otherwise.[3] Nevertheless, after reviewing both the cases set out in the database and those described from before the study period, it is clear that the field of consequences does in general correlate closely with the topic or topics of the claim and the field or fields of false understanding caused.

Factors That Shape the Scale, Severity and Duration of Consequences Caused

For measures that counter the consequences of false and misleading information to be both 'necessary and proportionate', as required by international humanitarian laws,[4] they must take account not only of the potential for consequences to occur but also of the number of those who may be affected, and the severity and duration of the effects that may be caused. However, to date, no reliable theoretical framework exists for determining the potential weight of such effects: the size, severity and duration of the storm.

What Shapes Scale of Consequences: Topic, Capacity to Act and Context

Based on a review of cases in the database, I identify one group of claims which caused consequences that were restricted to a specific individual, their friends and family. This happened in the case of the Zambian farmer distressed by the resurfacing of an earlier trauma, and in the killing of two men, and maiming of a third, falsely accused of endangering children in Ethiopia (Case 8.4). Other claims saw effects limited to specific groups, such as sufferers of a particular group, or individuals not specific to a particular group. Other claims affected large parts of society such as by influencing the outcome of a state election (Case 8.5) – or by influencing responses to climate change (Case 8.6). In these and other cases, the model identifies the topic, or focus, of the claim and the false understanding caused, as helping to shape the focus or scale of the observed or potential consequences.

Other factors play a part in shaping the scale of effects. This includes both how many people have a capacity and motivation to act on the claim in a way that affects themselves or others. If a false claim relates to a topic over which anyone may have agency, such as choosing to take up a supposed cure for a common medical condition, for example, the greater the number reached, the greater the numbers likely to be affected (Case 8.7). By contrast, if the claim relates to a rare health condition or an issue on which only a limited number of people can act for themselves or others, the number reached has less influence on the number affected than who is reached. Few people in South Africa in 2000 ever saw the false claim that appeared in articles in obscure academic journals that HIV was not the cause of AIDS, for example. The fact that one of those who did so was the president, and in a position to change public health policy, was what shaped the scale of consequences, not of the number of those persuaded by the claim but more the power of the person influenced to shape policy in ways that affected others (Case 8.8).

A third key factor shaping the numbers affected is the context or setting in which a false factual understanding spreads. Other things being equal, if a false claim spreads of wrongdoing by a minoritised group – Haitian immigrants eating 'cats and dogs' for example – its consequences are likely to be more widespread if it does so at a time of high, rather than low, tension, such as at an election or during social unrest.[6] Or if false information about the importance of handwashing spreads during the outbreak of a transmissible disease, more people are likely to be affected than if it spreads when there is no such disease in circulation (Case 8.9). Vulnerability to consequence is shaped in part by context or setting.

Factors Influencing Scale of Potential Consequences – Focus of Topic, Capacity to Act and Context

Case 8.4 – Scale of effects of false claim about two researchers' actions: affects the two men

Dawit Endeshaw, 'Mob action costs two researchers' lives', *The Reporter Ethiopia*, 27 October 2018, https://www.thereporterethiopia.com/6682/.

Case 8.5 – Scale of effects of claim about state election: state-wide effects – if claim affected poll

Tendai Dube, 'This video shows a shooting at a funeral in South Africa, not "thugs" working for a Nigerian governor', *AFPFactCheck*, 13 November 2019, https://factcheck.afp.com/video-shows-shooting-funeral-south-africa-not-thugs-working-nigerian-governor.

Case 8.6 – Scale of effects of false claims about climate change: worldwide – if claim affects global actions

Michael Tesler, 'Elite Domination of Public Doubts About Climate Change (Not Evolution)', *Political Communication*, 35(2). (2017), 306–26, https://doi.org/10.1080/10584609.2017.1380092.

Case 8.7 – Scale of effects when individuals can act on claim – shaped by the reach of claim

Anne-Sophie Faivre Le Cadre, 'Non, la tisane à l'artémisia et la noix de cola ne guérissent pas le paludisme', *AFPFactCheck*, 8 July 2019, https://factuel.afp.com/non-la-tisane-lartemisia-et-la-noix-de-cola-ne-guerissent-pas-le-paludisme.

Case 8.8 – Scale of effects when claim on policy topic – huge when affects president's understanding

Pride Chigwedere, George Seage, Sofia Gruskin, Tun-Hou Lee and M. Essex, 'Estimating the lost benefits of antiretroviral drug use in South Africa', *Journal of Acquired Immune Deficiency Syndrome*, 1.49.4 (2008), 410–15, https://doi.org/10.1097/qai.0b013e31818a6cd5.

Case 8.9 – Scale of effects influenced by context – greater during outbreak of transmissible disease

Reuters, 'False claim: Overuse of hand sanitizers and soaps leads to bacterial infections; overuse of face masks weakens the immune system', 15 May 2020, https://www.reuters.com/article/uk-factcheck-hand-sanitizer-bacteria/false-claim-overuse-of-hand-sanitizers-and-soaps-leads-to-bacterial-infections-overuse-of-face-masks-weakens-the-immune-system-idUSKBN22R2MV/.

Assessing the Likely Scale of Potential Consequences – From Specific Individuals to the Whole of Society

To establish, as far as possible, the potential scale of consequences, the model identifies four different, sometimes overlapping, groups who may be affected. These groups do not, in most cases, necessarily determine the number of those affected by the consequences of false information, but do influence the numbers. The scale of consequences, the model suggests, runs from (i) a specific individual or individuals, to (ii) individuals not specific to a particular group; (iii) members of a specific group or organisation, and finally; (iv) large parts of society or society as a whole.

False Claims That Affect a Specific Individual – Limited Number Affected by Consequences

The model identifies the potential consequences of false claims that focus on the identity or activities of a specific private individual or individuals, who are not seen as representing others, as likely restricted to the specific individuals concerned. Friends and family may be affected, but – in most cases – not more widely than that. The example, mentioned earlier, of the Zambian farmer distressed by a false claim that resurfaced an old trauma, is a case in point. Where a specific private individual is affected, and no inference is extended to others of similar identity, the focus, not the spread, of the claim affects the scale of effects. Greater spread of the claim may cause greater distress but won't change the number affected. (Case 8.10).

False Claims That Affect Individuals Not Specific to a Group – Numbers Vary With Claim Reach

The model identifies claims that relate to issues over which individuals – not specific to a particular group – have capacity to act, as having potential to cause consequences for individuals in general. As cases in the database demonstrate, this could mean a handful of people responding to scams or hoaxes,[7] or hundreds deciding to take an ineffective or dangerous health treatment for a common medical condition (Case 8.11). In such cases, the higher the number whose understanding is affected by the false claim, the greater the likely scale of effects, not limited by needing to be members of a particular demographic or social group.

False Claims That Affect a Specific Group or Organisation – Numbers Vary With Size of Group

Unlike the above cases, the model identifies claims as having potential to cause or contribute to consequences for members of a specific group or organisation, where the information relates to the actions of, or factors affecting, a particular group or organisation. As cases from the database demonstrate, this could be a claim about people living with a particular medical condition, such as diabetes,[8] the investors, customers, or staff of a particular business or organisation,[9] or members of a specific demographic or socio-economic group, such as Nigerians living in South Africa (Case 8.12). In such cases, the model suggests the number affected by the consequences is shaped not only by how many see and act on the claim, but also by the size of the group concerned.

False Claims That Affect a Large Part or Whole of Society – Numbers Vary With Topic, Spread

In addition to the above, the model also identifies claims whose consequences, if they occur, have potential to affect a large part or the whole of society. This would include, for example, claims which could influence the outcome of elections, or might affect public policy on topics from policing, to gender rights. At the international level, false information might contribute to fostering, or affecting the course of, a conflict, or climate change, with effects felt regionally or worldwide. In a case examined in the database, for example, a false claim that three African countries had decided to boycott a meeting in South Africa to protest recent violence put pressure on Nigeria to follow suit, affecting two countries' relations (Case 8.13). In cases such as these, the number affected is shaped primarily by the topic of the claim and capacity of those whose factual understanding is affected to act in ways that could affect society – be that influencing the outcome of an election, or the climate.

The Limits of 'Useful Forecast Skill' for the Scale of Consequences

As the meteorologist Edward Lorenz noted in 1972, differences of 'small amplitude' in factors contributing to outcomes in dynamic systems as complex as the weather, can make major differences not only in the likelihood but also in the scale of events. In applying any model to the potential outcomes of as complex a dynamic system as misinformation effects, it is important to be circumspect in assessing what meteorologists call our 'useful forecast skill'. The best that can be hoped for, statistician George Box suggested a few years after Lorenz, is that a model's findings are 'illuminating and useful'.

While it is possible, by applying the criteria set out in the model to the cases in the database, to confidently identify some claims likely to cause consequences limited to particular individuals or groups, in many cases, it is not possible to determine the extent to which the claim had or might have spread, or the context in which effects might follow, and hence the scale of potential effects. If the false claim, already discussed several times in the book, that foreign nationals were kidnapping schoolchildren from schools near Johannesburg, South Africa, led to violence, for example, the violence might plausibly have affected random individuals, members of the specific national groups named, or other immigrant groups, depending on how events unfolded (Case 8.14).

Identifying the Size of Individual or Group Potential Consequences May Affect

Case 8.10 – Some claims affect a specific individual or individuals

Mary Kulundu, 'Zambian farmer "greatly distressed2 by posts falsely identifying him as victim of South African violence', *AFPFactCheck*, 13 September 2019, https://factcheck.afp.com/zambian-farmer-greatly-distressed-posts-falsely-identifying-him-victim-south-african-violence.

Case 8.11 – Some claims affect individuals – not specific to any group

Tanya Khourie, 'Apricot seeds don't kill cancer cells, can have deadly side effects', *Africa Check*, 25 October 2019, https://africacheck.org/fact-checks/meta-programme-fact-checks/apricot-seeds-dont-kill-cancer-cells-can-have-deadly-side.

Case 8.12 – Some claims affect members of specific groups or organisations

Cayley Clifford, 'Still no data showing 800,000 Nigerians live in South Africa', *Africa Check*, 15 August 2019, https://africacheck.org/fact-checks/spotchecks/still-no-data-showing-800000-nigerians-live-south-africa.

Case 8.13 – Some claims affect a large part, or the whole, of society

Mayowa Tijani, 'No, the presidents of Rwanda, DR Congo and Malawi did not boycott the World Economic Forum in South Africa over anti-foreigner attacks', *AFPFactCheck*, 12 September 2019, https://factcheck.afp.com/no-presidents-rwanda-dr-congo-and-malawi-did-not-boycott-world-economic-forum-south-africa-over-anti.

Case 8.14 – The size of group likely affected by some claims is hard to determine

Tendai Dube, 'False kidnapping rumours spread during South Africa violence', *AFPFactCheck*, 9 September 2019, https://factcheck.afp.com/false-kidnapping-rumours-spread-during-south-africa-violence.

For this reason, where the means by which potential direct consequences may occur are clear, the model can be used to identify the potential scale of effects in terms of the four categories outlined. This has 'useful' value. Knowing, for example, that a claim might directly affect people living with a particular medical condition can tell us something of the numbers who may be affected. And knowing a claim might directly affect individuals in general – not specific to any particular group – may help us understand how many may be affected but only if we know how widely the claim has spread, and how many of those who have seen the claim might act on the false understanding, in what context.

For all these reasons, it is important when applying these criteria to be cautious in what can be confidently said. Where the means by which consequences may occur is unclear, it is important to recognise what we do and do not know. Our forecast ability can be useful but has limits.

Assessing the Likely Severity of Potential Consequences

To understand the weight of consequences or potential consequences of a claim, it is important not only to consider the number who may be affected, but also the severity of the effects or potential effects.

Other things being equal, most would accept that if an individual takes an ineffective medication for a mild medical condition, such as a blocked or stuffy nose, the consequences they suffer[10] will be less severe than if the condition is a debilitating or life-limiting disease.[11] Or if a claim provokes a single incident of verbal abuse of individuals, the consequences would normally be considered less severe than if it provokes physical violence. Assessing the relative severity of the same consequences in different contexts objectively is not straightforward, however. One consequence of false information is loss of 'face' or reputation – an outcome that may be seen, depending on the context, as almost a badge of honour by some but as profoundly harmful by others. What consequences weigh heavily on particular individuals may differ depending not only on their view of the effects but on their circumstances and stage of life.

Reviewing the range of consequences studied in the database, however, I argue that models for how to judge the severity of many types of outcomes do already exist, and it is on that basis that I assess the severity of effects in this model.

Lying for 'the Good of the State': Beneficial Consequences of False Information

While exposure to false information will often have negative consequences for some, its use has long been justified by proponents as a legitimate tool, if used in pursuit of a rightful cause. In ancient Greece, the philosopher Plato declared his approval of falsehoods that are 'helpful' to the state.[12] Religious minorities in many countries have long had to hide their faith to survive religious persecution.[13] Disinformation about Allied plans for D-Day helped shorten the Second World War in Europe, to the relief of most Europeans.[14] And, every day, people around the world tell 'prosocial' lies to spare others from emotional harm or dampen the risk of personal conflict.[15]

If the notion that certain falsehoods may be justified is widely accepted, the question of which lies in which circumstances are justified is more contested. Those using false information in cases examined in the database to promote a political or social goal may have believed their goals will benefit society overall. Interviews of separatists in Nigeria, for example, show many do support the use of disinformation (Case 8.15), and other controversial tactics, as a means to support their cause, but others disagree.[16]

The model I use thus identifies false information as having beneficial consequences for individuals or society overall only where it causes or contributes to behaviour with what would be universally recognised as positive effects, or discourages behaviour with negative outcomes, and causes with no or negligible negative effects for others. In September 2012, for example, the British health charity St John's Ambulance made a claim that overstated the number of lives that might be saved, each year, if more people knew First Aid skills. The most probable consequence of this, if any, would have been more people learning life-saving techniques than would have done so otherwise with no substantive negative consequences for themselves or others (Case 8.16).

Identifying False Claims As Beneficial Is Contested

Case 8.15 – Separatists often view their campaign as justified, making false claims beneficial

Jennifer Ojugbeli, '"Biafran Airlines" plane? No, photo of Lufthansa Airbus', *AfricaCheck*, 23 October 2019, https://africacheck.org/fact-checks/meta-programme-fact-checks/biafran-airlines-plane-no-photo-lufthansa-airbus.

Case 8.16 – A false claim that exaggerated the numbers saved if more learned first aid

FullFact, 'St John's Ambulance: do the numbers add up?', 20 September 2012, https://fullfact.org/health/st-john-ambulance-do-numbers-add/.

Reviewing cases in the database, using these criteria, I did not identify any false claim with the potential for beneficial consequences with either no or negligible negative effects for others, but I recognise the possibility that such claims may and do exist.

Rating Negative Consequences – From Mild to Severe

Rating the severity of different types of consequences objectively is difficult but in certain fields criteria have been developed – by the health, insurance and legal sectors among others – to triage cases and make assessments as objective as possible. Drawing on this principle, the model I propose in this study divides negative effects into three categories of severity: mild, moderate and severe.

Mild Consequences: Real but Modest and Easily Recovered

Case 8.17 – Treating cataracts with vegetable products has a real but recoverable negative effect

J. Ojugbeli, 'No, don't treat cataracts with vegetables!' *Africa Check*, 19 December 2019, https://africacheck.org/fact-checks/meta-programme-fact-checks/no-dont-treat-cataracts-vegetables.

Case 8.18 – Telecoms companies suffered vandalism but recovered

T. Willows, 'No, hazmat suits not needed to install 5G phone technology', *Africa Check.*, 13 August 2019, https://africacheck.org/fact-checks/meta-programme-fact-checks/no-hazmat-suits-not-needed-install-5g-phone-technology.

The model identifies consequences as 'mild' where they create a modest negative effect for the psychological, physical, or material well-being of an individual, group or society, or the integrity of a political process, and the negative effect is temporary or easily recoverable. Applying these criteria, a false claim that convinced individuals to use an ineffective, but not harmful, treatment for a medical condition such as cataracts is identified, for example, as causing a real but mild consequence, noting that the use of this treatment did not prevent later use of a more effective alternative (Case 8.17). The same finding was given when a large Telecoms company that suffered substantive but limited operational costs when vandals attacked some of its transmission towers, causing damage from which it could easily recover (Case 8.18).

Moderate Consequences: Severe but Short-Lived or Moderate But Longer-lasting Effects

Case 8.19 – This assault caused serious injuries from which the victim soon recovered

Mayowa Tijani, 'No, this video does not show Ivory Coast's ex-president Laurent Gbagbo being beaten by a mob', *AFPFactCheck*, 13 November 2019, https://factcheck.afp.com/no-video-does-not-show-ivory-coasts-ex-president-laurent-gbagbo-being-beaten-mob.

Case 8.20 – This financial policy caused limited but longer-lasting effects on the economy

Olugbenga Adanikin, 'Has Nigeria really achieved food security?' *ICIR/FactHub*, 19 August 2019, https://www.icirnigeria.org/fact-check-has-nigeria-really-achieved-food-security/.

By contrast, the model identifies claims as causing 'moderate' effects where the consequences – psychological, physical, material, or political – are either modest but longer in duration, or severe but short-term. Using these criteria, for example, an assault on an individual on the street from which the victim promptly recovered (Case 8.19), and the limited negative effects on the economy of a financial policy which was ultimately reversed (Case 8.20) are identified as moderate consequences.

Finally, the model identifies claims as causing 'severe' consequences if the effects are either moderate or severe in nature and long-lasting or permanent. Using these criteria, the assault on two health researchers and an assistant in Ethiopia, which led to the death of two men and permanent injury for a third, is identified as causing a severe consequence (Case 8.21). Contributing to a change in public health policy, authorising the public sale of a false medication for a fatal condition such as HIV/AIDS, is also identified as causing or contributing to severe consequences (Case 8.22).

Severe Consequences: Moderate or Severe, and Long-Lasting or Permanent

Case 8.21 – A crowd assault that left two men dead and one permanently maimed

Dawit Endeshaw, 'Mob action costs two researchers' lives', *The Reporter Ethiopia*, 27 October 2018, https://www.thereporterethiopia.com/6682/.

Case 8.22 – A change in public policy allowing the sale of a fake medication for a fatal disease

Black Feelings, 'Le vaccin enfin trouvé. Le professeur gabonais Mavoungou présente le vaccin contre le SIDA', November 2016, http://www.black-feelings.com/accueil/detail-actualite/article/le-professeur-gabonnais-mavoungou-presente-son-nouveau-vaccin-contre-le-sida.

The Duration of Consequences – Short-term and Long-term Effects

Duration of Consequences: Short-term or Reversible, Long-term and Permanent

Case 8.23 – A short-lived panic faded when parents realised fears were unfounded

Tendai Dube, 'False kidnapping rumours spread during South Africa violence', *AFPFactCheck*, 9 September 2019, https://factcheck.afp.com/false-kidnapping-rumours-spread-during-south-africa-violence.

Case 8.24 – The loss of wildlife killed by poachers on a false claim is likely permanent

Ruth Becker, 'Medical claims for rhino horn: you're better on an aspirin or biting your nails', *Africa Check*, 22 September 2012, https://africacheck.org/fact-checks/reports/medical-claims-rhino-horn-youre-better-aspirin-or-biting-your-nails.

Consequence accrues. The duration of effects influences their weight or gravity. Other things being equal, a lasting benefit brings greater reward than a transitory one. And lasting pain is a more weighty consequence than transitory pain. To judge the effect of different potential consequences, the model distinguishes between those that are short-term or reversible, and those that are long-term or irreversible.

The model identifies consequences as short-term where the effect is either shown, or likely to be, naturally limited in time, or easily and likely to be reversed. Applying these criteria to cases in the database, the panic caused when parents briefly believed foreign nationals were kidnapping children from schools in South Africa, for example, was naturally short-lived, ending as soon as the parents collected their children and found out the threat was not real (Case 8.23). By contrast, the model identifies consequences as long-term or irreversible, where the effects are permanent or opportunities to reverse them are limited. The rejection of safe and effective vaccines by the vaccine-hesitant is likely to be long-lasting, for example, as false understandings of vaccine effects are resistant to change.[17] And when false claims about rhino horn cause or contribute to the loss of a species, the effects are likely to be long-term or permanent in nature (Case 8.24).

Predicting Harm? The Limits of Our Forecasting Ability

Despite the massive amounts of data available on the factors that affect daily weather, our ability to predict tornadoes and tempests far into the future remains limited, as of today,[18] and even the most optimistic see little prospect of extending our useful forecast skill to a month or more, before 2040 at the earliest.[19] For all that we know about what shapes the weather, we still 'do not know how many butterflies there are, nor where they are all located, let alone which ones are flapping their wings at any instant', as Edward Lorenz noted in 1972.[20]

By contrast with the well-defined field of meteorology, misinformation effects occur across a great range of fields – from politics to public health, the economy and the environment – with effects subject to variables ranging from the topic and nature of the false claims that are spread, to the effect they do or do not have on factual understanding and attitude, the way they are received, as information or the sharing of a representative belief, the variables in the way that different individuals and groups respond to the same information, and differences in the capacity and motivation of those whose understanding is affected, to act on a false understanding caused.

With this many and more factors playing a role, and limits on the evidence of effects available, it is important to recognise – even with the often-hyped advances in the use of artificial intelligence to detect and assess false information – the limits to what we can know about the likelihood of particular false information to cause or contribute to specific consequences and the scale, severity and duration of the effects, if they do so.

Nevertheless, I argue that the model proposed above, based on a combination of evidence contained in the fact-checks in the database and the studies of misinformation effects discussed in Chapter 4, provides fact-checkers, researchers, policymakers and platforms with a useful means to identify false and misleading information that can be said, based on the balance of probabilities, to have, or not to have, a substantive potential to cause or contribute to specific substantive consequences for individuals and society. And, by the same process, it can be used to understand, in many cases, more than we otherwise do about the potential scale, severity and duration of these effects if they occur.

In the interests of freedom of speech – vital to the functioning of a good society – it is important for fact-checkers, researchers, platforms and policymakers to be cautious about attributing events and predicting effects of misinformation. At the same time. it is important also to recognise the evidence from history, the studies cited in Chapter 4 and elsewhere, and the consequences of false information examined in the database found to have caused or contributed to negative effects for individuals and society.

However, if carefully used, taking account of evidence on the many factors – of the type of communication, audience responses context, and political and social decision-making mechanisms – that shape the potential for false information to cause or contribute to meaningful consequences, I argue the model can enable those genuinely concerned by the effects of false information to better focus their efforts on identifying and countering the effects of false information that is or could be genuinely harmful for society. And it can also provide useful evidence and a powerful argument for all defenders of freedom of expression to better protect freedom of speech even when the information concerned is found to be in some way 'wrong'.

CONCLUSION

While unfettered speech may at times be abused to 'amplify division, sow distrust, and inflict serious harm', society should take a 'detached attitude' to the 'background noise of social media', Danish human rights lawyer Jacob Mchangama argues in his epic 514-page *Free Speech: A global history*. Attempts to shield citizens from 'hostile propaganda' cannot happen 'without compromising the egalitarian and liberal values of democracy', he argues.[1] To some critics, taking such an approach in the face of evidence that false information can and does lead to consequences for individuals and groups from physical abuse and violence to harms to public health would be a 'morally troubling choice'.[2]

*

I developed an interest in the consequences of misinformation more than twenty years ago when, having recently left my position as a reporter for the AFP news agency in west Africa, I learned of a surge of cases of polio in the region. Thousands of lives were affected, and many were lost, after false factual claims about a WHO and UNESCO polio vaccination campaign in Nigeria caused authorities in five northern states to ban the vaccinations, with disastrous results.[3] A decade later, I launched Africa Check to counter the sort of consequences caused or contributed to by this and other false claims, so often left unscrutinised in public debate and the media.

Four Ideas for Countering the Effects of Information Disorder

More than a decade on from starting out on that journey, I put forward four ideas that, I argue, can help fact-checkers, policymakers and platforms better understand the nature and consequences of the challenge faced today. Reviewing the cases of false or misleading information examined for this study, the factors that drove their emergence and effects, and evidence from earlier research, I argue, first, for the importance of taking a wider view of information disorder than the one commonly used by policymakers and platforms since 2017; not only exposure to various forms of false or misleading information, but also the lack of access to accurate information and the often partisan focus of information we all receive. Second, I argue that to counter this information disorder, it is necessary to act on the integrity of information not only online but also in offline settings, from print and broadcast media, to official halls of power, business meetings and community settings. Third, while this information disorder's effects often occur by distorting public understanding, it is important to consider the effects of false information directly influencing the understanding of policymakers and other members of the elite, whose decisions can affect not just their own lives but the lives of tens or hundreds of thousands of their citizens or more. And, fourth, I propose the model outlined above in this book – a series of questions and criteria summarised again below – that can be used by fact-checkers, researchers, policymakers and platforms to go beyond tired debates about misinformation effects to better understand which false claims do and which do not have a substantive potential to cause or contribute to specific substantive consequences for individuals and society, directly or over time by cumulative effect.

*

Setting out these ideas, I recognise that I enter a complex and much contested field – a debate starting with the notion of communication itself. The question of how individuals, and society, should understand communication has long been debated. It can be seen, as the late communications theorist James W. Carey argued in 1989, from distinctly different starting points: the 'transmission view of communication' and the 'ritual view'. The former sees communication primarily in terms of 'imparting ... sending ... or giving information to others'. The latter sees communication as less concerned with imparting information and more of a social or cultural act: 'the representation of shared beliefs'.[4]

Reviewing the different forms of communication in the database, it is clear that communication can be both of these things: both the straightforward, and somewhat mechanical 'transmission of information' and, in other circumstances, an act of association or sharing of beliefs and opinions serving social and cultural ends. To make sense of this, it is important to recognise the distinction between what the philosopher Dan Sperber identifies as 'factual' and 'representational' beliefs.[5] And I propose that much of the current debate over the consequences of false information – between academics, policymakers, and advocates of free speech[6] – arises, at least in part, from differences in the forms and contexts of information we have in mind, when we consider this debate.

Drawing my evidence from a sample of misinformation or disinformation identified by half-a-dozen fact-checking organisations, I set out cases that range from false claims spread in memes on social media or messaging platforms, used primarily to share common beliefs,[7] to false information about health cures, passed on by trusted community sources,[8] to false claims presented in Parliament,[9] and in official records,[10] and used to shape public policy decisions within the walls of government.

The actions people take, using this information, varies enormously. Human behaviour depends, of course, not on one but on many factors. Understanding the potential of false information to play a role in causing or contributing to events depends not only on analysing audience responses, but also understanding the context in which information spreads, the factual or symbolic understandings formed, and the means or mechanisms by which consequential decisions are or may be made.

Recognising the Wider Nature of Information Disorder

Understanding and responding appropriately to the challenge that information disorder poses starts with recognising that it is a broader, more complex problem than suggested by the most widely adopted definition. Information disorder, which I define as the disruption, or dysfunction of an information ecosystem that undermines factual understanding among the public and elite, is not restricted to exposure to false and misleading information. Rather, it includes exposure to false information, lack of easy public access to accurate information and the partisan focus of information to which the public is exposed.

As discussed in Chapter 3, lack of access to accurate information undermines public and elite factual understanding of events not only by denying the public, and often elites, accurate information, but also by making it harder to verify the accuracy of key claims. This is particularly a problem in countries with closed information economies – subject to Internet shutdowns and limited access to official information; however, even in open information societies, lack of timely access to information during security incidents and disasters has been shown to undermine understanding of critical events in ways that cause or contribute to harmful consequences for individuals and society.[11] Even when accurate information is available, cases in the study show it is often not trusted in the community, undermining its useful effect.[12]

At the same time, in many countries, the narrow selection of information available to many audiences causes false understandings to develop even when the individual reports they receive are accurate.[13] Presented with numerous images of trees, the audience sees a forest where one does not exist.[14]

And without countering all three challenges – false information, lack of access to accurate information, and the partisan focus of information available – society cannot effectively counter information disorder.

Recognising the Effects of False Information Offline and On Elite Understanding

Since 2016, the overwhelming majority of research into misinformation effects has focused on the effects of false information on public attitudes and opinions. Far less attention has been paid to the effects of false information, affecting the behaviour of what twentieth-century writer and philosopher Hannah Arendt termed 'the internal world of government'[15] – be it in politics, business, or other areas of policymaking.

The spread and consequences of online misinformation are clearly of great and growing importance. However, in this book, I also show with numerous examples that much consequential false or misleading emerges and has effects offline too – in print and broadcast media,[16] academic journals or think-tank reports,[17] political settings[18] and community contexts. As Yochai Benkler and colleagues at the Berkman Klein Center for the Internet and Society at Harvard University noted in 2020, 'contrary to the focus of most contemporary work on disinformation', a 'highly effective disinformation campaign' about voter fraud in the US presidential elections was driven primarily by elements of mainstream broadcast media and the political elite. 'Social media played only a secondary and supportive role,' the researchers found.[19]

And observing the consequences of policymaker responses to false information, from the decision to approve a fake AIDS vaccine in Democratic Republic of Congo,[20] to the misallocation of resources required for Lagos, Nigeria,[21] it is clear that, where a false claim causes a false understanding among elites on a topic on which they have decision-making powers, the consequences may be greater than those of false understandings on the same topic among the public. The capacity and motivation of those whose understanding is affected to act in a way that affects others is critical to the potential for and scale of consequence. It is a weakness of the misinformation research and policy field that the effects of exposure to false information on policymakers' decisions have been so little studied in recent years.

Considering the Effects of False Information On Factual Understanding and Attitude

If false information were to have no consequences beyond false understandings, the debate about the phenomenon might be of little more than theoretical interest. However, given the many consequences identified in this study alone, the questions posed here about what information disorder is, and what its effects are, clearly matter.

Since 2016, close to a hundred governments have introduced or amended laws and regulations to curb or penalise information they deem false, many of which laws have done little to resolve the problem and have made access to accurate information worse.[22] A better response, I argue, would be – whether it is fact-checkers, print and broadcast media, online platforms, educators, or policymakers who take action to counter information disorder – to take take account of all its elements through promoting information integrity: identifying and not removing but countering harmful false and misleading information with information that is accurate, improving public access to information that is reliable, and educating the public to distinguish between fact and fiction. Lacking such an approach, current strategies will continue to fail.

The effects of information, true or false, on human understanding have, of course, been disputed for many years. And when concern about the effects of false information surged in 2016, the same debate played out again to the despair of many media scholars.[23]

To understand the different positions, it is perhaps helpful to recognise not only the distinctions discussed above between different forms of understanding or belief, but also the different forms and settings of information and communication examined. It should not be a surprise, after all, if studies of the use of disinformation to mislead military commanders[24] come to different conclusions about the effects of false information than studies of false political information spread in the media or online to the general public.[25]

To further understand the differences in perspectives it is also, perhaps, useful to consider two distinct but ultimately compatible findings from research, both taken into account in the model I propose. One finds people commonly resistant to new information that runs contrary to their existing views or understanding; individuals hold on to false understandings despite strong disconfirmatory evidence, the research shows.[26] The other finds audiences susceptible to the persuasive effects of information, true or false, repeated over time; individuals adopt or accept a new understanding when a claim is repeated sufficiently often, even when the proposition is ostensibly implausible, one such study found.[27] Taken together, these findings may explain why single or limited exposure to information, true or false, may have limited effects on an individual's long-held understanding and attitudes, but repeated exposure to the same information may have significant effects on factual understandings and attitudes over the longer term.

The Potential of False Understandings to Cause or Contribute to Specific, Substantive Consequences

Since communications scholar Bernard Berelson suggested, somewhat dryly, in 1948, that all that researchers knew of communication effects was that 'some kinds of communication, on some kinds of issues, brought to the attention of some kinds of people … have some kinds of effects',[28] our understanding has advanced. In addition to a better understanding of the persistence of long-held beliefs and the effects of repetition on factual understanding, we have a wealth of evidence, discussed in Chapter 4, of the practical consequences that factual understandings have and have not caused in a wide range of fields, from factual information that did and did not affect the outcome of elections, to false information distorting international relations, affecting individual and public health, or contributing to violence and unrest.

What has remained unchanged by such research, to date, is what communications theorist Denis McQuail identified in 1983 as the 'great difficulty in predicting' these effects.[29] And, given the many variables involved in these events, it is still not possible today to predict the consequences of exposure to particular false information with even the limited precision of a two-week weather forecast. However, I have, in this book identified a theory about the process by which such effects do or do not occur that, I argue, can be used to help us understand better than we have done, to date, the potential for substantive consequences to take place and the potential scale, severity and duration of those effects, if they occur.

Looking Ahead: A Trial of Evaluating the Evidence of Misinformation Effects

Over six months in 2024, I worked with senior researchers at three leading fact-checking organisations – Cayley Clifford of Africa Check,

Estelle Peard of AFP and Joseph O'Leary of Full Fact – to test the utility, for fact-checking organisations, policymakers, and platforms, of the model set out in this book. Working with these colleagues, I developed two prototype tools – two sets of questions and criteria for fact-checkers and researchers to use to assess in a systematic way the potential of false information to cause or not to cause or contribute to specific substantive consequences.

The first tool, conceived to be used by fact-checkers when selecting claims to check, comprises a set of questions for fact-checkers to use, applying the criteria set out above, to determine – as best they can at the initial stage of selecting the claims to check – (i) whether or not the claim is or may be substantively false, (ii) if substantively false, whether the claim is believed to be true by sufficient people to cause or contribute to any particular consequence, and (iii) if it is, whether those who believe the claim to be true have both the capacity and motivation to cause the consequence concerned. At the end of that process, the fact-checkers or researchers have a better informed basis on which to decide which claims to check, taking the potential to cause or contribute to such consequences into account.

The second tool, to be used after a fact-check has been completed, comprises a longer list of questions and criteria – based on the factors identified in this study – to be used to answer those same core questions to assess, once all the information is in, whether the claim did, indeed, cause, or had a substantive potential to cause or have caused such an effect.

Using these tools, the fact-checkers examined the potential of a hundred claims identified by their colleagues as in some way false or misleading to cause or have caused or contributed to specific consequences, then or in future, if that or similar claims were repeated over time – finding some claims did and others did not.

Assessing the tools and the trial conducted with them, two doctoral researchers at University of Wisconsin-Madison – Elohim Monard-Rivas and Naomi Mine – supervised by Professor Lucas Graves, concluded in an independent report in October 2024, that using the claim selection tool prompted fact-checkers to better focus their efforts on claims with higher potential for consequences. Meanwhile, applying the tool after a fact-check had been completed, to assess whether there was a substantive potential for substantive consequences generated case studies and aggregate data that could be used in better identifying and countering what is potentially harmful misinformation.

The report noted a need for the very basic tools to be developed and iterate and for fact-checkers using them to receive special training, to increase the consistency with which the findings are reached. This could include changes to narrow users' choices based on previous answers, and prompts to remind users of the criteria to consider in reaching their conclusions, they suggested. If such tools are used, how they are used matters. If well applied, these tools can help both to counter the negative consequences caused by false information, and defend free speech, identifying false claims which do and do not have a substantive potential to cause or contribute to specific consequences and the weight of the potential effects, if they occur.

Under Article 19 of the Universal Declaration of Human Rights, freedom of expression – the freedom to state, argue, dispute and disagree – may be curtailed only where the information expressed causes or risks causing harm to 'the rights or reputation of individuals or institutions, public order or public health'.[30] Falsity, alone, is not adequate cause to remove or censor. Yet, in dozens of countries around the world, laws introduced since 2016 allow authorities to penalise publication of information they deem false on these grounds alone.[31] Having a means to identify information which does and does not have a substantive potential to cause or contribute to substantive consequences will not, in itself, change these laws and practices. It could, however, help those who wish to do so to focus on curbing real harm and help fight undue limitations on freedom of speech.

SUGGESTED FURTHER READING

Allport, Floyd and Milton Lepkin, 'Wartime Rumors of Waste and Special Privilege: Why Some People Believe Them', *Journal of Abnormal and Social Psychology*, 40(1) (1945), https://psycnet.apa.org/record/1945-01987-001.

Arendt, Hannah, 'Lying in Politics', in *Crises of the Republic* (New York: Harvest, 1972).

Bacon, Francis, *Novum Organum* (1620), https://oll.libertyfund.org/title/bacon-novum-organum.

Broedel, Hans Peter, *The Malleus Maleficarum and the construction of witchcraft: theology and popular belief* (Manchester: Manchester University Press, 2003).

Camargo, Chico Q. and Felix M. Simon, 'Mis-disinformation studies are too big to fail: Six suggestions for the field's future', *Harvard Misinformation Review*, 20 September 2022. https://doi.org/10.37016/mr-2020-106.

Carey, James, *Communication as Culture: Essays on media and society* (Boston, MA: Unwyn Hyman, 1989).

Cunliffe-Jones, Peter and Lucas Graves, 'Misinformation: how fact-checking journalism is evolving – and having a real impact on the world', *The Conversation*, 8 January 2024, https://theconversation.com/misinformation-how-fact-checking-journalism-is-evolving-and-having-a-real-impact-on-the-world-218379.

Egelhofer, Jana and Sophie Lecheler, 'Fake news as a two-dimensional phenomenon: A framework and research agenda', *Annals of the International Communication Association*, 43(2) (2019), 97–116. https://doi.org/10.1080/23808985.2019.1602782.

Entman, Robert M, 'Cascading Activation: Contesting the White House's Frame After 9/11', *Political Communication*, 20 (2003), 415–32, https://doi.org/10.1080/10584600390244176.

Festinger, Leon, Henry Riecken and Stanley Schachter, *When Prophecy Fails – A Social and Psychological Study of a Modern Group that Predicted the Destruction of the World* (Minneapolis: University of Minnesota, 1956).

Frankfurt, Harry G, *On Bullshit* (Princeton, NJ and Oxford: Princeton University Press, 2005).

Habgood-Coote, Joshua, 'The term "fake news" is doing great harm', *The Conversation*, 27 July 2018, https://theconversation.com/the-term-fake-news-is-doing-great-harm-100406.

Jerven, Morten, *Poor Numbers: How We are Misled by African Development Statistics and What to Do About It* (New York: Cornell University Press, 2013).

Kahneman, Daniel, *Thinking, Fast and Slow* (New York: Farrar, Strauss and Giroux, 2011).

Kaye, David, *Speech Police: The Global Struggle to Govern the Internet* (New York: Columbia Global Reports, 2019).

Klapper, Joseph, *The effects of mass communication,*(Glencoe, IL: Free Press, 1960)

Lasswell, Harold, *Propaganda technique in the world war*, (New York: Knopf, 1927).

Lazarsfeld, Paul, Bernard Berelson and Hazel Gaudet, *The people's choice* (New York: Columbia University Press, 1948).

Levine, Joshua, *Operation Fortitude: The greatest hoax of the Second World War* (London: Collins, 2012).

Marwick, Alice E, 'Why do people share fake news? A socio-technocratic model of media effects', Georgetown Law Technology Review. 2(2) (2018), 474–512. https://georgetownlawtechreview.org/wp-content/uploads/2018/07/2.2-Marwick-pp-474-512.pdf.

Mchangama, Jacob, *Free Speech: A global history from Socrates to social media* (London: Basic Books, 2022).

McNamara, Robert, *In Retrospect. The tragedy and lessons of Vietnam* (New York: Vintage Books, 1995).

McQuail, Denis, *McQuail's Media and Mass Communication Theory* (London: Sage Publications, 6th Edition, 2010).

Mercier, Hugo, *Not Born Yesterday. The Science of Who We Trust and What We Believe* (Princeton, NJ and Oxford: Princeton University Press, 2020).

Moore, Martin, *Democracy Hacked: How Technology is Destabilising Global Politics* (London: One World Publications, 2018).

Newey, Guy, 'Political Lying: A Defense', *Public Affairs Quarterly*, 11(2) (April 1997), 93–116. https://www.jstor.org/stable/40435986.

Perse, Elizabeth M, *Media effects and society* (Mahwah, NJ and London: Lawrence Erlbaum Associates Publishers, 2001).

Shultz, Richard and Roy Godson, *Dezinformatsia: Active Measures in Soviet Strategy* (Sterling, VA: Pergamon-Brassey's, 1984).

Van der Linden, Sander, *Foolproof – Why we fall for misinformation and how to build immunity* (London: 4th Estate, 2023).

Wardle, Claire and Hossein Derakhshan, 'Information Disorder: Toward an interdisciplinary framework for research and policy making', *Council of Europe*, 2017, https://rm.coe.int/information-disorder-toward-an-interdisciplinary-framework-for-researc/168076277c.

Williams, Bernard, *Truth and truthfulness. An essay in genealogy* (Princeton, NJ and Oxford: Princeton University Press, 2002).

APPENDICES

Appendix 1 – Link to the Database and Guidelines Used for This Study

This study is based on examination of existing scholarly research and evidence from a database, which I created between 2021 and 2023, of 250 examples of information identified as false or misleading by one or more of half-a-dozen fact-checking organisations, operating in sub-Saharan Africa in the second half of 2019.

See, below, the link to an online version of (i) the database and (ii) a set of extensive written guidelines that explain the criteria and evidence used in coming to the conclusions presented.

The database provides findings, in thirty categories on all 250 entries – many of which are referenced in the book. Alongside the findings, I provide – where considered useful – written explanations of the evidence and reason used in coming to the findings.

All references cited in the Appendices can be found in the main text's chapter endnotes.

- **Link** – https://westminsterresearch.westminster.ac.uk/item/wy086/database-for-fake-news-what-s-the-harm

Appendix 2 – Fields and Evidence of Specific Substantive Consequences

Fields and evidence of actual or potential specific consequences identified

In the database for this study, I identified false or misleading information as having caused, or had potential to cause or contribute to specific, substantive consequences in ten broad fields: (i) democracy and governance, (ii) international relations and cross border conflicts, (iii) physical health, (iv) mental health, (v) acts of abuse and discrimination, (vi) acts of violence in society from vigilante violence to civil unrest, and insurgencies, (vii) the justice system, (viii) business and the macro-economy, (ix) the environment and climate, and (x) individual financial loss, ID theft and digital harms.

The list of fields is, of course, open to interpretation. In many cases, the fields of consequence intersect with other factors such as individual characteristics of age, gender, or race, or broader factors of place and context. The selection is also not exhaustive, but based on fields of consequences, those identified represent findings based on the false claims examined in the database, which itself presents a snapshot of false information identified as circulating in that time and place. The evidence of proven consequences comes from findings in the fact-checks cited. The evidence of potential consequences comes from a combination of the fact-checks and existing academic research.

Broad field	Specific-field	Sub-field and audience	Evidence
1. Effects on democracy, governance	**Affects voting preferences during a limited election campaign**	Exposure of the public to political misinformation, during a typically brief election campaign, has limited potential, which is subject to a broad range of factors, **(i)** to influence how voters vote. **Notes** (i) In addition to factors common any claim (incl. audience pre-existing views, perceptions of source credibility, reach of source, etc.), particular factors include narrowness of race; whether the candidates, issues are new, or well-known to voters, or subject to pre-existing views. (iii) See Gunther et al. (2018) as listed in endnotes. (iv) See Kalla and Broockman, (2017); Guess et al. (2018 and 2020); McGregor and Kreiss (2020), as listed in endnotes.	Evidence from existing research is complex. Some found mis/disinformation in the US 2016 campaign may have affected how voters vote. **(ii)** Others argue effects are almost always limited, or nil, in the limited time available for persuasion in such campaigns **(ii)** save in rare cases including exceptionally close races, and little-known candidates, etc. I judge consequences can occur but unlikely and only in these rare and specific contexts, and subject to frequent repetition.

	Affects voter participation in an election and/or acceptance of result	Exposure of the public to political misinformation, during a typically brief election campaign, may have potential, subject to a broad range of factors, **(i)** to affect voters' political motivation and whether they vote. **Notes** (i) Note that in many countries in Latin America and in Australia, voting is mandatory. This alters the role of motivation effects.	While most studies find effects of misinformation during an election campaign to be limited, others find some potential to motivate or demotivate existing voters by relating to political desires or fears.
		Exposure of the public, during a limited election campaign, to misinformation re: the risks of participation in the election may have potential, subject to a wide variety of factors, **(i)** to affect voter participation – i.e., whether people vote. **Notes** (i) Beyond the range of factors common to all claims, particular factors include audience experience of previous incidents, making threats plausible. (ii) See Burchard (2015) and Shenga and Pereira (2019) as listed in endnotes.	Studies find that, where the risk of election violence is real, information about this risk – true or not – can affect whether or not people vote **(ii).**
		Exposure of the public, during a limited election campaign, to misinformation re: election rules/procedures may have potential, subject to a broad variety of factors, **(i)** to distort voter participation. **Notes** (i) Beyond factors common to all claims, such as source credibility, etc., factors particular to this effect include narrowness of election, low awareness. (i) Reports from election monitors, media suggests this may have affected some elections, but the evidence is limited.	Anecdotal evidence indicates this may occur but I have not identified specific studies. Research of this potential effect is needed **(ii).**

(Continued)

(*Continued*)

		Exposure of the public, during a limited election campaign, to misinformation re: likely election outcome and/or fairness may have potential, subject to a wide variety of factors, **(i)** to affect voter participation, acceptance of the result. **Notes** (i) Beyond factors common to all claims, particular factors include the closeness of the election, targeting of the information, and prior experience of rigged polls. (ii) See Jackson (1983) on the effect of US polling day predictions on turnout, and Shenga and Pereira (2019) on the effect of claims about election rigging in Africa, as listed in the endnotes.	Studies from the 1980s on have found that suggesting an election is effectively pre-set (e.g., a landslide or due to rigging) may have the effect of reducing voter participation, with potential to affect election outcomes depending on a variety of factors including closeness of the vote, and whether the effects are felt more by one side than another **(ii)**.
	Affects adherence to and/or application of public rules, laws and standards	Exposure of the public to misinformation re: public rules, laws and standards may have potential, subject to a broad range of factors, to affect adherence to the laws, standards. **Notes** (i) For example, a 2020 study of the effect on public behaviour of reports of Covid rule-breaking in the United Kingdom indicated public behaviour was sensitive to information about adherence.	Some studies indicate this effect may occur **(i)**, but more research of this potential effect is needed.
		Exposure of authorities to misinformation re: public rules, laws and standards may have potential, subject to a wide variety of factors, to distort application of those rules, laws and standards.	Media reports indicate this effect may occur but I have not identified specific studies. Research of this potential effect is needed.

	Affects use of public information, media as a guide for behaviour	Repeated exposure of the public, authorities to misinformation re the credibility of public information, media may have potential, subject to a broad variety of factors, **(i)** to affect the use of public information, media. **Notes** (i) Beyond factors common to all claims, a low trust culture and repetition play a role in the effect (ii) For example, Lazer et al. (2018) and Egelhofer and Lecheler (2019). (iii) See Hameleers et al. (2020) about effects of 'feeling disinformed' on public health behaviours, and Jungherr and Rauchfleisch (2024) on effects of 'alarmist disinformation discourse' on trust in democracy	Longitudinal studies are hard for many reasons, but studies have found that false claims that accurate information is 'fake' may have potential to undermine trust and use of accurate sources of information **(ii);** with possible negative consequences for society **(iii).**
	Affects participation in political movements, activity by creating false understanding of risks, likely outcomes	Exposure of the public to misinformation re: risks and/or outcome of participation in political movements, . protests, may have potential, subject to a wide variety of factors, **(i)** to affect participation in such movements and activity. **Notes** (i) Beyond factors common to the influence of any claim, particular factors include prior audience experience of policing of people involved in political movements, protests, making such threats appear plausible.	Studies of effects on elections suggest a similar potential effect on public participation in protest political movements. However, I have not identified specific studies of this effect for political movements. Research of this potential effect is needed.

(*Continued*)

(*Continued*)

	Affects political, social attitudes over long-term, with potential for future political, social effects	Repeated exposure of the public, authorities to political, social misinformation over the long term may have potential, subject to a broad range of factors, **(i)** to affect political, social attitudes and behaviour over time. **Notes** (i) Beyond the factors mentioned above, that play a part in any effects, a factor key to potential longitudinal effects is repetition. (ii) See, for example, Festinger et al. (1957), Nyhan and Reifler (2010), and others (iii) See for example, Allport and Lepkin (1945), Fazio et al. (2022), and Lacassagne et al. (2022) (iv) See, for example, Foos and Bischof (2021). All sources listed in the endnotes.	Longitudinal studies are hard to do for multiple reasons. And numerous studies show that individuals' core political and social attitudes are often slow to change **(ii).** At the same time, studies show repetition increases information's persuasive effect **(iii)** and may, over time, affect political and social attitudes **(iv).**
	Affects public policy outside election process Note I address how this effect relates to specific fields elsewhere in this table.	Where repeated exposure of the public to misinformation re: a policy issue affects public attitudes, it may have potential, subject to a wide variety of factors, **(i)** to affect public policy indirectly by creating or undermining public pressure on the issue **Notes** (i) Beyond the factors common to the effects of any claim, the effects of public opinion on policymakers' decisions depends on particularly the sensitivity of the political system and/or particular leaders to support. (ii) See, for example, this report from the World Economic Forum (2020), showing how public attitudes, affected by false information about climate change, influenced public policy. See the source listed in the endnotes.	Studies suggest that, where misinformation affects public views, this may affect public policy by creating, undermining real or perceived public pressure on the issue **(ii)**. More research of the potential effect is needed.

		Exposure of authorities to misinformation re: a policy issue may have potential, subject to a broad range of factors, **(i)** to affect public policy directly by misleading authorities on a reality of the issue. **Notes** (i) Beyond the other factors common to any claim, effects on policymakers' decisions are influenced by the particular decision-making process adopted. (ii) For example, in South Africa, then President Thabo Mbeki changed public health policy on AIDS treatment due partly to false information. See Chigwedere et al. (2008). In Nigeria, politicians banned polio vaccinations due in part to false information. See Jegede (2007). And during Covid, leaders from the United States and Brazil to Madagascar pursued ineffective health policies based, partly, on false information. See Pazzanese (2020), Milhorance (2021) and Ioussouf (2020), respectively. All sources detailed in the endnotes.	Numerous studies and reports show that false information may have the potential to affect public policy by misleading authorities directly, with substantive effects for society **(ii)**.

(*Continued*)

(*Continued*)

2. Effects on international relations, cross-border conflicts	**Affects international relations**	Exposure of the public to misinformation re: another country may have potential, subject to a wide range of factors, **(i)** to distort international relations, directly, through a voting process, or indirectly, by creating or undermining real or perceived public pressure on those relations **Notes** (i) Beyond factors common to all claims, a particular factor is knowledge of foreign affairs which differs in different countries and communities (ii) For example, a study found the US public more susceptible to media narratives on foreign affairs in 2003 than on 'most areas of domestic policy'. See Baum and Groeling (2010). Where foreign affairs are put to the vote this may affect relations. See Foos and Bischof (2021).	Studies suggest false information may affect public attitudes to other countries, **(ii)** and thus have potential to affect foreign relations, directly, where the issues are put to the vote, or indirectly via public pressure. More research of this potential effect is needed.
		Exposure of authorities to misinformation re: another country may have potential, subject to a wide range of factors, **(i)** to distort international relations by directly by misleading the authorities about a reality. **Notes** (i) Beyond factors common to all claims, the level of open knowledge about one or both countries is a factor in this potential effect.	Historians' accounts of international relations suggest false information may have often influenced political leaders about other countries directly; however, I have not identified specific studies. Research of this potential effect is needed.
		Exposure of business leaders, the public, to misinformation re: another country has potential, subject to a variety of factors, to affect relations at a business, individual level. **Notes** (i) For example, false claims of attacks on Nigerians in South Africa in 2019 affected SA-owned business operations in Nigeria.	Examples in the database of this study indicates this effect may occur, **(i)** but I have not identified specific studies. Research of this effect is needed.

	Affects occurrence of and/or distorts course of cross-border conflicts	Exposure of the public to misinformation re: another country's actions, capabilities may have potential, subject to a wide variety of factors, **(i)** to cause or contribute to the occurrence or outcome of cross-border conflicts by affecting public support. **Notes** (i) Beyond factors common to all information effects, particular factors include the degree to which political/military authorities feel the need to take public opinion into account. (ii) See Lasswell (1927) for an early twentieth-century perspective on the effects of 'propaganda' influencing public support for US entry into the First World War. See Baum and Groeling (2010) and others on the susceptibility of public opinion to elite narratives. See sources listed in the endnotes.	Studies suggest media may have a role in influencing the occurrence of and/or course of wars and conflicts by affecting support and/or participation **(ii)**.
		Exposure of political, military leaders to misinformation re: another country's actions or capabilities may have potential, subject to a broad range of factors, **(i)** to cause or contribute to the occurrence or outcome of cross-border conflicts by misleading them re: a reality. **Notes** (i) Beyond the factors common to the effects of any claim, particular factors include the level of knowledge political, military elites have on the other country. The less they have, the more vulnerable they are to false information. (ii) For example, during the Second World War, German military commanders diverted troops from where they were needed in France after being misled by Allied disinformation efforts. See Levine (2012). And during the US war on Vietnam, false claims in internal reports influenced many key decisions. See McNamara (1995) and Arendt (1972). See sources listed in the endnotes	Numerous histories have found that false information, in public or within government, may have potential to play a direct role in the occurrence and course of conflicts by misinforming leaders about a reality **(ii)**.

(Continued)

(*Continued*)

3. Effects on physical health	**Affects individual physical health by affecting behaviour**	Exposure of the public to health misinformation may have potential, subject to a wide range of factors, **(i)** to affect individuals' health behaviour in a way that causes direct harm to health of self or others **Notes** (i) Beyond factors common to all claims, particular factors include both levels of health literacy and the access to reliable, affordable healthcare. (Often, people unable to afford effective healthcare are more susceptible to cheap, unproven alternatives) (ii) See, for example, Aghababaeian et al. (2022) on the effects of false claims that alcohol was a reliable treatment for Covid-19, and Cunliffe-Jones (2020) on the effects of false claims about purported treatments for conjunctivitis, in Nigeria. See these sources listed in the endnotes.	Many studies have identified the effects on public health of false information that promotes directly harmful health behaviour **(ii)**.
		Exposure of the public to health misinformation may have potential, subject to a wide range of factors, **(i)** to affect health behaviour in a way that causes indirect harm to health. **Notes** (i) Beyond factors common to all claims, particular factors include both those mentioned above (health literacy; access to reliable healthcare). (ii) See studies of effects of false health information that: (1) misled audiences about causes, consequences, prevalence of particular health conditions. (2) misled audiences about the health effects of particular behaviours. (3) discouraged use of effective medication by promoting ineffective alternatives. See Thielman et al. (2014). (4) discouraged use of effective medication by promoting false fears of effective treatment. See Larson (2018) and Motta and Stecula (2021). (5) discouraged use of effective medication by promoting false fear of health workers. See Allen et al. (2015).	Numerous studies have identified the effect of false information on individuals' health where the behaviour promoted is indirectly harmful to health **(ii)**.

	Affects sexual behaviour with negative health effects	Exposure of the public to misinformation re: natural disasters, physical risks may have potential, subject to a variety of factors, **(i)** to cause physical harm. **Notes** (i) Beyond factors common to all claims, particular factors include access to accurate information on the incident and 'urgency' of the decision (reduces scrutiny). (ii) See, for example, a study by Torpan et al. (2021) on the effects of false information misdirecting the public on their safety during a natural disaster or security incident. The study is listed in the endnotes.	Studies have found misinformation unrelated to health issues can encourage physically dangerous behaviour in particular settings or contexts **(ii)**. More research of this potential effect is needed.
		Exposure of the public to misinformation re: sexual health may have potential, subject to a variety of factors, **(i)** to cause, contribute to sexual behaviour with negative health effects. **Notes** (i) Beyond factors common to all claims, social and cultural factors may play a particular role in shaping the potential for such effects. (ii) See, for example, a 2003 study of the effects on sexual behaviour of a myth then widespread in parts of South Africa that sex with a virgin child could cure a man of AIDS.	Studies have found false information has potential to promote sexual behaviour with negative health effects, including claims underplaying risky behaviour, or that harmful activities have health benefits. More research of the potential for this effect is needed.

(*Continued*)

(Continued)

	Affects public health policy in ways with negative effects on public health	Repeated exposure of the public to health misinformation may have potential, subject to a wide range of factors, **(i)** to negatively affect public health by, over time, creating or undermining public support for health policy **Notes** (i) Beyond factors common to all claims, particular factors include repetition and differences in levels of trust in health authorities in given audiences. (ii) See Jegede (2007) on public distrust in polio vaccinations in Nigeria in 2002–03 and Larson (2018) on distrust in vaccines more widely. See Allen et al. (2015) on distrust in public health workers in Sierra Leone. See details in the endnotes	Longitudinal studies are hard to do for many reasons, however multiple studies show false information about public health – from vaccine campaigns to interventions a public health crisis – can undermine support for public health policy **(ii)**.
		Exposure of politicians, health authorities to health misinformation may have potential, subject to a variety of factors, **(i)** to negatively affect public health by misleading them about a reality. **Notes** (i) Beyond factors common to all claims, particular factors include low levels of trust in mainstream medical industry in particular countries and political settings. (For example, particular distrust in South Africa of messaging around AIDS and race; distrust in Nigeria in drugs companies given experience with Pfizer in 1996.) (ii) In South Africa, then president Thabo Mbeki changed public health policy on AIDS treatment due, partly, to exposure to false information. See Chigwedere et al. (2008). Nigerian politicians banned polio vaccinations due in part to exposure to false information. See Jegede (2007). During Covid, leaders from the United States and Brazil to Madagascar pursued ineffective health policies based, in part, on false information See Pazzanese (2020), Milhorance (2021) and Ioussouf, (2020), respectively.	Numerous studies and reports show that false health information may have potential to affect public health policy by misleading authorities directly, with substantive effects for society **(ii)**.

4. Effects on mental health	**Causes or contributes directly to chronic fear or distress for individuals**	Repeated exposure of individuals or groups to misinformation causing chronic fear or distress has potential, subject to a variety of factors, **(i)** to harm the mental health of the object/s of the misinformation by causing or contributing to chronic fear. **Notes** (i) Beyond other factors, mental health effects can vary greatly depending on individual characteristics and prior trauma. (ii) See Karnatovskaia et al. (2020) and others on the effects of chronic fear, distress on individuals' physical and mental health. Sources detailed in the endnotes.	Individuals exposed repeatedly to false information can experience chronic fear, identified as where it lasts for more than a month. Studies identify chronic fear as causing potential long-term harm to physical and mental health **(ii)**.
	Affects behaviour and/or public policy toward mental health	Exposure of politicians, employers, health authorities to misinformation re: mental health may have potential, subject to a variety of factors, **(i)** to distort mental health policies directly by misleading them about a reality. **Notes** (i) Beyond factors common to all claims, particular factors include existing social understandings of mental health issues, shaping understanding among decision-makers.	Media reports indicate false information on the prevalence, nature and causes of poor mental health may have potential to affect public policy in this field, but I have not identified specific studies. More research of this potential effect is needed.
5. Effects on acts of abuse, discrimination	**Used to enact and/or justify acts of abuse, discrimination**	Exposure of the public to misinformation re: character of an individual or demographic group may have potential, subject to a variety of factors, **(i)** to be used to enact and/or justify acts of abuse or discrimination toward that individual or group. **Notes** (i) Beyond factors common to all claims, particular factors include perceived acceptability of abuse, discrimination as a social norm. (ii) Numerous studies and reports, including entries in the database of this study, identify false information spread online, or in the offline community, as causing or contributing to abuse and discrimination of individuals and groups.	Numerous studies and reports detail occasions where misinformation is used to justify and/or enact abuse, discrimination, e.g. false claims chanted as abuse **(ii)**.

(Continued)

(*Continued*)

		Repeated exposure of the public to misinformation re: character of an individual or demographic group has potential, subject to a variety of factors, **(i)** to cause or contribute, over time, to shaping attitudes that cause or contribute to abuse, discrimination of the group. **Notes** (i) Beyond factors common to all claims, particular factors include repetition of the claims over time, and social acceptance of abuse, discrimination as a norm. (ii) See, for example, Festinger et al. (1957), Nyhan and Reifler (2010), and others. (iii) See, for example, Allport and Lepkin (1945), Fazio et al. (2022), and Lacassagne et al. (2022). (iv) For example, where individuals' attitudes to a particular group or community are then triggered by false information. See Wilmot (2024). Sources are listed in the endnotes.	Longitudinal studies are hard to do and studies show that core political and social attitudes are often slow to change, **(ii)** but repetition increases information's persuasive effect, **(iii)** and may have potential to contribute to this effect **(iv)**. More research of this potential effect is needed.
	Affects public policies related to abuse discrimination	Repeated exposure of the public to misinformation re: character of a demographic group has potential, subject to a variety of factors, **(i)** to affect policies that affect discrimination by, over time, affecting real or perceived public support for policy. **Notes** (i) Beyond factors common to all claims, particular factors include repetition of the claims over time, social acceptance of discrimination as a norm and the susceptibility of decision-makers to perceived public opinion. (ii) Numerous media and other research reports in many countries show policymakers express false understandings about particular individuals or communities. The extent to which they do this as a direct understanding or in response to perceived public attitudes requires research.	Longitudinal studies are hard to do but the studies noted above suggest repeated exposure to misinformation can affect social attitudes over time. Numerous media reports suggest this may apply to attitudes among policymakers as much as it does to attitudes among members of the public. **(ii)** More research of the potential of this effect to shape policy is needed.

6. Effects on violence in society – vigilanteviolence, civil unrest and insurgencies	**Causes or contributes to violence in civil society**	Exposure of the public to misinformation re: the character or actions of an individual or individuals has potential, subject to a wide variety of factors, **(i)** to cause to cause or contribute to vigilante violence. **Notes** (i) Beyond factors common to all claims, particular factors include both levels of public distrust in authorities to ensure justice and/or protect their community and the social/cultural acceptance of vigilante action. See Banaji et al. (2019), for discussion of this effect. (ii) See Banaji et al. (2019) on vigilante murders in India in 2018, and Endeshaw (2018), on vigilante murders in Ethiopia in 2018. See details in endnotes.	Numerous studies and reports show that the spread of false information re: the behaviour or character of an individual or individuals has caused or contributed to vigilante violence **(ii)**.
		Exposure of the public to political misinformation to misinformation re: character and actions of political, religious or ethnic groups has potential, subject to a broad range of factors, **(i)** to cause, contribute to broad political and civil violence. **Notes** (i) Beyond factors common to all claims, particular factors include pre-existing socio-cultural and political tensions, level of security. (ii) See, for example, Ellis-Peterson (2018), on the role of false information about the Rohingya in Myanmar in contributing to violence in 2017. See Adegoke and BBC Africa Eye (2018) on the role of false claims that an ethnic minority presented a threat to another group in Nigeria in causing civil violence in 2018. See details of source in the endnotes	Numerous studies find political misinformation and/or related to demographic groups may cause, contribute to broad political and civil violence **(ii)**.

(Continued)

(*Continued*)

	Affects the occurrence and/or distorts course of insurgencies	Exposure of the public to misinformation re: actions, capabilities of parties to an insurgency may have potential, subject to a wide range of factors, **(i)** to influence the occurrence and/or course of an insurgency by affecting public support and/or participation **Notes** (i) Beyond factors common to all claims, particular factors include the level of political/social opposition and the access to open information about the conflict. (ii) See, for example, evidence of how both the UK government and the supporters of the Irish Republican Army spread disinformation about their opponents to seek to undermine support for their opponent during their conflict.	Reports from many conflicts show both insurgents and authorities have sought to use false information to undermine public support for the other side. **(ii)** I have not identified specific studies of their effectiveness.
		Exposure of authorities, insurgency leaders to misinformation re: the actions or capabilities of the other side may have has potential, subject to a broad range of factors, **(i)** to influence the occurrence or course of an insurgency by misleading them re: a reality. **Notes** (i) Beyond factors common to all claims, particular factors include the level of knowledge the different parties have of their opponents – insurgents or authorities. (ii) See McNamara, (1995) and Arendt (1972) on the role of false information about the actions of insurgent in Vietnam. Details of sources in the endnotes.	Accounts by participants and observers of the US war on Vietnam suggest false information about the actions, capabilities of the Viet Cong insurgents, spread through official channels to US authorities, influenced US policy. **(ii)** I have not identified specific studies of this issue in other insurgencies.

7. Effects on justice system	**Affects the course or outcome of particular court cases**	Exposure of authorities in the justice system to misinformation re: a particular court case may have potential, subject to a range of factors, **(i)** to affect the course or outcome of the case. **Notes** (i) Beyond factors common to all claims, particular factors in the court context include the processes used by different courts to identify and counter effects of public misinformation. (ii) See, for example, Loftus (2005) and Frenda et al. (2011). Sources are in the endnotes.	Numerous studies, conducted over three decades, have found false information spread in online and offline media may have potential to affect witness statements and court decisions **(ii)**.
	Affects public policies related to the justice system	Repeated exposure of the public to misinformation re: the justice system may have potential, subject to a wide variety of factors, **(i)** to distort justice policies by undermining or firming public support for a policy. (i) Beyond factors common to all claims, particular factors include both repetition of the claims and the sensitivity of the authorities to public attitudes (ii) See, for example, Foos and Bischof (2021).	Studies listed above suggest repeated exposure to misinformation can affect the public's social attitudes over time. **(ii)** I have not identified specific studies. More research of this potential effect is needed.
		Exposure of authorities to misinformation re: the operation of the justice system may have potential, subject to a broad range of factors, **(i)** to distort justice policies directly by misleading them about a reality. **Notes** (i) Beyond factors common to all claims, particular factors include the level of understanding of the justice system shown by those overseeing policies in the sector.	Media reports indicate false information about the operation of the justice system may have potential to affect public policies re: the justice system, but I have not identified specific studies. Research is needed.

(Continued)

(*Continued*)

8. Effects on business operations, macro-economy	**Affects the operations of business or the business sector**	Exposure of the public to misinformation re: the actions, effects of a business or the business sector may have potential, subject to a wide variety of factors, **(i)** to affect the operations of that business or sector. **Notes** (i) Beyond factors common to all claims, particular factors include the sensitivity of the particular business, sector, or market to the understanding of those (e.g., the public, market traders, other businesses) whose understanding is affected by the false claim. (ii) See reports of effects on businesses such as a run on a bank. See Katwala (2019). See Hilts (1996) on the effects of tobacco firm disinformation on the economic performance of that sector. See studies of wider financial effects: Baily et al. (2016) and Berton and Pitt (2018).	Numerous reports and studies suggest that false information related to business operations, effects, market conditions and other economic factors may have potential to affect the operations of the businesses targeted and wider society **(ii)**.
	Affects macro-economic activity, performance	Repeated exposure of the public to misinformation re: the status of the economy may have potential, subject to a wide range of factors, **(i)** to distort macro-economic activity by misleading the public about a reality. **Notes** (i) Beyond factors common to all claims, particular factors include market mechanisms put in place to counter negative effects (e.g., trading 'brakes' on market falls). (ii) Economic history has many examples of economic booms and crashes due, in part, to false information from the 'South Sea Bubble' of the 1720s to the sub-prime collapse of 2008.	Evidence from economic history indicates false information about the status of the economy may have potential to affect macro-economic activity by affecting public understanding and activity. **(ii)** I have not identified specific studies of this as a broad effect. Research of this potential effect is needed.

		Exposure of business leaders and/or political and economic authorities to misinformation re: the status of the economy may have potential, subject to a wide variety of factors, **(i)** to distort economic policy by misleading them about a reality. **Notes** (i) Beyond factors common to all claims, particular factors include the access to accurate information and level of economic understanding of business, political and economic leaders.	Evidence from economic history indicates this false information may have potential to affect the understanding of business, political and economic leaders about the status of the economy, with resulting effects on the economy. Research of this potential effect is needed.
9. Effects on environment climate	**Affects public behaviour, public policy on climate change**	Repeated exposure of the public to misinformation on climate change has potential, subject to a broad range of factors, **(i)** to affect public behaviour that affects climate change. **Notes** (i) Beyond factors common to all claims, particular factors include both repetition of the false claims, over time, and levels of trust in authorities. (ii) See, for example, World Economic Forum (2020).	Many studies show false information re: climate change has undermined support for climate mitigation policies **(ii)**. Research of effects on behaviour is needed.
		Repeated exposure of the public to misinformation on climate change may have potential, subject to a variety of factors, **(i)** to affect climate policy firming or undermining public pressure. **Notes** (i) Beyond factors common to all claims, particular factors include the repetition of the false claims and policymakers' sensitivity to perceived public opinion. (ii) See Tesler (2018), World Economic Forum (2020).	Numerous studies have found misinformation about climate change have affected public policy by affecting public opinion **(ii)**.

(Continued)

(*Continued*)

		Exposure of authorities to misinformation on climate change has potential, subject to a broad range of factors, **(i)** to distort climate policies by misleading authorities about a reality. **Notes** (i) Beyond factors common to all claims, particular factors include the decision-making processes adopted and level of factual understanding of climate science among political and social elites.	Numerous studies have identified mistaken factual understandings of climate science among political and social elites. I have not identified studies demonstrating this to be genuine misunderstanding. More research of this issue is needed.
	Affects public behaviour, public policy on protection of wildlife, biodiversity	Exposure of the public to misinformation about the nature and effects of environmental and wildlife products may have potential, subject to a wide variety of factors, **(i)** to affect demand for the products. **Notes** (i) Beyond factors common to all claims, particular factors, in some such cases, include social and cultural understandings of particular wildlife products. (ii) See, for example, Becker (2012), listed in the endnotes, on the effects of the false claim that rhino horn powder has medicinal properties, underpinning demands for rhino horn products in South East Asia.	Media reports indicate false factual understandings of the nature and effects of particular products affects demand. **(ii)** I have not identified specific studies of this effect. More research of this potential effect is needed.
		Repeated exposure of the public to misinformation on wildlife, biodiversity has potential, subject to a broad range of factors, **(i)** to affect public policy by creating or undermining public pressure. **Notes** (i) Beyond factors common to all claims, particular factors include the affective nature of much misinformation related to wildlife, biodiversity issues.	Media reports suggest false information about wildlife and biodiversity may affect public policy on the issues. **(ii)** I have not identified specific studies. More research is needed.

		Exposure of authorities to misinformation on wildlife, biodiversity may have potential, subject to a range of factors, **(i)** to affect public policy by misleading authorities on a reality. **Notes** (i) Beyond factors common to all claims, particular factors include the affective nature of much misinformation related to wildlife, biodiversity issues, and the decision-making processes of policymakers.	Media reports suggest false information about wildlife and biodiversity may affect public policy on the issues. **(ii)** I have not identified specific studies. More research is needed.
10. Effects of financial loss, career harm, ID theft, digital harms for individuals, organisations	**Affects an individual's work opportunities, professional standing and/or career**	Exposure of the public to misinformation re: the character, actions, rights of an individual or individuals may have potential, subject to a variety of factors, **(i)** to affect their work opportunities, professional standing and/or career **Notes** (i) Beyond factors common to all claims, particular factors include the sensitivity of the individual's work opportunities or career to public opinion. (ii) See, for example, a report by Mary Kulundu (2019), listed in endnotes, on the effects of a false claim that a US missionary underwent FGM in Kenya had on the woman's career.	Media reports, including examples identified in the database of this study, demonstrate that false information may have potential to have this effect. **(ii)** But I have not identified specific studies.

(*Continued*)

(*Continued*)

	Causes or contributes to financial loss, identity theft and/or digital harms to individuals, organisations	Exposure of the public to hoaxes and certain types of clickbait which use false information to engage audiences may have potential, subject to a range of factors, **(i)** to cause individuals or organisations financial loss, identity theft and/or various forms of digital harm such as exposure to malware, computer viruses to individuals, organisations. **Notes** (i) Beyond factors common to all claims, particular factors include the need of particular audience members for the reward offered by the hoax or their vulnerability to malware or viruses. For example, people with well-paid full-time employment are unlikely to respond to hoax job advertisements. People with good online security are less likely to fall victim to a computer virus in a clickbait-style report. (ii) See, for example: Brett Horner (2019), listed in the endnotes.	Studies and reports have identified misinformation – from fake job ads to clickbait – causing financial loss, IF theft and/or digital harms. **(ii)** More research of this effect is needed.

Appendix 3 – Factors Affecting the Field and Weight of Consequences that Occur

When a false claim contributes to a specific effect, a range of factors shape the field, and weight of consequences caused. The table below sets out factors, evidence and examples.

Factors that Influence the Field of the Consequences

Factors shaping field of effects	How these factors influence the field of effects	Example
The topic of the claim shapes the field of false understanding	The **topic or topics of the claim** affect the field or fields in which false understanding is created. The false understanding determines the consequences that follow.	For example, a false claim related to a particular health condition causes people to take a treatment for that particular health condition that is harmful.
The context in which the claim circulates	The **context in which the claim circulates** affects the field of consequences that follow.	For example, a false claim that relates to the behaviour of politicians reduces trust amid a health crisis and thus affects public health.

Factors that Influence the Scale of Consequences

Factors shaping scale of effects	How these factors influence the scale of effects	**Example**
The focus of the topic shapes the focus of the consequences	The claim is focused on **a specific private individual or individuals.** Its consequences focus on that individual.	For example, a false claim about the behaviour of a specific individual causes distress to that individual and family.

(*Continued*)

(*Continued*)

Factors shaping scale of effects	How these factors influence the scale of effects	Example
	The claim is focused on an issue which relates to **individuals in general – not specific to a particular individual or group** – or over which they have agency to cause effects. It affects individuals in general.	For example, a false claim related to a medical treatment for a common health condition causes individuals in general – not specific to any particular group – to take an inappropriate treatment.
	The claim is focused on an issue which relates to or affects **a specific group or groups of individuals, businesses, or organisations.** It affects that group.	For example, a false claim related to an issue that would only affect a particular social or demographic group, a business or organisation, affects only people in that group or organisation.
	The topic of the claim relates to an issue which affects, or potential to affect, **large parts of society, or society as a whole.** It affects part of all of society as a whole.	For example, the claim relates to issues affecting areas of public policy, and affects society as a whole, or global issues such as conflict or climate change, and affects the world as a whole.

NOTES

Acknowledgements

1 Peter Cunliffe-Jones, Assane Diagne, Alan Finlay and Anya Schiffrin. *Bad Law – Legal and Regulatory Responses to Misinformation in Eleven African Countries 2016–2020,* https://www.uwestminsterpress.co.uk/site/chapters/m/10.16997/book53.b/ In *Review Of Misinformation Across Sub-Saharan Africa 2016–2020: A Study Of And Policy Framework For 'Media Literacy' In Schools And Legal/Regulatory Responses* (London: University of Westminster Press, 2021).

2 Respectively, the then-Director of Reporters Without Borders for West Africa, in Senegal, an Internet and media rights researcher and lecturer with the University of the Witwatersrand, in South Africa, and the Director of the Technology, Media and Communications Specialization at the School of International and Public Affairs at Columbia University, United States.

3 Benin, Burkina Faso, Côte d'Ivoire, Ethiopia, Kenya, Malawi, Niger, Nigeria, Senegal, South Africa and Uganda. Between 2016 and 2020, the number of laws related to 'false' information rose in those countries from seventeen to thirty-one.

4 Peter Cunliffe-Jones, Sahite Gaye, Wallace Gichunge, Chido Onumah, Cornia Pretorius and Anya Schiffrin. *The State of Media Literacy in Sub-Saharan Africa 2020 and a Theory of Misinformation Literacy,* https://www.uwestminsterpress.co.uk/site/chapters/m/10.16997/book53.a/, In *Review Of Misinformation Across Sub-Saharan Africa 2016-2020: A Study Of And Policy Framework For 'Media Literacy' In Schools And Legal/Regulatory Responses* (London: University of Westminster Press, 2021).

5 Respectively, a Researcher and Lecturer at the Centre d'Études des Sciences et des Techniques de l'Information (CESTI) at University of Dakar, Senegal, the Founder and Executive Director of the Centre for Media & Information Literacy in Kenya, the Coordinator of the African Centre for Media & Information

Literacy, at Abuja, Nigeria, a Researcher and Lecturer at North West University, at Potschefstroom, South Africa, and then Director of the Technology, Media and Communications Specialization at the School of International and Public Affairs, at Columbia University, United States.

Introduction

1 World Economic Forum, 'Global Risks Report 2024', 10 January 2024 https://www.weforum.org/publications/global-risks-report-2024/

2 Martin Moore, *Democracy Hacked: How Technology is Destabilising Global Politics* (London: One World Publications, 2018), 107–35.

3 David Kaye, *Speech Police: The Global Struggle to Govern the Internet* (New York: Columbia Global Reports, 2019).

4 Israel Junior Borges do Nascimento, Ana Beatriz Pizarro, Jussara M Almeida, Natsasha Azzopardi-Muscat, Marcos Andre Concalves, Maria Björklunde and David Novillo-Ortiz, 'Infodemics and health misinformation: a systematic review of reviews', *Bulletin of the World Health Organization*. 100(9) (2022), 544–61. https://doi.org/10.2471/BLT.21.287654.

5 Peter Cunliffe-Jones, Assane Diagne, Alan Finlay and Anya Schiffrin, *Bad Law – Legal and Regulatory Responses to Misinformation in Eleven African Countries 2016–2020* www.uwestminsterpress.co.uk/site/chapters/m/10.16997/book53.b/, in *Review Of Misinformation Across Sub-Saharan Africa 2016–2020: A Study Of And Policy Framework For 'Media Literacy' In Schools And Legal/Regulatory Responses* (London: University of Westminster Press, 2021).

6 Center for News Technology & Innovation, 'Most "Fake News" Legislation Risks Doing More Harm Than Good Amid a Record Number of Elections in 2024', last accessed 10 June 2024 https://innovating.news/article/most-fake-news-legislation-risks-doing-more-harm-than-good-amid-a-record-number-of-elections-in-2024/.

7 Lucas Graves and Alexios Mantzarlis, 'Amid Political Spin and Online Misinformation, Fact Checking Adapts', *The Political Quarterly*, 91(3) (2020), 585–91, https://doi.org/10.1111/1467-923X.12896.

8 Sander Van der Linden *Foolproof – Why We Fall for Misinformation and How to Build Immunity* (London: 4th Estate, 2023).

9 Alice Huguet, Jennifer Kavanagh, Garrett Baker and Marjory S Blumenthal, 'Exploring Media Literacy Education as a Tool for Mitigating Truth Decay', *Rand Corporation*, 11 July 2019 www.rand.org/pubs/research_reports/RR3050.html

10 Peter Cunliffe-Jones, Sahite Gaye, Wallace Gichunge, Chido Onumah, Cornia Pretorius and Anya Schiffrin. 'The State of Media Literacy in Sub-Saharan Africa 2020 and a Theory of Misinformation Literacy',

https://www.uwestminsterpress.co.uk/site/chapters/m/10.16997/book53.a/ In *Review Of Misinformation Across Sub-Saharan Africa 2016–2020: A Study Of And Policy Framework For 'Media Literacy' In Schools And Legal/Regulatory Responses* (London: University of Westminster Press, 2021).

11 Chico Q. Camargo and Felix M. Simon, 'Mis-disinformation studies are too big to fail: Six suggestions for the field's future', *Harvard Misinformation Review*, 20 September 2022, https://doi.org/10.37016/mr-2020-106.

12 Lucas Graves, 'Lessons from an extraordinary year: Four heuristics for studying mediated misinformation in 2020 and beyond', in *The Routledge Companion to Media Disinformation and Populism*, eds Howard Tumbler and Silvio Waisbord (London: Routledge, 2021), https://doi.org/10.4324/9781003004431.

13 I provide details on 250 of these entries in the database, which can be seen in Appendix 1, and links to 152 entries which related or were similar to claims already examined.

14 Lucas Graves, *Deciding What's True: The Rise of Political Fact-checking in American Journalism* (New York: Columbia University Press, 2016), 7.

15 The author was one of the two co-authors of the IFCN Code of Principles in 2016, with Phoebe Arnold of the UK fact-checking organisation Full Fact, and led a review and update of the code in 2019–20.

16 Graves, *Deciding What's True*, 70–71.

17 Herman Wasserman and Dani Madrid-Morales, 'An exploratory study of "fake news" and media trust in Kenya, Nigeria and South Africa', *African Journalism Studies*, 40(1) (August 2019), 107–23, https://doi:10.1080/23743670.2019.1627230.

18 Jeffrey Conroy-Krutz, 'Africans are concerned about ills of social media but oppose government restrictions", *The Conversation*, 1 June 2020, https://theconversation.com/africans-are-concerned-about-ills-of-social-media-but-oppose-government-restrictions-137653

19 Cameron Martel, Jennifer Allen, Gordon Pennycook and David G. Rand, 'Crowds Can Effectively Identify Misinformation at Scale', *Perspectives on Psychological Science*, 19(2) (August 2023), https://doi.org/10.1177/17456916231190388.

20 James Carey, *Communication as Culture: Essays on Media and Society* (Boston, MA: Unwyn Hyman, 1989).

21 Dan Sperber, 'Apparently irrational beliefs', in *Rationality and Relativism*, eds Martin Hollis and Steven Lukes (Cambridge.MA: MIT Press, 1982), 171–2, https://www.dan.sperber.fr/wp-content/uploads/1982_apparently-irrational-beliefs.pdf

22 Claire Wardle and Hossein Derakhshan, 'Information Disorder: Toward an interdisciplinary framework for research and policy making', *Council of Europe*, 2017, https://rm.coe.int/information-disorder-toward-an-interdisciplinary-framework-for-researc/168076277c.

23 Gillian Murphy, Constance De Saint Laurent, Megan Reynolds, Omar Aftab, Karen Hegarty, Yuning Sun and Ciara M. Greene, 'What do we study when we study misinformation? A scoping review of experimental research (2016–2022)', *Harvard Misinformation Review*, 15 November 2023, https://misinforeview.hks.harvard.edu/article/what-do-we-study-when-we-study-misinformation-a-scoping-review-of-experimental-research-2016-2022/.

24 Hannah Arendt, 'Lying in Politics', in *Crises of the Republic* (New York: Harvest, 1972), 35.

Part 1 – Introduction

1 BBC News, 'What is 2017's word of the year?', 2 November 2017, www.bbc.co.uk/news/uk-41838386.

2 Center for News Technology & Innovation, 'Most "Fake News" Legislation Risks Doing More Harm Than Good', 5 April 2024, https://innovating.news/article/most-fake-news-legislation-risks-doing-more-harm-than-good-amid-a-record-number-of-elections-in-2024/.

3 Alice Huguet, Jennifer Kavanagh, Garrett Baker and Marjory S. Blumenthal, 'Exploring Media Literacy Education as a Tool for Mitigating Truth Decay', *Rand Corporation*, 11 July 2019, www.rand.org/pubs/research_reports/RR3050.html.

4 An annual count by the Reporters Lab at Duke University found that the number of fact-checking websites active grew from 152 in 2015 to 457 in 2022, before falling back slightly to 439 in 2024. See Marc Stencel, Erica Ryan and Joel Luther, 'With half the planet going to the polls in 2024, fact-checking splutters', *Duke Reporters Lab*, 30 May 2024, https://reporterslab.org/with-half-the-planet-going-to-the-polls-in-2024-fact-checking-sputters/.

5 Sander Van der Linden, *Foolproof – Why We Fall For Misinformation and How to Build Immunity* (London: 4th Estate, 2023).

6 Between 2016 and 2021, citations of academic articles with the term 'fake news' in the title increased from 331 to 5,671; a leap of more than 1,600 per cent in six years.

7 Chico Q. Camargo and Felix M. Simon, 'Mis-disinformation Studies Are Too Big to Fail: Six Suggestions for the Field's Future', *Harvard Misinformation Review*, 20 September 2022, https://doi.org/10.37016/mr-2020-106.

8 Jon Bateman, Elonnai Hickock, Laura Courchesne, Isra Thange and Jacob N Shapiro, 'Measuring the Effects of Influence Operations: Key Findings and Gaps from Empirical Research', *Carnegie Endowment*, 28 June 2021, https://carnegieendowment.org/2021/06/28/measuring-effects-of-influence-operations-key-findings-and-gaps-from-empirical-research-pub-84824.

9 Camille François, 'Actors, Behaviors, Content: A Disinformation ABC', Graphika & Berkman Klein Center for Internet & Society at Harvard University, 20 September 2019, https://www.ivir.nl/publicaties/download/ABC_Framework_2019_Sept_2019.pdf.

10 Magda Osman, 'Disinformation Is Often Blamed for Swaying Elections – the Research Says Something Else', *The Conversation*, 26 January 2024, https://theconversation.com/disinformation-is-often-blamed-for-swaying-elections-the-research-says-something-else-221579.

Chapter 1

1 Martin Moore, *Democracy Hacked: How Technology is Destabilising Global Politics* (London: One World Publications, 2018).

2 Peter Pomerantsev, *This is Not Propaganda. Adventures in the War Against Reality* (London: Faber & Faber, 2019).

3 Hannah Arendt, 'Lying in Politics', in *Crises of the Republic* (New York: Harvest, 1972).

4 Hugo Mercier, Not Born Yesterday. The Science of Who We Trust and What We Believe (Princeton, NJ and Oxford: Princeton University Press, 2020).

5 Ceren Budak, Brendan Nyhan, David M. Rothschild, Emily Thorson and Duncan J. Watts, 'Misunderstanding the harms of online misinformation', *Nature*, 630 (2024), 45–53, https://doi.org/10.1038/s41586-024-07417-w.

6 James Carey, *Communication as Culture: Essays on media and society* (Boston, MA: Unwyn Hyman, 1989).

7 Dan Sperber, 'Apparently irrational beliefs' in *Rationality and Relativism*, edited by Martin Hollis and Steven Lukes (Cambridge, MA: MIT Press, 1982), 171–2, https://www.dan.sperber.fr/wp-content/uploads/1982_apparently-irrational-beliefs.pdf.

8 Rick Noack, 'The ugly history of "*Lügenpresse*", a Nazi slur shouted at a Trump rally', *Washington Post*, 24 October 2016, https://www.washingtonpost.com/news/worldviews/wp/2016/10/24/the-ugly-history-of-luegenpresse-a-nazi-slur-shouted-at-a-trump-rally/.

9 Callum Borchers, 'Trump claims falsely (again), that he coined the term "fake news"', *Washington Post*, 26 October 2017, https://www.washingtonpost.com/news/the-fix/wp/2017/10/26/trump-falsely-claims-again-that-he-coined-the-term-fake-news/.

10 Merriam Webster, 'The real story of fake news', 2017, https://www.merriam-webster.com/words-at-play/the-real-story-of-fake-news.

11 James Jacoby, 'The Facebook dilemma – Interview with Craig Silverman', *PBS Frontline*, 20 April 2018, https://www.pbs.org/wgbh/frontline/interview/craig-silverman/.

12 J. E. Tandoc, C. W. Lim, R. Ling, 'Defining "Fake News"', *Digital Journalism*, 6(2) (2018), 137–53, https://www.tandfonline.com/doi/abs/10.1080/21670811.2017.1360143.

13 Richard Lloyd Parry, 'Rohingya ethnic cleansing is fake news, says Burma army', *The Times*, 15 November 2017, https://www.thetimes.co.uk/article/rohingya-ethnic-cleansing-is-fake-news-says-burma-army-580hbxw6r.

14 Jean Le Roux, 'Nigerian army dismisses Lekki Toll Gate massacre as "fake news"', *DFR Lab*, 22 October 2020, https://medium.com/dfrlab/nigerian-army-dismisses-lekki-toll-gate-massacre-as-fake-news-6e4665eed6d7.

15 Joshua Habgood-Coote, 'The term "fake news" is doing great harm', *The Conversation*, 27 July 2018, https://theconversation.com/the-term-fake-news-is-doing-great-harm-100406.

16 Madeleine de Cock Buning, 'A multi-dimensional approach to disinformation. Report of the independent High Level Group on Fake News and Online Disinformation', *European Commission*, 8 March 2018, https://digital-strategy.ec.europa.eu/en/library/final-report-high-level-expert-group-fake-news-and-online-disinformation.

17 David Lazer, Matthew Baum, Yochai Benkler, Adam Berinsky, Kelly Greenhill, Filippo Menczer, Miriam Metzger et al., 'The science of fake news: addressing fake news requires a multidisciplinary effort', *Science*, 2018, 3591094–6 , https://doi.org:10.1126/science.aao2998.

18 Harry G. Frankfurt, *On Bullshit* (Princeton, NJ and Oxford: Princeton University Press, 2005).

19 The first evidence of the term in English appears in a 1587 text by clergyman Abraham Fleming. See https://www.oed.com/dictionary/misinformation_n?tl=true.

20 Emily Vraga and Leticia Bode, 'Defining Misinformation and Understanding its Bounded Nature: Using Expertise and Evidence for Describing Misinformation', *Political Communication*, 37(1) (2020), 136–44, https://doi.org/10.1080/10584609.2020.1716500.

21 James Kuklinski, Jennifer Quirk, Paul Jerit, David Schwieder and Robert Rich, 'Misinformation and the Currency of Democratic Citizenship', *Journal of Politics*, 62(3) (2003), https://doi.org/10.1111/0022-3816.00033.

22 Bernard Williams, *Truth and truthfulness. An essay in genealogy* (Princeton, NJ and Oxford: Princeton University Press, 2002), 1.

23 Brendan Nyhan and Jason Reifler, 'When corrections fail: The persistence of political misperceptions', *Political Behavior*, 32(2) (2010), 303–30, https://doi.org:10.1007/s11109-010-9112-2.

24 Claire Wardle and Hossein Derakhshan, 'Information Disorder: Toward an interdisciplinary framework for research and policy making', *Council of Europe*, 2017,

https://rm.coe.int/information-disorder-toward-an-interdisciplinary-framework-for-researc/168076277c.

25 Sacha Altay, Manon Berriche, Hendrik Heuer, Jonas Farkas, Steven Rathje, 'A survey of expert views on misinformation: Definitions, determinants, solutions, and future of the field', *Harvard Misinformation Review*, 27 July 2023, https://misinforeview.hks.harvard.edu/article/a-survey-of-expert-views-on-misinformation-definitions-determinants-solutions-and-future-of-the-field/.

26 Kalina Bontcheva and Julie Posetti, eds, *Balancing Act: Countering Digital Disinformation while respecting Freedom of Expression*, ITU & UNESCO, September 2020, https://www.broadbandcommission.org/Documents/working-groups/FoE_Disinfo_Report.pdf.

27 From emails to the author from leaders of fact-checking organisations in September 2023.

28 Readers can access the database through a link provided in Appendix 1.

29 See Sperber, 'Apparently irrational beliefs', 171–2.

30 Center for News Technology & Innovation, 'Most 'Fake News' Legislation Risks Doing More Harm Than Good', 5 April 2024, https://innovating.news/article/most-fake-news-legislation-risks-doing-more-harm-than-good-amid-a-record-number-of-elections-in-2024/.

31 Richard Shultz and Roy Godson, *Dezinformatsia: Active Measures in Soviet Strategy* (McLean, VA: Pergamon-Brassey's, 1984).

32 Harold Lasswell, *Propaganda technique in the world war* (New York: Knopf, 1927), 9.

33 Garth Jowett and Victoria O'Donnell, *Propaganda and Persuasion* (London: Sage, 1999).

34 See (i) Leon Festinger, Henry Riecken and Stanley Schachter, *When Prophecy Fails – A Social and Psychological Study of a Modern Group that Predicted the Destruction of the World* (Minneapolis: University of Minnesota, 1956). (ii) For more recent work, see Nyhan and Reifler, 'When corrections fail'.

35 See: (i) Nathan Walter, Jonathan Cohen, R. Lance Holbert and Yasmin Morag, 'A Meta-Analysis of What Works and for Whom', *Political Communication*, 37(3) (October 2019), 350–75, https://doi.org/10.1080/10584609.2019.1668894. (ii) For a study across multiple countries, see Ethan Porter and Tom Wood 'The global effectiveness of fact-checking: Evidence from simultaneous experiments in Argentina, Nigeria, South Africa, and the United Kingdom,' *Proceedings of the National Academy of Science* 118(37) (2021), https://doi:10.1073/pnas.2104235118.

36 Philip Hilts, *Smokescreen: The truth behind the tobacco industry cover-up*, (Reading, MA: Addison-Wesley, 1996), 8–22.

37 James Hoggan and Richard Littlemore, *Climate cover-up: The crusade to deny global warming*. (Vancouver: Greystone Books, 2009), 61–72.

38 de Cock Buning, 'A multi-dimensional approach to disinformation'.

39 Plato, *Republic*, translated by Robin Waterfield (Oxford: Oxford University Press, 1993), 78.

40 Arendt, 'Lying in Politics', 4.

41 Peter Oborne, *The rise of political lying* (London: Free Press, 2005), 130.

42 Joshua Levine, *Operation Fortitude: The greatest hoax of the Second World War* (London: Collins, 2012).

43 Xinyan Zhao and Stephanie Tsang, 'How People Process Different Types of Health Misinformation: Roles of Content Falsity and Evidence Type', *Health Communication*, 39(4) (2023), 741–53, https://doi.org/10.1080/10410236.2023.2184452.

44 Evelyn Douek, 'What Does "Coordinated Inauthentic Behavior" Actually Mean?', *Slate*, 2 July 2020, https://slate.com/technology/2020/07/coordinated-inauthentic-behavior-facebook-twitter.html.

45 Floyd Allport and Milton Lepkin, 'Wartime Rumors of Waste and Special Privilege: Why Some People Believe Them', *Journal of Abnormal and Social Psychology*, 40(1) (1945), https://psycnet.apa.org/record/1945-01987-001.

46 Lisa Fazio, Raunak Pillai and Deep Patel, 'The effects of repetition on belief in naturalistic settings', *Journal of Experimental Psychology*, 151(10) (2022), 2604–13, https://pubmed.ncbi.nlm.nih.gov/35286116/.

47 Doris Lacassagne, Jeremy Bena and Olivier Corneille, 'Is Earth a perfect square? Repetition increases the perceived truth of highly implausible statements', *Cognition*, 223 (2022), https://doi.org/10.1016/j.cognition.2022.105052.

Chapter 2

1 Chico Q. Camargo and Felix M. Simon, 'Mis-disinformation studies are too big to fail: Six suggestions for the field's future', *Harvard Misinformation Review*. 20 September 2022, https://doi.org/10.37016/mr-2020-106.

2 Alana Schetzer, 'Governments are making fake news a crime, but it could stifle free speech', *The Conversation*, 7 July 2019, https://theconversation.com/governments-are-making-fake-news-a-crime-but-it-could-stifle-free-speech-117654.

3 Gabrielle Lim and Samantha Bradshaw, 'Chilling legislation: Tracking the impact of "fake news" laws on press freedom internationally', *Center for International Media Assistance*, 19 July 2023, https://www.cima.ned.org/publication/chilling-legislation/.

4 Lisa O'Carroll, 'How the EU Digital Services Act affects Facebook, Google and others', *The Guardian*, 25 August 2023, https://www.theguardian.com/world/2023/aug/25/how-the-eu-digital-services-act-affects-facebook-google-and-others.

5 Paul Sandle, 'UK's Online Safety Bill finally passed by parliament', *Reuters*, 19 September 2023, https://www.reuters.com/world/uk/uks-online-safety-bill-passed-by-parliament-2023-09-19/.

6 See EU Commissioner Věra Jourová's statement posted on X, then known as Twitter: https://twitter.com/VeraJourova/status/1537388143284043776, 16 June 2022.

7 Lucas Graves and Alexios Mantzarlis, 'Amid Political Spin and Online Misinformation, Fact Checking Adapts', *The Political Quarterly*, 91(3) (2020), 585–91, https://doi.org/10.1111/1467-923X.12896.

8 Renee Hobbs, 'Defining digital literacy', *Media Ed Lab*, 10 February 2019. https://mediaedlab.com/2019/02/10/defining-digital-literacy-2/.

9 John Paul Stonard, 'Opinion: The dazzling lies of art', *Tate etc.*, 8 February 2019, https://www.tate.org.uk/tate-etc/issue-45-spring-2019/opinion-dazzling-lies-art-john-paul-stonard.

10 Eve MacDonald, 'The fake news that sealed the fate of Antony and Cleopatra', *The Conversation*, 13 January 2017, https://theconversation.com/the-fake-news-that-sealed-the-fate-of-antony-and-cleopatra-71287.

11 Jacob Soll, 'The long and brutal history of fake news', *Politico*, 18 December 2016, https://www.politico.com/magazine/story/2016/12/fake-news-history-long-violent-214535/.

12 Jacob Mchangama, *Free Speech: A global history from Socrates to social media*, (London: Basic Books, 2022), 63.

13 Mchangama, *Free Speech*, 66.

14 Robert G. Parkinson, 'Fake news? That's a very old story', *Washington Post*, 25 November 2016, https://www.washingtonpost.com/opinions/fake-news-thats-a-very-old-story/2016/11/25/c8b1f3d4-b330-11e6-8616-52b15787add0_story.html.

15 Kevin Young, 'Moon Shot: Race, a Hoax, and the Birth of Fake News', *The New Yorker*, 21 October 2017, https://www.newyorker.com/books/page-turner/moon-shot-race-a-hoax-and-the-birth-of-fake-news.

16 W. Joseph Campbell, 'The Halloween myth of the War of the Worlds panic', *BBC News*, 30 October 2011, https://www.bbc.co.uk/news/magazine-15470903.

17 Stuart Thompson and Yuliya Parshina-Kottas, '*The War in Ukraine, as Seen on Russian TV*', 6 May 2022, https://www.nytimes.com/interactive/2022/05/06/technology/russian-propaganda-television.html.

18 Mchangama, *Free Speech*, 1, 76 and 225.

19 Ibn Khaldun, *The Muqaddimah: An Introduction to History,* trans Franz Rosenthal, (New York: Princeton University Press, 1989).

20 John F. Burns, 'Vorster', *New York Times*, 10 June 1979, https://www.nytimes.com/1979/06/10/archives/was-the-system-vindicated-or-does-it-stand-accused-vorster.html.

21 Stephen Ellis, 'The Historical Significance of South Africa's Third Force', *Journal of Southern African Studies*, 24(2) (1998), 261–99, https://www.tandfonline.com/doi/abs/10.1080/03057079808708577.

22 Paul Erasmus, *Confessions of a Stratcom hitman* (Johannesburg: Jacana Media, 2021), 104.

23 Simone Monasebian, 'The Pre-Genocide Case Against Radio-Télévision Libre des Milles Collines', in *The media and the Rwanda Genocide*, edited by Allan Thompson (London: Pluto Press, 2007), 308–30.

24 Monasebian, 'The Pre-Genocide Case Against Radio-Télévision Libre des Milles Collines'.

25 Ayodele Jegede, 'What Led to the Nigerian Boycott of the Polio Vaccination Campaign?', *PLOS Medicine*, 4(3) (March 2007), https://doi.org/10.1371/journal.pmed.0040073.

26 Jeanne Lenzer, 'Secret report surfaces showing that Pfizer was at fault in Nigerian drug tests', *British Medical Journal*, 332(1233) (2006), https://doi.org/10.1136/bmj.332.7552.1233-a.

27 News24.com, 'Vaccine boycott spreads polio', 11 February 2004, https://www.news24.com/news24/vaccine-boycott-spreads-polio-20040211.

28 WHO Regional Committee for Africa, Polio eradication in the African Region: progress report, *World Health Organization*, 2011, https://apps.who.int/iris/handle/10665/1861.

29 Pride Chigwedere, George Seage, Sofia Gruskin, Tun-Hou Lee and M. Essex, 'Estimating the lost benefits of antiretroviral drug use in South Africa', *Journal of Acquired Immune Deficiency Syndrome*, 49(4) (2008), 410–15, https://doi.org/10.1097/qai.0b013e31818a6cd5.

30 Nicoli Nattrass, 'AIDS and the Scientific Governance of Medicine in Post-Apartheid Africa', *African Affairs*, 107(427) (2008), 157–76, https://academic.oup.com/afraf/article/107/427/157/30448.

31 Harry G. Frankfurt, *On Bullshit* (Princeton, NJ and Oxford: Princeton University Press, 2005), 62.

32 Craig Silverman, 'Facebook says its fact checking program helps reduce the spread of a fake story by 80%', *BuzzFeed News*, 12 October 2017, https://www.buzzfeednews.com/article/craigsilverman/facebook-just-shared-the-first-data-about-how-effective-its.

33 Yochai Benkler, Casey Tilton, Bruce Etling, Hal Roberts, Justin Clark, Robert Faris, Jonas Kaiser and Carolyn Schmitt, 'Mail-In Voter Fraud: Anatomy of a Disinformation Campaign', Berkman Klein Center, Harvard University,

1 October 2020, https://cyber.harvard.edu/publication/2020/Mail-in-Voter-Fraud-Disinformation-2020.

34 Ceren Budak, Brendan Nyhan, David M. Rothschild, Emily Thorson and Duncan J. Watts, 'Misunderstanding the harms of online misinformation', *Nature*, 630 (2024), 45–53, https://doi.org/10.1038/s41586-024-07417-w.

35 Gillian Murphy, Constance De Saint Laurent, Megan Reynolds, Omar Aftab, Karen Hegarty, Yuning Sun and Ciara M. Greene, 'What do we study when we study misinformation? A scoping review of experimental research (2016–2022)', *Harvard Misinformation Review*, 15 November 2023, https://misinforeview.hks.harvard.edu/article/what-do-we-study-when-we-study-misinformation-a-scoping-review-of-experimental-research-2016-2022/.

36 Laura Eggertson, 'Lancet retracts 12-year-old article linking autism to MMR vaccine', *Canadian Medical Association Journal*, 182(4) (March 2010), 199–200, https://doi:10.1503/cmaj.109-3179.

37 Chigwedere et al., 'Estimating the lost benefits of antiretroviral drug use in South Africa'.

38 Kelsey Piper, 'The staggering death toll of scientific lies', *Vox*, 26 August 2024, https://www.vox.com/future-perfect/368350/scientific-research-fraud-crime-jail-time.

39 Claire Wilson, 'The replication crisis has spread through science – can it be fixed?', *New Scientist*, 6 April 2022, https://www.newscientist.com/article/mg25433810-400-the-replication-crisis-has-spread-through-science-can-it-be-fixed/.

40 UN News, 'Fake medicines kill almost 500,000 sub-Saharan Africans a year: UNODC report', 1 February 2023, https://news.un.org/en/story/2023/02/1133062.

41 Mayowa Tijani, 'This photo has been edited to falsely show Nigerian separatist leader Nnamdi Kanu addressing the European Parliament', *AFPFactCheck*, 20 September 2019, https://factcheck.afp.com/photo-has-been-edited-falsely-show-nigerian-separatist-leader-nnamdi-kanu-addressing-european.

42 Dawit Endeshaw, 'Mob action costs two researchers' lives', *The Reporter Ethiopia*, 27 October 2018, https://www.thereporterethiopia.com/6682/.

43 Taryn Khourie, 'Over 2,000 phoney marriages reported in South Africa, but only 1,160 "truly fraudulent"', *Africa Check*, 16 July 2019, https://africacheck.org/fact-checks/reports/over-2000-phoney-marriages-reported-south-africa-only-1160-truly-fraudulent.

44 Jon Cartwright, 'AIDS contrarian ignored warnings of scientific misconduct', *Nature*, 4 May 2010, https://www.nature.com/articles/news.2010.210.

Chapter 3

1 Claire Wardle and Hossein Derakhshan, 'Information Disorder: Toward an interdisciplinary framework for research and policy making', *Council of Europe*, 2017, https://rm.coe.int/information-disorder-toward-an-interdisciplinary-framework-for-researc/168076277c.

2 Dan Williams, 'Should we trust misinformation experts to decide what counts as misinformation?', *Conspicuous Cognition*, 14 February 2024, https://www.conspicuouscognition.com/p/should-we-trust-misinformation-experts.

3 Nirmal Kandel, 'Information Disorder Syndrome and its Management', *Journal of Nepal Medical Association*, 58(224) (2020), 220–85, https://doi.org/10.31729/jnma.4968.

4 Herman Wasserman, ed, Azamat Ababakirov, Ahmed Ashour, Ramathi Bandaranayake, Ruwanka Silva and Dominique Diouf, 'Meeting the challenges of information disorder in the Global South', *IDRC*, 2022, https://idl-bnc-idrc.dspacedirect.org/handle/10625/60954.

5 James Carey *Communication as Culture: Essays on media and society* (Boston, MA: Unwyn Hyman, 1989), 15, 18.

6 Dan Sperber, 'Apparently irrational beliefs' in *Rationality and Relativism*, ed. Martin Hollis and Steven Lukes (Cambridge, MA: MIT Press, 1982), 149–80, https://www.dan.sperber.fr/wp-content/uploads/1982_apparently-irrational-beliefs.pdf.

7 Francis Bacon, *Novum Organum* (1620), https://oll.libertyfund.org/title/bacon-novum-organum.

8 Hannah Arendt, 'Lying in Politics', in *Crises of the Republic* (New York: Harvest, 1972), 8.

9 Hugo Mercier, *Not Born Yesterday. The Science of Who We Trust and What We Believe* (Princeton, NJ and Oxford: Princeton University Press, 2020), xiv–xv.

10 Paul Lazarsfeld, Bernard Berelson and Hazel Gaudet, *The People's Choice* (New York: Columbia University Press, 1948).

11 Joseph Klapper, *The effects of mass communication* (Glencoe, IL: Free Press, 1960), 12–15, 60.

12 Leon Festinger, Henry Riecken and Stanley Schachter, *When Prophecy Fails – A Social and Psychological Study of a Modern Group that Predicted the Destruction of the World* (Minneapolis: University of Minnesota, 1956).

13 Brendan Nyhan and Jason Reifler, 'When corrections fail: The persistence of political misperceptions', *Political Behavior*, 32(2) (2010), 303–30, https://doi.org:10.1007/s11109-010-9112-2.

14 Sten Torpan, Sten Hansson, Mark Rhinard, Austeja Kazemekaityte, Pirjo Jukarainen, Sunniva Frislid Meyer, Abriel Schieffelers, Gabriella Lovasz and Kati

Orru, 'Handling false information in emergency management: A cross-national comparative study of European practices', *International Journal of Disaster Risk Reduction*, 57 (2021), 102–15, https://www.sciencedirect.com/science/article/pii/S2212420921001175.

15 Torpan et al., 'Handling false information in emergency management'.

16 Torpan et al., 'Handling false information in emergency management'.

17 Anthony Lane, 'Eight Minutes of Terror at London Bridge', *The New Yorker*, 4 June 2017, www.newyorker.com/news/news-desk/eight-minutes-of-terror-at-london-bridge.

18 Denise R. Allen, Romel Lacson, Amos Gborie, Manisha Patel and Michael Beach, 'Understanding Why Ebola Deaths Occur at Home in Urban Montserrado County, Liberia', *Centre for Disease Control and Prevention*, June 2015, www.ebola-anthropology.net/wp-content/uploads/2015/07/FINAL-Report-to-Liberia-MoH-Understanding-Why-Ebola-Deaths-Occur-at-Home-Liberia.pdf.

19 At the first meeting of groups seeking to establish fact-checking operations in Africa, in Johannesburg in November 2017, the author asked all participants to name their biggest challenge. Without exception, they all identified lack of easy access to accurate information.

20 Nic Newman, Richard Fletcher, Craig T. Robertson, Amy R Arguedas and Rasmus Kleis Nielsen, 'Reuters Institute Digital News Report', *Reuters Institute for the Study of Journalism*, 2024, https://reutersinstitute.politics.ox.ac.uk/sites/default/files/2024-06/RISJ_DNR_2024_Digital_v10%20lr.pdf.

21 Dani Madrid-Morales, Herman Wasserman, Gregory Gondwe, Khulekani Ndlovu, Etse Sikanu, Melissa Tully, Emeka Umejei and Chikezie Uzuegbunam, 'Motivations for Sharing Misinformation. A Comparative Study in Six Sub-Saharan African Countries', *International Journal of Communication*, 15 (2021), 1200–19, https://ijoc.org/index.php/ijoc/article/view/14801/3378.

22 Jeffrey Conroy-Krutz and Josephine Appiah-Nyamekye Sanny, 'How free is too free? Across Africa, media is on the defensive', *Afrobarometer Policy Paper Number 56* (May 2019), http://afrobarometer.org/sites/default/files/publications/Policy%20papers/ab_r7_policypaperno56_support_for_media_freedom_declines_across_africa_1.pdf.

23 Maria Celeste Wagner and Pablo J. Boczkowski, 'The Reception of Fake News: The Interpretations and Practices That Shape the Consumption of Perceived Misinformation', *Digital Journalism*, 7 (August 2019), https://doi.org/10.1080/21670811.2019.1653208.

24 See (i) Heidi Larson, 'The Biggest Pandemic Risk? Viral Misinformation', *Nature* 562, (2018), 309, https://doi.org/10.1038/d41586-018-07034-4. (ii) And World Economic Forum, '3 charts that show how attitudes to climate science vary

around the world', 22 January 2020, https://www.weforum.org/agenda/2020/01/climate-science-global-warming-most-sceptics-country/.

25 *The Guardian*, '"It's the real me": Nigerian president denies dying and being replaced by a clone', 3 December 2018, https://www.theguardian.com/world/2018/dec/03/its-real-me-nigerian-president-denies-dying-and-being-replaced-by-clone.

26 Elizabeth M. Perse, *Media effects and society* (Mahwah, NJ and London: Lawrence Erlbaum Associates Publishers, 2001), 99.

27 Alice E. Marwick, 'Why do people share fake news? A socio-technocratic model of media effects', *Georgetown Law Technology Review*. 2(2) (2018), 474–512. https://georgetownlawtechreview.org/wp-content/uploads/2018/07/2.2-Marwick-pp-474-512.pdf.

28 BBC News, 'South Africa rejects Donald Trump's tweet on farmer killings', 23 August 2018, https://www.bbc.co.uk/news/world-africa-45282088.

29 Nechama Brodie, 'Using Mixed-Method Approaches to Provide New Insights into Media Coverage of Femicide', *University of the Witwatersrand*, 2019, http://wiredspace.wits.ac.za/handle/10539/29294.

30 Sara Tiegreen and Elana Newman, 'Violence: Comparing Reporting and Reality', *Dart Center for Journalism and Trauma*, 18 February 2009, https://dartcenter.org/content/violence-comparing-reporting-and-reality.

31 Claudia Paola Lagos Lira and Patsili Toledo, 'The Media and Gender-Based Murders of Women: Notes on the Cases in Europe and Latin America', *Heinrich Böll Stiftung*, 24 July 2014, https://eu.boell.org/en/2014/07/24/media-and-gender-based-murders-women-notes-cases-europe-and-latin-america.

32 Tendai Dube, 'No, this video doesn't show a real Cape Town shootout – the scene was staged', *AFPFactCheck*, 23 July 2019, https://factcheck.afp.com/no-video-doesnt-show-real-cape-town-shootout-scene-was-staged.

33 Allwell Okpi, 'No, daggers seized by police in Nigeria's Kano state not for "killing Christians"', *Africa Check*, 19 August 2019, https://africacheck.org/fact-checks/spotchecks/no-daggers-seized-police-nigerias-kano-state-not-killing-christians.

34 Segun Olakoyenikan, 'No, these pictures do not show weapons from France going to Boko Haram insurgents in Nigeria', *AFPFactCheck*, 30 December 2019, https://factcheck.afp.com/no-these-pictures-do-not-show-weapons-france-going-boko-haram-insurgents-nigeria.

35 James Carey *Communication as Culture: Essays on media and society* (Boston, MA: Unwyn Hyman, 1989), 18.

36 Sperber, 'Apparently irrational beliefs', 171–2.

37 Daniel Kahneman, *Thinking, Fast and Slow* (New York: Farrar, Strauss and Giroux, 2011), 20–30.

38 Gordon Pennycook and David G. Rand, 'Lazy, not biased: Susceptibility to partisan fake news is better explained by lack of reasoning than by motivated reasoning', *Cognition*, 188 (2019), 39–50 https://www.sciencedirect.com/science/article/abs/pii/S001002771830163X.

39 Mathias Osmundsen, Alexander Bor, Vahlstrup, Peter Bjerregaard, Anja Bechmann and Michael Bang Petersen, 'Partisan Polarization Is the Primary Psychological Motivation behind Political Fake News Sharing on Twitter', *American Political Science Review*, 115(3) (2021), 999–1015, https://doi.org/10.1017/s0003055421000290.

40 Tom Buchanan and James Kempley, 'Individual differences in sharing false political information on social media: Direct and indirect effects of cognitive-perceptual schizotypy and psychopathy', *Personality and Individual Differences*, 182 (2021), https://doi.org/10.1016/j.paid.2021.111071.

41 Madrid-Morales et al., 'Motivations for Sharing Misinformation'.

42 *The Guardian*, '"It's the real me"'.

43 Mark Tran, 'Nigeria's President Yar'Adua dies', *The Guardian*, 6 May 2010, https://www.theguardian.com/world/2010/may/06/yaradua-nigeri-dies-president.

44 See: (i) Thomas E. Powell, Hajo G. Boomgaarden, Knut de Swert and Claes H. de Vreese, 'A clearer picture: The contribution of visuals and text to framing effects', *Journal of Communication*, 65(6) (2015), 997–1017, https://doi.org/10.1111/jcom.12184. (ii) Paul Messaris and Linus Abraham, 'The role of images in framing news stories', in *Framing public life. Perspectives on Media and Our Understanding of the Social World*, edited by Stephen Reese, Oscar Gandy and August Grant (Mahwah, NJ and London: Lawrence Erlbaum Associates Publishers, 2001), 215–26.

45 Floyd Allport and Milton Lepkin, 'Wartime Rumors of Waste and Special Privilege: Why Some People Believe Them', *Journal of Abnormal and Social Psychology*, 40(1) (1945), https://psycnet.apa.org/record/1945-01987-001.

46 Lisa Fazio, Raunak Pillai and Deep Patel, 'The effects of repetition on belief in naturalistic settings', *Journal of Experimental Psychology*, 151(10) (2022), 2604–13, https://pubmed.ncbi.nlm.nih.gov/35286116/.

47 See (i) William J. Brady, Julian A. Wills, John T. Jost, Joshua A. Tucker and Jay J. Van Bavel, 'Emotion Shapes the Diffusion of Moralized Content in Social Networks', *Proceedings of the National Academy of Sciences*, 114(28) (2017), 7313–18. https://doi.org/10.1073/pnas.1618923114. (ii) Nyhan and Reifler, 'When corrections fail'.

48 Cecilie S. Traberg, Trisha Harjani, Jon Roozenbeek and Sander Van der Linden, 'The persuasive effects of social cues and source effects on misinformation susceptibility', *Scientific Reports*, 2024, https://doi.org/10.1038/s41598-024-54030-y.

49 In 2012, an investigation by the Erasmus Medical School in the Netherlands found that one of its most eminent researchers, Don Poldermans, had used 'fictitious data' in formulating European guidelines for the treatment of patients prior to surgery. His prominence in the field gave his findings credibility. Some researchers believe the misleading guidelines may have resulted in hundreds of thousands of excess deaths: Kelsey Piper, 'The staggering death toll of scientific lies', *Vox*, 26 August 2024, https://www.vox.com/future-perfect/368350/scientific-research-fraud-crime-jail-time.

50 Martin Moore, *Democracy Hacked: How Technology is Destabilising Global Politics* (London: One World Publications, 2018), 107–35.

51 Israel Junior Borges do Nascimento, Ana Beatriz Pizarro, Jussara M Almeida, Natsasha Azzopardi-Muscat, Marcos Andre Concalves, Maria Björklunde and David Novillo-Ortiz, 'Infodemics and health misinformation: a systematic review of reviews', *Bulletin of the World Health Organization*, 100(9) (2022), 544–61. https://doi.org/10.2471/BLT.21.287654.

52 Harold Lasswell, *Propaganda technique in the world war* (New York: Knopf, 1927), 14.

53 Moore, *Democracy Hacked*, 103.

54 Zeba Siddiqui and Ruma Paul, 'Facebook, Twitter remove fake news sites in Bangladesh ahead of election', *Reuters*, 21 December 2018, https://www.reuters.com/article/us-bangladesh-election-facebook-idUSKCN1OJ2N3.

55 Melanie Smith, 'Archives: Facebook finds "coordinated and inauthentic behavior" in the Philippines; suspends a set of pro-government pages ahead of May elections', *Graphika*, 29 March 2019, https://medium.com/graphika-team/archives-facebook-finds-coordinated-and-inauthentic-behavior-in-the-philippines-suspends-a-set-d02f41f527df.

56 Andrew Cave, 'Deal that undid Bell Pottinger: Inside story of the South Africa scandal', *The Guardian*, 5 September 2017, https://www.theguardian.com/media/2017/sep/05/bell-pottingersouth-africa-pr-firm.

57 Abdi Latif Dahir, '"We'd stage the whole thing": Cambridge Analytica was filmed boasting of its role in Kenya's poll', *Quartz Africa*, 20 March 2018, https://qz.com/africa/1233084/channel-4-news-films-cambridge-analytica-execs-saying-they-staged-kenya-uhuru-kenyatta-elections/.

58 Carole Cadwalladr, 'Cambridge Analytica's ruthless bid to sway the vote in Nigeria', The Guardian, 21 March 2018, https://www.theguardian.com/uk-news/2018/mar/21/cambridge-analyticas-ruthless-bid-to-sway-the-vote-in-nigeria.

59 Mary Kulundu, 'Ignore these "polling figures" on the popularity of Kenya's possible presidential contenders – they didn't really come from IPSOS', *AFPFactCheck*, 3 July 2019, https://factcheck.afp.com/ignore-these-polling-figures-popularity-kenyas-possible-presidential-contenders-they-didnt-really.

60 Tendai Dube, 'This video shows a shooting at a funeral in South Africa, not "thugs" working for a Nigerian governor', *AFPFactCheck*, 13 November 2019, https://factcheck.afp.com/video-shows-shooting-funeral-south-africa-not-thugs-working-nigerian-governor.

61 Jennifer Ojugbeli, 'No, Nigerian politician Melaye hasn't won Kogi West senator's seat – election declared inconclusive', *Africa Check*, 20 November 2019, https://africacheck.org/fact-checks/meta-programme-fact-checks/no-nigerian-politician-melaye-hasnt-won-kogi-west-senators.

62 Select Committee on Intelligence, 'Final report on Russian active measures, campaigns and interference in the 2016 US election', *US Senate*, 2020, https://www.intelligence.senate.gov/sites/default/files/documents/report_volume5.pdf.

63 Mark Scott, Laura Kayali and Laurens Cerulus, 'European Commission accuses China of peddling disinformation', *Politico EU*, 10 June 2020, https://www.politico.eu/article/european-commission-disinformation-china-coronavirus/.

64 Twitter, 'Disclosing networks to our state-linked information operations archive', 8 October 2020, https://blog.twitter.com/en_us/topics/company/2020/disclosing-removed-networks-to-our-archive-of-state-linked-information.

65 *Time*, 'Yanks to the rescue: The secret story of how American advisers helped Yeltsin win', 15 July 1996, https://archive.org/details/TimeUSMeddlingOnRussia/page/n1/mode/2up.

66 Peter Pomerantsev, *This is Not Propaganda. Adventures in the War Against Reality* (London: Faber & Faber, 2019).

67 Philip Hilts, *Smokescreen: The truth behind the tobacco industry cover-up*, (Reading, MA: Addison-Wesley, 1996).

68 James Hoggan and Richard Littlemore, *Climate cover-up: The crusade to deny global warming* (Vancouver: Greystone Books, 2009), 61–72.

69 Amit Katwala, 'The Metro Bank hoax shows the immense power of fake news on WhatsApp', *Wired*, 14 May 2019, https://www.wired.co.uk/article/metro-bank-share-price-whats-app-hoax.

70 Pierre Berthon and Leyland Pitt, 'Brands, Truthiness and Post-Fact: Managing Brands in a Post Rational World', *Journal of Macro-Marketing*, 38(2) (2018), https://doi.org/10.1177/0276146718755869.

71 Simon Constable, 'How the Enron scandal changed American business forever', *Time*, 2 December 2021, https://time.com/6125253/enron-scandal-changed-american-business-forever/.

72 Zeke Faux, *Number Go Up. Inside Crypto's Wild Rise and Staggering Fall* (New York: Random House, 2023).

73 Moore, *Democracy Hacked*, 154.

74 See (i) Soroush Vosoughi, Deb Roy and Sinan Aral, 'The spread of true and false news online', *Science*, 359 (March 2018), 1146–51. https://doi.org/10.1126/science.aap9559. (ii) Mike Isaac, 'Facebook Wrestles With the Features It Used to Define Social Networking', *New York Times*, 29 October 2021, https://www.nytimes.com/2021/10/25/technology/facebook-like-share-buttons.html.

75 Naomi Nix and Sarah Ellison, 'Following Elon Musk's lead, Big Tech is surrendering to disinformation', *Washington Post*, 25 August 2023, https://www.washingtonpost.com/technology/2023/08/25/political-conspiracies-facebook-youtube-elon-musk/.

76 Yochai Benkler, Casey Tilton, Bruce Etling, Hal Roberts, Justin Clark, Robert Faris, Jonas Kaiser and Carolyn Schmitt, 'Mail-In Voter Fraud: Anatomy of a Disinformation Campaign', Berkman Klein Center, Harvard University, 1 October 2020, https://cyber.harvard.edu/publication/2020/Mail-in-Voter-Fraud-Disinformation-2020.

77 Yariv Tsfati, Hajo G. Boomgaarden, J. Stromback, A. Vliegenthart, A. Damstra and E. Lindgren, 'Causes and consequences of mainstream media dissemination of fake news: literature review and synthesis', *Annals of the International Communication Association*, 44(2) (2020), 157–73, https://doi:10.1080/23808985.2020.1759443.

78 Stuart Thompson and Yuliya Parshina-Kottas, 'The War in Ukraine, as Seen on Russian TV', 6 May 2022, https://www.nytimes.com/interactive/2022/05/06/technology/russian-propaganda-television.html.

79 Nic Newman, Richard Fletcher, Craig T. Robertson, Amy R Arguedas, Rasmus Kleis Nielsen, 'Reuters Institute Digital News Report', *Reuters Institute for the Study of Journalism*, 2024, https://reutersinstitute.politics.ox.ac.uk/sites/default/files/2024-06/RISJ_DNR_2024_Digital_v10%20lr.pdf.

80 Denise R. Allen, Romel Lacson, Amos Gborie, Manisha Patel, Michael Beach, 'Understanding Why Ebola Deaths Occur at Home in Urban Montserrado County, Liberia', *Centre for Disease Control and Prevention*, June 2015, http://www.ebola-anthropology.net/wp-content/uploads/2015/07/FINAL-Report-to-Liberia-MoH-Understanding-Why-Ebola-Deaths-Occur-at-Home-Liberia.pdf.

81 Ogala Emmanuel and Nnenna Ibeh, 'Ebola sparks panic across Nigeria as citizens scramble for salt-water bath "remedy"', *Premium Times*, 8 August 2014. https://www.premiumtimesng.com/news/166257-ebola-sparks-panic-across-nigeria-as-citizens-scramble-for-salt-water-bath-remedy.html#sthash.Ge0bomNI.dpbs.

82 Jamie Hitchen, 'The WhatsApp rumours that infused Sierra Leone's tight election', *African Arguments*, April 2018, https://africanarguments.org/2018/04/10/the-whatsapp-rumours-infused-sierra-leone-tight-election-social-media/.

83 Madalitso Wills Kateta, 'From corruption to the "mark of the beast" – why countries like Malawi are struggling against Covid', *The Guardian*, 6 January 2022, https://www.theguardian.com/commentisfree/2022/jan/06/malawi-fight-covid-government-corruption-vaccination.

84 Richard Lee Rogers and Nicolette Powe, 'COVID-19 Information Sources and Misinformation by Faith Community', *Inquiry*, https://doi.org/10.1177/00469580221081388.

85 Morten Jerven, *Poor numbers: How We are Misled by African Development Statistics and What to Do About It* (New York: Cornell University Press, 2013), xi.

86 UNESCO, 'Commitment versus action in Africa. Implement is as important as adoption of Access to Information laws', 20 April 2023, https://www.unesco.org/reports/access-to-information/2021/en/africa-ati-case-study.

87 Zach Rosson, Felicia Anthonio and Carolyn Tackett, 'Weapons of control, shields of impunity. Internet shutdowns in 2022', *Access Now*, 2023, https://www.accessnow.org/wp-content/uploads/2023/05/2022-KIO-Report-final.pdf

88 Michelle Amazeen, 'The misinformation recognition and response model: an emerging theoretical framework for investigating antecedents to and consequences of misinformation recognition', *Human Communication Research*, 50(2) (April 2024), 218–29, https://doi.org/10.1093/hcr/hqad040.

89 Peter Cunliffe-Jones and Guy Berger. 'Opinion: The next chapter for fact-checking: information integrity', *Poynter*, 5 December 2024, https://www.poynter.org/ifcn/2024/the-next-chapter-for-fact-checking-information-integrity/.

Part 2 – Introduction

1 Alana Schetzer, 'Governments are making fake news a crime, but it could stifle free speech', *The Conversation*, 7 July 2019, https://theconversation.com/governments-are-making-fake-news-a-crime-but-it-could-stifle-free-speech-117654.

2 See: (i) Lisa O'Carroll, 'How the EU Digital Services Act affects Facebook, Google and others', *The Guardian*, 25 August 2023, https://www.theguardian.com/world/2023/aug/25/how-the-eu-digital-services-act-affects-facebook-google-and-others. (ii) Paul Sandle, 'UK's Online Safety Bill finally passed by parliament', *Reuters*, 19 September 2023, https://www.reuters.com/world/uk/uks-online-safety-bill-passed-by-parliament-2023-09-19/.

3 Craig Silverman, 'Facebook says its fact checking program helps reduce the spread of a fake story by 80%', *BuzzFeed News*, 12 October 2017, https://www.buzzfeednews.com/article/craigsilverman/facebook-just-shared-the-first-data-about-how-effective-its.

4 Vishwam Sankaran, 'Twitter launches Community Notes feature that lets people add context to Tweets', *The Independent*, 12 December 2022, https://www.independent.co.uk/tech/twitter-community-notes-tweet-context-b2243311.html.

5 Reuters, 'TikTok to automatically remove content that violates policy', 9 July 2021, https://www.reuters.com/technology/tiktok-automatically-remove-content-that-violates-policy-2021-07-09/.

6 Center for News Technology & Innovation, 'Most "Fake News" Legislation Risks Doing More Harm Than Good', 5 April 2024, https://innovating.news/article/most-fake-news-legislation-risks-doing-more-harm-than-good-amid-a-record-number-of-elections-in-2024/.

7 Marc Stencel, Erica Ryan and Joel Luther, 'With half the planet going to the polls in 2024, fact-checking splutters', *Duke Reporters Lab*, 30 May 2024. https://reporterslab.org/with-half-the-planet-going-to-the-polls-in-2024-fact-checking-sputters/.

8 Camille François, 'Actors, Behaviors, Content: A Disinformation ABC', *Graphika* and the Berkman Klein Center for Internet & Society at Harvard University, 20 September 2019, https://www.ivir.nl/publicaties/download/ABC_Framework_2019_Sept_2019.pdf.

9 Jacob Mchangama, *Free Speech: A global history from Socrates to social media* (London: Basic Books, 2022), 8.

10 C. W. Anderson, 'Fake news is not a virus. On platforms and their effects', *Communications Theory*, 31(1) (2021), https://doi.org/10.1093/ct/qtaa008, 42–61.

11 See (i) Ullrich Ecker, Jon Roozenbeek, Sander van der Linden, Li Qian Tay, John Cook, Naomi Oreskes and Stephen Lewandowsky, 'Misinformation poses a bigger threat to democracy than you might think', *Nature*, 5 June 2024, https://www.nature.com/articles/d41586-024-01587-3, and (ii) Ceren Budak, Brendan Nyhan, David M. Rothschild, Emily Thorson and Duncan J. Watts, 'Misunderstanding the harms of online misinformation', *Nature*, 630 (2024), 45–53, https://doi.org/10.1038/s41586-024-07417-w.

Chapter 4

1 Max Read, 'Donald Trump Won Because of Facebook', *Intelligencer – New York Magazine*, 9 November 2016, https://nymag.com/intelligencer/2016/11/donald-trump-won-because-of-facebook.html.

2 Harold Lasswell, *Propaganda technique in the world war* (New York: Knopf, 1927), 2–3.

3 Lasswell, *Propaganda technique in the world war*, 187.

4 Alan Rusbridger, 'This is a key moment in the public's view of mainstream news', *The Guardian*, 3 May 2020, https://www.theguardian.com/commentisfree/2020/may/03/this-is-a-key-moment-in-the-publics-view-of-mainstream-news.

5 Bernard Berelson, 'Communications and Public Opinion', in *Communications in Modern Society: Fifteen studies of the mass media*, edited by W. Schramm, (Champaign: University of Illinois Press, 1948), 172.

6 Denis McQuail, *McQuail's Media and Mass Communication Theory* (London: Sage Publications, 6th Edition, 2010), 454.

7 Paul Lazarsfeld, Bernard Berelson and Hazel Gaudet, *The people's choice* (New York: Columbia University Press, 1948), 151.

8 Joseph Klapper, *The effects of mass communication* (Glencoe, IL: Free Press, 1960), 12–22.

9 Elizabeth M. Perse, *Media effects and society* (Mahwah, NJ and London: Lawrence Erlbaum Associates Publishers, 2001), 1.

10 C. W. Anderson, 'Fake news is not a virus. On platforms and their effects', *Communications Theory*, 31(1) (2021), 42–61, https://doi.org/10.1093/ct/qtaa008.

11 Read, 'Donald Trump Won Because of Facebook'.

12 Richard Gunther, Paul Beck and Erik Nisbet, 'Fake News May Have Contributed to Trump's 2016 Victory', Ohio State University, March 2018, https://www.documentcloud.org/documents/4429952-Fake-News-May-Have-Contributed-to-Trump-s-2016.html.

13 Margaret Sullivan, 'Facebook has a huge truth problem. A high-priced "oversight board" won't fix it', *Washington Post*, 14 May 2020, https://www.washingtonpost.com/lifestyle/media/facebook-has-a-huge-truth-problem-a-high-priced-oversight-board-wont-fix-it/2020/05/14/c5b53cba-95d9-11ea-9f5e-56d8239bf9ad_story.html.

14 Shannon C. McGregor and Daniel Kreiss, 'Americans are too worried about political misinformation', *Slate*, 30 October 2020, https://slate.com/technology/2020/10/misinformation-social-media-election-research-fear.html.

15 Craig Silverman, 'This Analysis Shows How Viral Fake Election News Stories Outperformed Real News On Facebook', *Buzzfeed News*, 16 November 2016, https://www.buzzfeednews.com/article/craigsilverman/viral-fake-election-news-outperformed-real-news-on-facebook#.qqE7PoA2Ql.

16 Martin Moore, *Democracy Hacked: How Technology is Destabilising Global Politics* (London: One World Publications, 2018), 107–35.

17 Carole Cadwalladr, 'The Great British Brexit robbery. How our democracy was hijacked', *The Guardian*, 7 May 2017, https://www.theguardian.com/technology/2017/may/07/the-great-british-brexit-robbery-hijacked-democracy.

18 Moore, *Democracy Hacked*, 127–8.

19 Admire Mare and Trust Matsilele, 'Hybrid Media System and the July 2018 Elections in "Post-Mugabe" Zimbabwe', in *Social Media and Elections in Africa, Volume 1 Theoretical Perspectives and Election Campaigns*, edited by Martin Ndlela

and Winston Mano (London: Palgrave MacMillan, 2020), 147–76. https://www.palgrave.com/gp/book/9783030305529.

20 Idayat Hassan and Jamie Hitchen, 'Nigeria's "propaganda secretaries"', *Mail & Guardian*, 18 April 2019, https://mg.co.za/article/2019-04-18-00-nigerias-propaganda-secretaries/.

21 Joshua Kalla and David Broockman, 'The minimal persuasive effects of campaign contact in general elections: Evidence from 49 field experiments', *American Political Science Review*, 28 September 2017, https://doi.org/10.1017/S0003055417000363.

22 Andrew Guess, Brendan Nyhan and Jason Reifler, 'Exposure to untrustworthy websites in the 2016 US election', *Nature Human Behaviour*, 4(5) (2018), 472–80, https://doi.org/10.1038/s41562-020-0833-x.

23 Andrew Guess, Dominique Lockett, Benjamin Lyons, Jacob Montgomery, Brendan Nyhan and Jason Reifler, '"Fake news" may have limited effects beyond increasing beliefs in false claims', *Harvard Misinformation Review*, 14 January 2020, https://misinforeview.hks.harvard.edu/article/fake-news-limited-effects-on-political-participation/.

24 Shannon C. McGregor and Daniel Kreiss, 'Americans are too worried about political misinformation', *Slate*, 30 October 2020, https://slate.com/technology/2020/10/misinformation-social-media-election-research-fear.html.

25 Elizabeth Gibney, 'The scant science behind Cambridge Analytica's controversial marketing techniques', *Nature*, 29 March 2018, https://www.nature.com/articles/d41586-018-03880-4.

26 Oberire Apuke and Ivo Apollo, 'Public perception of the role of Facebook usage in political campaigns in Nigeria', *International Journal of Community Development & Management Studies*, 1 (2017), https://www.informingscience.org/Articles/v1p085-102Apuke4069.pdf.

27 Mare and Matsilele, 'Hybrid Media System and the July 2018 Elections in "Post-Mugabe" Zimbabwe'.

28 Hugo Mercier, *Not Born Yesterday. The Science of Who We Trust and What We Believe* (Princeton, NJ and Oxford: Princeton University Press, 2020), 14.

29 Guess, Nyhan and Reifler, 'Exposure to untrustworthy websites in the 2016 US election'.

30 Shannon C. McGregor and Daniel Kreiss, 'Americans are too worried about political misinformation', *Slate*, 30 October 2020, https://slate.com/technology/2020/10/misinformation-social-media-election-research-fear.html.

31 John Jackson, 'Election night reporting and voter turnout', *American Journal of Political Science*, 20 (1983), 615–35. https://www.jstor.org/stable/2110886.

32 Seymour Sudman, 'Do exit polls influence voting behavior', *Public Opinion Quarterly*, 50(3) (1986), 331–9, https://www.jstor.org/stable/2748722.

33 Ullrich Ecker, Jon Roozenbeek, Sander van der Linden, Li Qian Tay, John Cook, Naomi Oreskes and Stephen Lewandowsky, 'Misinformation poses a bigger threat to democracy than you might think', *Nature*, 5 June 2024, https://www.nature.com/articles/d41586-024-01587-3.

34 Stephanie Burchard, *Electoral violence in sub-Saharan Africa. Causes and consequences* (Boulder, CO: Lynne Rienner, 2015), 18.

35 Carlos Shenga and Amilcar Pereira, A. 'The Effect of Electoral Violence on Electoral Participation in Africa', *Cadernos de Estudos Africanos*, 38 (2019), https://doi.org/10.4000/cea.4459.

36 Dominic Penna, 'Tory fury as election of new 1922 Committee chairman mired in chaos', *Daily Telegraph*, 9 July 2024, https://www.telegraph.co.uk/politics/2024/07/09/tory-chaos-as-bob-blackman-elected-1922-committee/.

37 Florian Foos and Daniel Bischof, 'Tabloid Media Campaigns and Public Opinion: Quasi-Experimental Evidence on Euroscepticism in England', *American Political Science Review*, 116(1) (2021), 19–37, https://doi.org/10.1017/S000305542100085X.

38 Moore, *Democracy Hacked*, 127–8.

39 Lasswell, *Propaganda technique in the world war*, 214–18.

40 Matthew Baum and Tim Groeling, *War Stories: the causes and consequences of public views of war* (Princeton, NJ and Oxford: Princeton University Press, 2010), 3.

41 Emails to the author and: United Nations, 'Security Council Adopts Sweeping Resolution 2717 (2023) Outlining Peacekeepers' Gradual, Responsible, Sustainable Withdrawal from Democratic Republic of Congo', 19 December 2023, https://press.un.org/en/2023/sc15538.doc.htm

42 Lucas Graves, 'Lessons from an extraordinary year: Four heuristics for studying mediated misinformation in 2020 and beyond', in *The Routledge Companion to Media Disinformation and Populism*, edited by Howard Tumbler and Silvio Waisbord (London: Routledge, 2021), https://doi.org/10.4324/9781003004431.

43 Israel Junior Borges do Nascimento, Ana Beatriz Pizarro, Jussara M Almeida, Natsasha Azzopardi-Muscat, Marcos Andre Concalves, Maria Björklunde and David Novillo-Ortiz, 'Infodemics and health misinformation: a systematic review of reviews', *Bulletin of the World Health Organization*, 100(9) (2022), 544–61. https://doi.org/10.2471/BLT.21.287654.

44 Hamidreza Aghababaeian, Lara Hamdanieh and Abbas Ostadtaghizadeh, 'Alcohol intake in an attempt to fight COVID-19: A medical myth in Iran', *Alcohol*, 88 (2022), 29–32, https://doi.org/10.1016/j.alcohol.2020.07.006.

45 Peter Cunliffe-Jones, 'From Church and Mosque to WhatsApp—Africa Check's Holistic Approach to Countering "Fake News"', *The Political Quarterly*, 91(3) (July–September 2020), https://onlinelibrary.wiley.com/doi/full/10.1111/1467-923X.12899.

46 Nathan Thielman, Jan Ostermann, Kathryn Whetten, Rachel Itemba, Dafrosa Itemba, Venance Maro, Brian Pence and Elizabeth Reddy, 'Reduced Adherence to Antiretroviral Therapy among HIV-infected Tanzanians Seeking Cure from the Loliondo Healer', *Journal of Acquired Immune Deficiency Syndrome*, 65(3) (2014), 104–9, https://doi.org/10.1097/01.qai.0000437619.23031.83.

47 Rachel Schraer, 'HIV: The misinformation still circulating in 2021', *BBC News*, 1 December 2021 https://www.bbc.co.uk/news/59431598.

48 Heidi Larson, 'The Biggest Pandemic Risk? Viral Misinformation', *Nature* 562 (2018), 309, https://doi.org/10.1038/d41586-018-07034-4.

49 Matthew Motta and Dominik Stecula, 'Quantifying the effect of Wakefield et al. (1998) on skepticism about MMR vaccine safety in the U.S.', *PLOS One*, 19 August 2021, https://doi.org/10.1371/journal.pone.0256395.

50 Deutsche Welle, 'Ebola burial team attacked', 20 September 2014, https://www.dw.com/en/ebola-burial-team-attacked-in-sierra-leone/a-17937340#.

51 Donna McKay, Michele Heisler, Ranit Mishouri, Howard Catton and Otmar Kloiber, 'Attacks against health-care personnel must stop, especially as the world fights COVID-19', *The Lancet* (395), 6 June 2020, https://www.thelancet.com/journals/lancet/article/PIIS0140-6736(20)31191-0/fulltext.

52 Samantha Brooks and Neil Greenberg, 'Psychological impact of being wrongfully accused of criminal offences: A systematic literature review', *Medicine, Science & the Law*, 61(1) (2020), https://doi.org/10.1177/0025802420949069.

53 Martin Chulov, 'How Syria's disinformation wars destroyed the co-founder of the White Helmets', *The Guardian*, 27 October 2020, https://www.theguardian.com/news/2020/oct/27/syria-disinformation-war-white-helmets-mayday-rescue-james-le-mesurier.

54 Ecker et al., 'Misinformation poses a bigger threat to democracy than you might think'.

55 Shakuntala Banaji, Ram Bhat, Anushi Agarwal, Nihal Passsanha and Mukti Pravin, 'WhatsApp vigilantes: An exploration of citizen reception and circulation of WhatsApp misinformation linked to mob violence in India', London School of Economics, 2019, https://www.lse.ac.uk/media-and-communications/assets/documents/research/projects/WhatsApp-Misinformation-Report.pdf.

56 BBC News, 'Rwandans jailed for "hate media"', 3 December 2003, http://news.bbc.co.uk/1/hi/world/africa/3288267.stm.

57 David *Kaye, Speech Police: The Global Struggle to Govern the Internet* (New York: Columbia Global Reports, 2019), 28–30.

58 Steven Frenda, Rebecca M. Nichols and Elizabeth F. Loftus, 'Current Issues and Advances in Misinformation Research', *Current Directions in Psychological Science*, 20(1) (2021), https://doi.org/10.1177/0963721410396620.

59 Elizabeth F. Loftus, 'Planting misinformation in the human mind. A 30-year investigation of the malleability of memory', *Learning and memory*, 12 (2005), 361–6, https://doi.org/10.1101/lm.94705.

60 Odanga Madung and Brian Obilo, 'Fellow Research: Inside the shadowy world of disinformation-for-hire in Kenya', *Mozilla Foundation*, 2 September 2021, https://foundation.mozilla.org/en/blog/fellow-research-inside-the-shadowy-world-of-disinformation-for-hire-in-kenya/.

61 Philip Hilts, *Smokescreen: The truth behind the tobacco industry cover-up*, (Reading, MA: Addison-Wesley, 1996).

62 Amit Katwala, 'The Metro Bank hoax shows the immense power of fake news on WhatsApp', *Wired*, 14 May 2019, https://www.wired.co.uk/article/metro-bank-share-price-whats-app-hoax.

63 Martin Baily, Robert Litan and Matthew Johnson, 'The Origins of the Financial Crisis', *Brookings Institute*, November 2008, https://www.brookings.edu/wp-content/uploads/2016/06/11_origins_crisis_baily_litan.pdf.

64 Michael Tesler, 'Elite Domination of Public Doubts About Climate Change (Not Evolution)', *Political Communication*, 35(2) (2017), 306–26. https://doi.org/10.1080/10584609.2017.1380092.

65 World Economic Forum, '3 charts that show how attitudes to climate science vary around the world', 22 January 2020, https://www.weforum.org/agenda/2020/01/climate-science-global-warming-most-sceptics-country/.

66 Ruth Becker, 'Medical claims for rhino horn: you're better on an aspirin or biting your nails', *Africa Check*, 22 September 2012, https://africacheck.org/fact-checks/reports/medical-claims-rhino-horn-youre-better-aspirin-or-biting-your-nails.

67 Sten Torpan, Sten Hansson, Mark Rhinard, Austeja Kazemekaityte, Pirjo Jukarainen, Sunniva Frislid Meyer, Abriel Schieffelers, Gabriella Lovasz and Kati Orru, 'Handling false information in emergency management: A cross-national comparative study of European practices', *International Journal of Disaster Risk Reduction*, 57 (2021), 102–15, https://www.sciencedirect.com/science/article/pii/S2212420921001175.

68 Robert M. Entman, 'Cascading Activation: Contesting the White House's Frame After 9/11', *Political Communication*, 20 (2003), 415–32, https://doi.org/10.1080/10584600390244176.

69 Pride Chigwedere, George Seage, Sofia Gruskin, Tun-Hou Lee and M Essex, 'Estimating the lost benefits of antiretroviral drug use in South Africa', *Journal of Acquired Immune Deficiency Syndrome*, 49(4) (2008), 410–15, https://doi.org/10.1097/qai.0b013e31818a6cd5.

70 Ayodele Jegede, 'What Led to the Nigerian Boycott of the Polio Vaccination Campaign?', *PLOS Medicine*, 4(3) (March 2007), https://doi.org/10.1371/journal.pmed.0040073.

71 Raissa Ioussouf, 'Madagascar president's herbal tonic fails to halt Covid-19 spike', *BBC News*, 14 August 2020, https://www.bbc.co.uk/news/world-africa-53756752.

72 Sun Tzu, *The Art of War*, translated by Samuel B. Griffith (Oxford: Oxford University Press, 1963), 146.

73 Joshua Levine, *Operation Fortitude: The greatest hoax of the Second World War* (London: Collins, 2012).

74 Robert McNamara, *In Retrospect. The tragedy and lessons of Vietnam* (New York: Vintage Books, 1995), 47–8.

75 Alex Wickham and Camille Cjis, 'Putin advisers mislead Russian leader about Ukraine war status, UK intelligence says', *Politico EU*, 31 March 2022, https://www.politico.eu/article/russia-advisers-president-vladimir-putin-war-ukraine-military-uk-intelligence/.

76 Vincent Ng'ethe, 'No, adolescents don't account for half of new HIV infections in Kenya', *Africa Check*, 29 August 2019, https://africacheck.org/fact-checks/reports/no-adolescents-dont-account-half-new-hiv-infections-kenya.

77 Motunrayo Joel and David Ajikobi, 'What a waste: Fact-checking four claims about Nigeria's garbage problem', *Africa Check*, 26 July 2019, https://africacheck.org/fact-checks/reports/what-waste-fact-checking-four-claims-about-nigerias-garbage-problem.

78 Kelsey Piper, 'The staggering death toll of scientific lies', *Vox*, 26 August 2024, https://www.vox.com/future-perfect/368350/scientific-research-fraud-crime-jail-time.

Chapter 5

1 Joseph Klapper, *The effects of mass communication* (Glencoe, IL: Free Press, 1960), 13.

2 James Carey *Communication as Culture: Essays on media and society* (Boston, MA: Unwyn Hyman, 1989), 25–6.

3 Tendai Dube, 'This video shows a shooting at a funeral in South Africa, not "thugs" working for a Nigerian governor', *AFPFactCheck*, 13 November 2019, https://factcheck.afp.com/video-shows-shooting-funeral-south-africa-not-thugs-working-nigerian-governor

4 Kemi Busari, 'Investigation: "Baba Aisha Herbal Medicine": The deadly concoction consumed by many Nigerians', *Premium Times*, 10 June 2023, https://www.premiumtimesng.com/health/health-investigations/603560-investigation-baba-aisha-herbal-medicine-the-deadly-concoction-consumed-by-many-nigerians.html

5 Temilade Onilede, 'Picture on Buhari's Death Is False!', *Dubawa*, 26 August 2019, https://dubawa.org/picture-on-buharis-death-is-false/.

6 *The New Yorker*, 10 July 1971. Quoted in: Hannah Arendt, 'Lying in Politics', in *Crises of the Republic* (New York: Harvest, 1972), 18.

7 Martin Moore, *Democracy Hacked: How Technology is Destabilising Global Politics* (London: One World Publications, 2018), 107–35.

8 Callum Borchers, 'Trump falsely claims (again) that he coined the term "fake news"', *Washington Post*, 26 October 2017, https://www.washingtonpost.com/news/the-fix/wp/2017/10/26/trump-falsely-claims-again-that-he-coined-the-term-fake-news/.

9 Michael P. Lynch, 'Fake News and the Internet Shell Game', *New York Times*, 28 November 2016, https://www.nytimes.com/2016/11/28/opinion/fake-news-and-the-internet-shell-game.html.

10 Katherine Ognyanova, David Lazer, Ronald E. Robertson and Christo Wilson, 'Fake news exposure is linked to lower trust in media, higher trust in government when your side is in power', *Harvard Misinformation Review*, 2 June 2020, https://misinforeview.hks.harvard.edu/article/misinformation-in-action-fake-news-exposure-is-linked-to-lower-trust-in-media-higher-trust-in-government-when-your-side-is-in-power/.

11 Michal Kosinski, David Stilwell and Thore Graepel, 'Private traits and attributes are predictable from digital records of human behavior', *PNAS* 110(15) (2013), 5802–5. https://www.pnas.org/doi/10.1073/pnas.1218772110.

12 Rachel Schraer and Jack Goodman, 'Ivermectin: How false science created a Covid "miracle" drug', *BBC News*, 6 October 2021, https://www.bbc.co.uk/news/health-58170809.

13 Dawit Endeshaw, 'Mob action costs two researchers' lives', *The Reporter Ethiopia*, 27 October 2018, https://www.thereporterethiopia.com/6682/.

14 Denis McQuail, *McQuail's Media and Mass Communication Theory* (London: Sage Publications, 6th Edition, 2010), 454.

15 Klapper, *The effects of mass communication*, 14.

16 While millions of people saw and believed false claims that a notorious paedophile ring operated from a particular pizza parlour in Washington, DC, only one person acted on those claims, travelling to the restaurant and attacking it with an assault rifle. See Matthew Haag and Maya Salam, 'Gunman in "Pizzagate" Shooting Is Sentenced to 4 Years in Prison', *New York Times*, 22 June 2017, https://www.nytimes.com/2017/06/22/us/pizzagate-attack-sentence.html.

17 Ayodele Jegede, 'What Led to the Nigerian Boycott of the Polio Vaccination Campaign?', *PLOS Medicine*, 4(3) (March 2007), https://doi.org/10.1371/journal.pmed.0040073.

18 Pride Chigwedere, George Seage, Sofia Gruskin, Tun-Hou Lee and M. Essex, 'Estimating the lost benefits of antiretroviral drug use in South Africa', *Journal of Acquired Immune Deficiency Syndrome*, 49(4) (2008), 410–15, https://doi.org/10.1097/qai.0b013e31818a6cd5.

19 Christina Pazzanese, 'Calculating possible fallout of Trump's dismissal of face masks', *Harvard Gazette*, 27 October 2020, https://news.harvard.edu/gazette/story/2020/10/possible-fallout-from-trumps-dismissal-of-face-masks/.

20 Raissa Ioussouf, 'Madagascar president's herbal tonic fails to halt Covid-19 spike', *BBC News*, 14 August 2020, https://www.bbc.co.uk/news/world-africa-53756752.

21 Kelsey Piper, 'The staggering death toll of scientific lies', *Vox*, 26 August 2024, https://www.vox.com/future-perfect/368350/scientific-research-fraud-crime-jail-time.

Chapter 6

1 Gillian Murphy, Constance De Saint Laurent, Megan Reynolds, Omar Aftab, Karen Hegarty, Yuning Sun and Ciara M Greene, 'What do we study when we study misinformation? A scoping review of experimental research (2016–2022)', *Harvard Misinformation Review*, 15 November 2023, https://misinforeview.hks.harvard.edu/article/what-do-we-study-when-we-study-misinformation-a-scoping-review-of-experimental-research-2016-2022/.

2 Pride Chigwedere, George Seage, Sofia Gruskin, Tun-Hou Lee and M. Essex, 'Estimating the lost benefits of antiretroviral drug use in South Africa', *Journal of Acquired Immune Deficiency Syndrome*, 49(4) (2008), 410–15, https://doi.org/10.1097/qai.0b013e31818a6cd5.

3 Ayodele Jegede, 'What Led to the Nigerian Boycott of the Polio Vaccination Campaign?', *PLOS Medicine*, 4(3) (March 2007), https://doi.org/10.1371/journal.pmed.0040073.

4 Kelsey Piper, 'The staggering death toll of scientific lies', *Vox*, 26 August 2024, https://www.vox.com/future-perfect/368350/scientific-research-fraud-crime-jail-time.

5 Robert McNamara, *In Retrospect. The tragedy and lessons of Vietnam* (New York: Vintage Books, 1995).

6 Alex Wickham and Camille Cjis, 'Putin advisers mislead Russian leader about Ukraine war status, UK intelligence says', *Politico EU*, 31 March 2022, https://www.politico.eu/article/russia-advisers-president-vladimir-putin-war-ukraine-military-uk-intelligence/.

7 Donald J. Abrams, Starley B. Shade, Paul Couey, Joseph M. McCune, Joan Lo, Peter Bacchetti, Barbara Chang, Lori Epling, Teri Liegler and Robert M. Grant, 'Dehydroepiandrosterone (DHEA) effects on HIV replication and host immunity: a randomized placebo-controlled study', *AIDS Research and Human Retroviruses*, 23(1) (2007), 77–85, https://doi.org/10.1089/aid.2006.0170.

8 Chigwedere et al., 'Estimating the lost benefits of antiretroviral drug use in South Africa'.

9 Motunrayo Joel and David Ajikobi, 'What a waste: fact-checking four claims about Nigeria's garbage problem,' *Africa Check*, 26 July 2019, https://africacheck.org/fact-checks/reports/what-waste-fact-checking-four-claims-about-nigerias-garbage-problem.

10 L. V. Karnatovskaia, M. M. Johnson, K. Varga, J. A. Highfield, B. D. Wolfrom, K. L. Philbrick, E. Wesley, E. Ely, J. C. Jackson, O. Gajic, S. R. Ahmad, A. S. Niven, 'Stress and Fear: Clinical Implications for Providers and Patients (in the Time of COVID-19 and Beyond)', *Mayo Clinical Proceedings*, 95(11) (2020), 2487–98, https://doi.org/10.1016/j.mayocp.2020.08.028.

11 Karnatovskaia et al., 'Stress and Fear'.

12 MSF, 'Access to healthcare in Cameroon severely limited as violence and unrest rule', 29 July 2021, https://www.msf.org/violence-continues-cameroon-access-healthcare-remains-seriously-limited.

13 Chigwedere et al., 'Estimating the lost benefits of antiretroviral drug use in South Africa'.

14 Raissa Ioussouf, 'Madagascar president's herbal tonic fails to halt Covid-19 spike', *BBC News*, 14 August 2020, https://www.bbc.co.uk/news/world-africa-53756752.

15 Flavia Milhorance, 'Brazil could have stopped 400,000 Covid deaths with better response, expert says', *The Guardian*, 29 June 2021, https://www.theguardian.com/global-development/2021/jun/29/brazil-coronavirus-deaths-jair-bolsonaro.

16 Celia Hatton, 'Nobel Prize winner Tu Youyou helped by ancient Chinese remedy', *BBC News*, 6 October 2015, https://www.bbc.co.uk/news/blogs-china-blog-34451386.

17 See (i) Ullrich Ecker, Jon Roozenbeek, Sander van der Linden, Li Qian Tay, John Cook, Naomi Oreskes and Stephen Lewandowsky, 'Misinformation poses a bigger threat to democracy than you might think', *Nature*, 5 June 2024, https://www.nature.com/articles/d41586-024-01587-3, and (ii) Ceren Budak, Brendan Nyhan, David M. Rothschild, Emily Thorson and Duncan J. Watts, 'Misunderstanding the harms of online misinformation', *Nature*, 630 (2024), 45–53, https://doi.org/10.1038/s41586-024-07417-w.

Part 3 – Introduction

1 The original quotation was 'All models are wrong.' It was expanded in 1978 to add the part about some models being useful. See George Box, 'Robustness in the Strategy of Scientific Model Building', *Robustness in Statistics*, 1979, 201–36, https://doi.org/10.1016/B978-0-12-438150-6.50018-2.

2 An annual count by the Reporters Lab at Duke University found that the number of fact-checking websites active grew from 152 in 2015 to 457 in 2022, before falling back slightly to 439 in 2024. See Marc Stencel, Erica Ryan and Joel Luther, 'With half the planet going to the polls in 2024, fact-checking splutters', *Duke Reporters Lab*, 30 May 2024, https://reporterslab.org/with-half-the-planet-going-to-the-polls-in-2024-fact-checking-sputters/.

3 Zhijiang Guo, Michael Schlichtkrull and Andreas Vlachos, 'A Survey on Automated Fact-Checking', *Transactions of the Association for Computational Linguistics*, 10, 9 February 2022, https://direct.mit.edu/tacl/article/doi/10.1162/tacl_a_00454/109469/A-Survey-on-Automated-Fact-Checking.

4 Gabrielle Lim and Samantha Bradshaw, 'Chilling legislation: Tracking the impact of 'fake news' laws on press freedom internationally', *Center for International Media Assistance*, 19 July 2023, https://www.cima.ned.org/publication/chilling-legislation/.

5 Peter Cunliffe-Jones, Assane Diagne, Alan Finlay and Anya Schiffrin. *Bad Law – Legal and Regulatory Responses to Misinformation in Eleven African Countries 2016–2020.* https://www.uwestminsterpress.co.uk/site/chapters/m/10.16997/book53.b/, In *Review Of Misinformation Across Sub-Saharan Africa 2016-2020: A Study Of And Policy Framework For 'Media Literacy' In Schools And Legal/Regulatory Responses* (London: University of Westminster Press, 2021).

6 Jacob Mchangama, *Free Speech: A global history from Socrates to social media*, (London: Basic Books, 2022), 8, 386.

Chapter 7

1 Denis McQuail, *McQuail's Media and Mass Communication Theory* (London: Sage Publications, 6th Edition, 2010), 454.

2 Edward N. Lorenz, 'Predictability: does the flap of a butterfly's wings in Brazil set off a tornado in Texas?', *American Association Advancement of Science*, 1972, https://mathsciencehistory.com/wp-content/uploads/2020/03/132_kap6_lorenz_artikel_the_butterfly_effect.pdf.

3 In earlier versions of his talk, Lorenz imagined a seagull's wings creating the effect. He changed to the more poetic image on a friend's advice. https://www.bbvaopenmind.com/en/science/leading-figures/when-lorenz-discovered-the-butterfly-effect/

4 Lorenz, 'Predictability: does the flap of a butterfly's wings in Brazil set off a tornado in Texas?'.

5 Lorenz, 'Predictability'.

6 Stanley G. Benjamin, John M. Brown, Gilbert Brunet, Peter Lynch, Kazuo Saito and Thomas W. Schlatter, '100 Years of Progress in Forecasting and NWP Applications', *Journal of the American Meteorological Society*, 2018, https://journals.ametsoc.org/view/journals/amsm/59/1/amsmonographs-d-18-0020.1.xml.

7 Gillian Murphy, Constance De Saint Laurent, Megan Reynolds, Omar Aftab, Karen Hegarty, Yuning Sun and Ciara M Greene, 'What do we study when we study misinformation? A scoping review of experimental research (2016–2022)', *Harvard Misinformation Review*, 15 November 2023, https://misinforeview.hks.harvard.edu/article/what-do-we-study-when-we-study-misinformation-a-scoping-review-of-experimental-research-2016-2022/.

8 Motunrayo Joel and David Ajikobi, 'What a waste: fact-checking four claims about Nigeria's garbage problem', *Africa Check*, 26 July 2019, https://africacheck.org/fact-checks/reports/what-waste-fact-checking-four-claims-about-nigerias-garbage-problem.

9 Pride Chigwedere, George Seage, Sofia Gruskin, Tun-Hou Lee and M Essex, 'Estimating the lost benefits of antiretroviral drug use in South Africa', *Journal of Acquired Immune Deficiency Syndrome*, 49(4) (2008), 410–15, https://doi.org/10.1097/qai.0b013e31818a6cd5.

10 Dawit Endeshaw, 'Mob action costs two researchers' lives', *The Reporter Ethiopia*, 27 October 2018, https://www.thereporterethiopia.com/6682/.

11 Tendai Dube, 'South African police deny claims that Longwe Twala was arrested for the murder of Senzo Meyiwa', *AFPFactCheck*, 22 November 2019, https://factcheck.afp.com/south-african-police-deny-claims-longwe-twala-was-arrested-murder-senzo-meyiwa.

12 MSF, 'Access to healthcare in Cameroon severely limited as violence and unrest rule', 29 July 2021, https://www.msf.org/violence-continues-cameroon-access-healthcare-remains-seriously-limited.

13 Mayowa Tijani, 'This is an old picture that does not show a reprisal for recent xenophobic violence in South Africa', *AFPFactCheck*, 4 September 2019, https://factcheck.afp.com/old-picture-does-not-show-reprisal-recent-xenophobic-violence-south-africa.

14 Ange Kasongo, 'Non, la RDC n'a pas signé un accord avec la firme russe Russell', *AFPFactuel*, 29 October 2019, https://factuel.afp.com/non-la-rdc-na-pas-signe-un-accord-avec-la-firme-russe-russell.

15 Taryn Khourie, 'Apricot seeds don't kill cancer cells, can have deadly side effects', *Africa Check*, 25 October 2019, https://africacheck.org/fact-checks/meta-programme-fact-checks/apricot-seeds-dont-kill-cancer-cells-can-have-deadly-side.

16 Dominic Penna, 'Tory fury as election of new 1922 Committee chairman mired in chaos', *Daily Telegraph*, 9 July 2024, https://www.telegraph.co.uk/politics/2024/07/09/tory-chaos-as-bob-blackman-elected-1922-committee/.

17 Michael P Lynch, 'Fake News and the Internet Shell Game', *New York Times*, 28 November 2016, https://www.nytimes.com/2016/11/28/opinion/fake-news-and-the-internet-shell-game.html.

18 Michael Hameleers, Toni Van der Meer and Anna Brosius, 'Feeling 'disinformed' reduces compliance with COVID-19 guidelines', *Harvard Misinformation Review*, 31 May 2020, https://misinforeview.hks.harvard.edu/article/feeling-disinformed-lowers-compliance-with-covid-19-guidelines-evidence-from-the-us-uk-netherlands-and-germany/.

19 Chigwedere et al., 'Estimating the lost benefits of antiretroviral drug use in South Africa'.

20 Thabo Mbeki, 'A brief commentary on the question of HIV and AIDS by Thabo Mbeki', *UNISA/SA History Online*, 7 March 2016, https://www.sahistory.org.za/archive/brief-commentary-question-hiv-and-aids-thabo-mbeki-7-march-2016.

21 Ayodele Jegede, 'What Led to the Nigerian Boycott of the Polio Vaccination Campaign?', *PLOS Medicine*, 4(3) (March 2007), https://doi.org/10.1371/journal.pmed.0040073.

22 Taryn Khourie, 'Apricot seeds don't kill cancer cells, can have deadly side effects', *Africa Check*, 25 October 2019, https://africacheck.org/fact-checks/meta-programme-fact-checks/apricot-seeds-dont-kill-cancer-cells-can-have-deadly-side

23 Allwell Okpi, 'No, daggers seized by police in Nigeria's Kano state not for "killing Christians"', *Africa Check*, 19 August 2019, https://africacheck.org/fact-checks/spotchecks/no-daggers-seized-police-nigerias-kano-state-not-killing-christians.

24 Jennifer Ojugbeli, 'No, Nigerian politician Melaye hasn't won Kogi West senator's seat – election declared inconclusive', 20 November 2019, https://africacheck.org/fact-checks/meta-programme-fact-checks/no-nigerian-politician-melaye-hasnt-won-kogi-west-senators.

25 Grace Gichuhi, 'No, Carrefour not selling half-price maize after toxin ban', *Africa Check*, 19 November 2019, https://africacheck.org/fact-checks/meta-programme-fact-checks/no-carrefour-kenya-not-selling-half-price-maize-after-toxin.

26 Matthew Haag and Maya Salam, 'Gunman in "Pizzagate" Shooting Is Sentenced to 4 Years in Prison', *New York Times*, 22 June 2017, https://www.nytimes.com/2017/06/22/us/pizzagate-attack-sentence.html.

27 Manvir Singh, 'Don't believe what they're telling you about misinformation', *The New Yorker*, 14 April 2024, https://www.newyorker.com/magazine/2024/04/22/dont-believe-what-theyre-telling-you-about-misinformation.

28 Monique Ngo Mayag, 'Le virus Ebola arrivé à Kinshasa? La Croix-Rouge et les autorités démentent', *AFPFactuel*, 1 August 2019, https://factuel.afp.com/le-virus-ebola-arrive-kinshasa-la-croix-rouge-et-les-autorites-dementent.

29 Amit Katwala, 'The Metro Bank hoax shows the immense power of fake news on WhatsApp', *Wired*, 14 May 2019, https://www.wired.co.uk/article/metro-bank-share-price-whats-app-hoax.

30 Dawit Endeshaw, 'Mob action costs two researchers' lives', *The Reporter Ethiopia*, 27 October 2018, https://www.thereporterethiopia.com/6682/.

31 Jennifer Ojugbeli, 'No, Nigerian politician Melaye hasn't won Kogi West senator's seat – election declared inconclusive', 20 November 2019, https://africacheck.org/fact-checks/meta-programme-fact-checks/no-nigerian-politician-melaye-hasnt-won-kogi-west-senators.

32 Matthew Haag and Maya Salam, 'Gunman in "Pizzagate" Shooting Is Sentenced to 4 Years in Prison', *New York Times*, 22 June 2017, https://www.nytimes.com/2017/06/22/us/pizzagate-attack-sentence.html.

33 Anne-Sophie Faivre Le Cadre, 'Deux 'oiseaux-sorcières' tombés du ciel au Congo? Non, des femmes atteintes d'encéphalopathie au Togo', *AFPFactuel*, 7 August 2019, https://factuel.afp.com/deux-oiseaux-sorcieres-tombes-du-ciel-au-congo-non-des-femmes-atteintes-dencephalopathie-au-togo.

34 Dawit Endeshaw, 'Mob action costs two researchers' lives', *The Reporter Ethiopia*, 27 October 2018, https://www.thereporterethiopia.com/6682/.

35 Heidi Larson, 'The Biggest Pandemic Risk? Viral Misinformation', *Nature*, 562 (2018), 309–309, https://doi.org/10.1038/d41586-018-07034-4.

36 Grace Gichuhi, 'Kenyan gospel music star Ringtone Apoke is alive and well', *Africa Check*, 12 July 2019, https://africacheck.org/fact-checks/meta-programme-fact-checks/kenyan-gospel-music-star-ringtone-apoko-alive-and-well.

37 Robert M. Entman, 'Cascading Activation: Contesting the White House's Frame After 9/11', *Political Communication*, 20 (2003), 415–32, https://doi.org/10.1080/10584600390244176.

38 Khourie, 'Apricot seeds don't kill cancer cells, can have deadly side effects'.

39 Several studies show that voter expectations of electoral rigging may dampen participation by supporters of the side that make the accusation. See Carlos Shenga and Amilcar Pereira, 'The Effect of Electoral Violence on Electoral Participation in Africa', *Cadernos de Estudos Africanos*, 38 (2019), https://doi.org/10.4000/cea.4459.

40 Benjamin et al., '100 Years of Progress in Forecasting and NWP Applications'.

41 Ullrich Ecker, Jon Roozenbeek, Sander van der Linden, Li Qian Tay, John Cook, Naomi Oreskes and Stephen Lewandowsky, 'Misinformation poses a bigger threat to democracy than you might think', *Nature*, 5 June 2024, https://www.nature.com/articles/d41586-024-01587-3.

42 The International Fact-Checking Network Code of Principles. Last reviewed August 2024. https://ifcncodeofprinciples.poynter.org/the-commitments. The author led work in 2016 to establish the code and led a review of the code in 2019–20.

43 Michal Kosinski, David Stilwell and Thore Graepel, 'Private traits and attributes are predictable from digital records of human behavior', *PNAS*, 110(15) (2013), 5802–5. https://www.pnas.org/doi/10.1073/pnas.1218772110.

44 Dani Madrid-Morales, Herman Wasserman, Gregory Gondwe, Khulekani Ndlovu, Etse Sikanu, Melissa Tully, Emeka Umejei and Chikezie Uzuegbunam, 'Motivations for Sharing Misinformation. A Comparative Study in Six Sub-Saharan African Countries', *International Journal of Communication*, 15 (2021), 1200–19, https://ijoc.org/index.php/ijoc/article/view/14801/3378.

45 Thomas E. Powell, Hajo G. Boomgaarden, Knut de Swert and Claes H. de Vreese, 'A clearer picture: The contribution of visuals and text to framing effects', *Journal of Communication*, 65(6) (2015), 997–1017, https://doi.org/10.1111/jcom.12184.

46 William J. Brady, Julian A. Wills, John T. Jost, Joshua A. Tucker and Jay J. Van Bavel, 'Emotion Shapes the Diffusion of Moralized Content in Social Networks', *Proceedings of the National Academy of Sciences*, 114(28) (2017), 7313–18. https://doi.org/10.1073/pnas.1618923114.

47 Brendan Nyhan and Jason Reifler, 'When corrections fail: The persistence of political misperceptions', *Political Behavior*, 32(2) (2010), 303–30, https://doi.org:10.1007/s11109-010-9112-2.

48 Cecilie S. Traberg, Trisha Harjani, Jon Roozenbeek and Sander Van der Linden, 'The persuasive effects of social cues and source effects on misinformation susceptibility', *Scientific Reports*, 2024, https://doi.org/10.1038/s41598-024-54030-y.

49 Lisa Fazio, Raunak Pillai and Deep Patel, 'The effects of repetition on belief in naturalistic settings', *Journal of Experimental Psychology*, 151(10) (2022), 2604–13, https://pubmed.ncbi.nlm.nih.gov/35286116/.

50 Anne-Sophie Faivre Le Cadre, 'Non, la tisane à l'artémisia et la noix de cola ne guérissent pas le paludisme', *AFPFactCheck*, 8 July 2019, https://factuel.afp.com/non-la-tisane-lartemisia-et-la-noix-de-cola-ne-guerissent-pas-le-paludisme.

51 Jegede, 'What Led to the Nigerian Boycott of the Polio Vaccination Campaign?'.

52 Anne-Sophie Faivre Le Cadre, 'Deux "oiseaux-sorcières" tombés du ciel au Congo?'.

53 Endeshaw, 'Mob action costs two researchers' lives'.

54 Shakuntala Banaji, Ram Bhat, Anushi Agarwal, Nihal Passsanha and Mukti Pravin, 'WhatsApp vigilantes: An Exploration of citizen reception and circulation of WhatsApp misinformation linked to mob violence in India', London School of Economics, 2019, https://www.lse.ac.uk/media-and-communications/assets/documents/research/projects/WhatsApp-Misinformation-Report.pdf.

55 Claire Wilmot, 'Did Russian disinformation fuel the Southport protests', *The Bureau of Investigative Journalism*, 2 August 2024, https://www.thebureauinvestigates.com/stories/2024-08-02/did-russian-disinformation-fuel-the-southport-protests/.

56 Tendai Dube, 'False kidnapping rumours spread during South Africa violence', *AFPFactCheck*, 9 September 2019, https://factcheck.afp.com/false-kidnapping-rumours-spread-during-south-africa-violence.

57 Lorenz, 'Predictability'.

Chapter 8

1 Andrew Guess, Dominique Lockett, Benjamin Lyons, Jacob Montgomery, Brendan Nyhan and Jason Reifler, '"Fake news" may have limited effects beyond increasing beliefs in false claims', *Harvard Misinformation Review*, 14 January 2020, https://misinforeview.hks.harvard.edu/article/fake-news-limited-effects-on-political-participation/.

2 World Economic Forum, 'Global Risks Report 2024', 10 January 2024, https://www.weforum.org/publications/global-risks-report-2024/.

3 Philip Hilts, *Smokescreen: The truth behind the tobacco industry cover-up*, (Reading, MA: Addison-Wesley, 1996).

4 Article 19 of the 1966 Universal Declaration of Human Rights permits restrictions to freedom of speech in a limited number of cases only where 'necessary' to prevent identified harms or infringement of recognised rights: https://www.ohchr.org/en/professionalinterest/pages/ccpr.aspx.

5 Mary Kulundu, 'Zambian farmer "greatly distressed" by posts falsely identifying him as victim of South African violence', *AFPFactCheck*, 13 September

2019, https://factcheck.afp.com/zambian-farmer-greatly-distressed-posts-falsely-identifying-him-victim-south-african-violence.

6 Obed Manuel, 'Bomb threats followed Trump's false claims about Springfield. Some Haitians may leave', *National Public Radio*, 19 September 2024, https://www.npr.org/2024/09/19/nx-s1-5114047/springfield-ohio-haitian-migrants-trump-safety-concerns.

7 Mayowa Tijani, 'This is a scam to get your details – MTN is not giving 122gb to customers in Nigeria', *AFPFactCheck*, 15 October 2019, https://factcheck.afp.com/scam-get-your-details-mtn-not-giving-122gb-customers-nigeria.

8 Monique Ngo Mayag, 'Le corossol n'est pas un remède miracle contre le diabète', *AFPFactuel*, 12 November 2019, https://factuel.afp.com/le-corossol-nest-pas-un-remede-miracle-contre-le-diabete.

9 Amit Katwala, 'The Metro Bank hoax shows the immense power of fake news on WhatsApp', *Wired*, 14 May 2019, https://www.wired.co.uk/article/metro-bank-share-price-whats-app-hoax.

10 Anirudh Parthasarathy, 'Fact check: Think twice before sticking garlic up your nose to clear a block', *The Hindu*, 23 March 2022, https://www.thehindu.com/sci-tech/health/fact-check-think-twice-before-sticking-garlic-up-your-nose-to-clear-a-block/article65248667.ece.

11 Denise R. Allen, Romel Lacson, Amos Gborie, Manisha Patel, Michael Beach, 'Understanding Why Ebola Deaths Occur at Home in Urban Montserrado County, Liberia', *Centre for Disease Control and Prevention*, June 2015, http://www.ebola-anthropology.net/wp-content/uploads/2015/07/FINAL-Report-to-Liberia-MoH-Understanding-Why-Ebola-Deaths-Occur-at-Home-Liberia.pdf.

12 Plato, *Republic*, translated by Robin Waterfield (Oxford: Oxford University Press, 1993), 78.

13 Peter Oborne, *The rise of political lying* (London: Free Press, 2005), 116.

14 Joshua Levine, *Operation Fortitude: The greatest hoax of the Second World War* (London: Collins, 2012).

15 Emma Levine and Matthew Lupoli, 'Prosocial lies: Causes and consequences', *Current Opinion in Psychology*, 43 (2022), 335–40, https://doi.org/10.1016/j.copsyc.2021.08.006.

16 Disinformation Team, 'Ipob: Nigerian "media warriors" call for killings on social media over Biafra', *BBC News*, 12 May 2022, https://www.bbc.co.uk/news/world-africa-61354014.

17 Heidi Larson, 'The Biggest Pandemic Risk? Viral Misinformation', *Nature*, 562 (2018), 309, https://doi.org/10.1038/d41586-018-07034-4.

18 Stanley G. Benjamin, John M. Brown, Gilbert Brunet, Peter Lynch, Kazuo Saito and Thomas W. Schlatter, '100 Years of Progress in Forecasting and NWP Applications', *American Meteorological Society*, 2018, https://journals.ametsoc.org/view/journals/amsm/59/1/amsmonographs-d-18-0020.1.xml.

19 Robin McKie, 'The perfect storm for small talk? Weather forecasters aim at long-range accuracy', *The Guardian*, 18 February 2024, https://www.theguardian.com/science/2024/feb/18/the-perfect-storm-for-small-talk-weather-forecasters-aim-at-long-range-accuracy.

20 Edward N. Lorenz, 'Predictability: does the flap of a butterfly's wings in Brazil set off a tornado in Texas?', *American Association Advancement of Science*, 1972, https://mathsciencehistory.com/wp-content/uploads/2020/03/132_kap6_lorenz_artikel_the_butterfly_effect.pdf.

Conclusion

1 Jacob Mchangama, *Free Speech: A global history from Socrates to social media* (London: Basic Books, 2022), 387–8.

2 Ullrich Ecker, Jon Roozenbeek, Sander van der Linden, Li Qian Tay, John Cook, Naomi Oreskes and Stephen Lewandowsky, 'Misinformation poses a bigger threat to democracy than you might think', *Nature*, 5 June 2024, https://www.nature.com/articles/d41586-024-01587-3.

3 Ayodele Jegede, 'What Led to the Nigerian Boycott of the Polio Vaccination Campaign?', *PLOS Medicine*, 4(3) (March 2007), https://doi.org/10.1371/journal.pmed.0040073.

4 James Carey *Communication as Culture: Essays on media and society* (Boston, MA: Unwyn Hyman, 1989), 15, 18.

5 Dan Sperber, 'Apparently irrational beliefs' in *Rationality and Relativism*, edited by Martin Hollis and Steven Lukes (Cambridge, MA: MIT Press, 1982), 149–80, https://www.dan.sperber.fr/wp-content/uploads/1982_apparently-irrational-beliefs.pdf.

6 See these two competing articles from *Nature* in 2024: (i) Ecker et al., 'Misinformation poses a bigger threat to democracy than you might think', and (ii) Ceren Budak, Brendan Nyhan, David M. Rothschild, Emily Thorson and Duncan J. Watts, 'Misunderstanding the harms of online misinformation', *Nature*, 630 (2024), 45–53, https://doi.org/10.1038/s41586-024-07417-w.

7 Africa Check, 'No, organ donors not alive when organs harvested. This harmful meme risks lives', 4 July 2019, https://africacheck.org/fact-checks/meta-programme-fact-checks/no-organ-donors-not-alive-when-organs-harvested-harmful-meme.

8 Ogala Emmanuel and Nnenna Ibeh, 'Ebola sparks panic across Nigeria as citizens scramble for salt-water bath "remedy"', *Premium Times*, 8 August 2014, https://www.premiumtimesng.com/news/166257-ebola-sparks-panic-across-nigeria-as-citizens-scramble-for-salt-water-bath-remedy.html#sthash.Ge0bomNI.dpbs.

9 Cayley Clifford, 'South Africa's police recruitment drive based on dubious UN standard', *Africa Check*, 17 July 2019, https://africacheck.org/fact-checks/spotchecks/south-africas-police-recruitment-drive-based-dubious-un-standard.

10 Motunrayo Joel and David Ajikobi, 'What a waste: Fact-checking four claims about Nigeria's garbage problem', *Africa Check*, 26 July 2019, https://africacheck.org/fact-checks/reports/what-waste-fact-checking-four-claims-about-nigerias-garbage-problem.

11 Sten Torpan, Sten Hansson, Mark Rhinard, Austeja Kazemekaityte, Pirjo Jukarainen, Sunniva Frislid Meyer, Abriel Schieffelers, Gabriella Lovasz and Kati Orru, 'Handling false information in emergency management: A cross-national comparative study of European practices', *International Journal of Disaster Risk Reduction*, 57 (2021), 102–15, https://www.sciencedirect.com/science/article/pii/S2212420921001175.

12 Heidi Larson, 'The Biggest Pandemic Risk? Viral Misinformation', *Nature*, 562 (2018), 309, https://doi.org/10.1038/d41586-018-07034-4.

13 Alice E. Marwick, 'Why do people share fake news? A socio-technocratic model of media effects', *Georgetown Law Technology Review*, 2(2) (2018), 474–512, https://georgetownlawtechreview.org/wp-content/uploads/2018/07/2.2-Marwick-pp-474-512.pdf.

14 Katlego Disemelo, "'Is Johannesburg the world's largest man-made forest? The claim is a myth"', *Africa Check*, 23 May 23, 2013, https://africacheck.org/fact-checks/reports/johannesburg-worlds-largest-man-made-forest-claim-myth.

15 Hannah Arendt, 'Lying in Politics', in *Crises of the Republic* (New York: Harvest, 1972).

16 Allwell Okpi, 'No data shows 30% of Nigerian men "not biological fathers of their children"', *Africa Check*, 9 July 2019, https://africacheck.org/fact-checks/reports/no-data-shows-30-nigerian-men-not-biological-fathers-their-children.

17 Cayley Clifford, 'No evidence "nearly half of all child deaths in Africa stem from hunger"', *Africa Check*, 10 September 2019, https://africacheck.org/fact-checks/reports/no-evidence-nearly-half-all-child-deaths-africa-stem-hunger.

18 Cayley Clifford, 'South Africa's police recruitment drive based on dubious UN standard', *Africa Check*, 17 July 2019, https://africacheck.org/fact-checks/spotchecks/south-africas-police-recruitment-drive-based-dubious-un-standard.

19 Yochai Benkler, Casey Tilton, Bruce Etling, Hal Roberts, Justin Clark, Robert Faris, Jonas Kaiser and Carolyn Schmitt, 'Mail-In Voter Fraud: Anatomy of a Disinformation Campaign', Berkman Klein Center, Harvard University, 1 October 2020, https://cyber.harvard.edu/publication/2020/Mail-in-Voter-Fraud-Disinformation-2020.

20 Charlotte Durand and Monique Ngo Mayag, 'Un médicament pour guérir du sida? Un faux, depuis interdit dans plusieurs pays', *AFPFactuel*, 6 July 2019, https://factuel.afp.com/un-medicament-pour-guerir-du-sida-un-faux-depuis-interdit-dans-plusieurs-pays.

21 Joel and Ajikobi, 'What a waste: fact-checking four claims about Nigeria's garbage problem'.

22 Center for News Technology & Innovation, 'Most "Fake News" Legislation Risks Doing More Harm Than Good', 5 April 2024, https://innovating.news/article/most-fake-news-legislation-risks-doing-more-harm-than-good-amid-a-record-number-of-elections-in-2024/.

23 C. W. Anderson, 'Fake news is not a virus. On platforms and their effects', *Communications Theory*, 31(1) (2021), 42–61, https://doi.org/10.1093/ct/qtaa008.

24 Joshua Levine, *Operation Fortitude: The greatest hoax of the Second World War* (London: Collins, 2012).

25 Andrew Guess, Dominique Lockett, Benjamin Lyons, Jacob Montgomery, Brendan Nyhan and Jason Reifler, '"Fake news" may have limited effects beyond increasing beliefs in false claims', *Harvard Misinformation Review*, 14 January 2020, https://misinforeview.hks.harvard.edu/article/fake-news-limited-effects-on-political-participation/.

26 Brendan Nyhan and Jason Reifler, 'When corrections fail: The persistence of political misperceptions', *Political Behavior*, 32(2) (2010), 303–30, https://doi.org:10.1007/s11109-010-9112-2.

27 Doris Lacassagne, Jeremy Bena and Olivier Corneille, 'Is Earth a perfect square? Repetition increases the perceived truth of highly implausible statements', *Cognition*, 223 (2022), https://doi.org/10.1016/j.cognition.2022.105052.

28 Bernard Berelson, 'Communications and Public Opinion' in *Communications in Modern Society, Fifteen studies of the mass media*, edited by W. Schramm, (Champaign, IL: University of Illinois Press, 1948), 172.

29 Denis McQuail, *McQuail's Media and Mass Communication Theory* (London: Sage Publications, 6th Edition, 2010), 454.

30 Article 19 of the Universal Declaration of Human Rights (1966), https://www.ohchr.org/en/professionalinterest/pages/ccpr.aspx.

31 Gabrielle Lim and Samantha Bradshaw, 'Chilling legislation: Tracking the impact of "fake news" laws on press freedom internationally', *Center for International Media Assistance*, 19 July 2023, https://www.cima.ned.org/publication/chilling-legislation/.